THIS DOG
WILL CHANGE
YOUR LIFE

ELIAS WEISS FRIEDMAN

THE DOGIST

WITH

BEN GREENMAN

BALLANTINE BOOKS

NEW YORK

THIS
DOG
WILL
CHANGE
YOUR
LIFE

Ballantine Books
An imprint of Random House
A division of Penguin Random House LLC
1745 Broadway, New York, NY 10019
randomhousebooks.com
penguinrandomhouse.com

BALLANTINE BOOKS & colophon are registered trademarks
of Penguin Random House LLC.

Hardback ISBN 978-0-593-87207-9
Ebook ISBN 978-0-593-87208-6

Printed in Canada on acid-free paper

2 4 6 8 9 7 5 3 1

First Edition

BOOK TEAM: Production editor: Cara DuBois • Managing editor: Pam Alders •
Production manager: Jenn Backe • Copy editor: Annette Szlachta-McGinn •
Proofreaders: Josh Karpf, Tess Rossi, Jennifer Sale, Tricia Wygal

Book design by Caroline Cunningham
Title-page hand lettering and title-page and part-title dog collage:
Reed Barrow and Hunter Barrow
Dog pawprint icon: Mariam/Adobe Stock

The authorized representative in the EU for product safety and
compliance is Penguin Random House Ireland, Morrison Chambers,
32 Nassau Street, Dublin D02 YH68, Ireland. https://eu-contact.penguin.ie

FOR ELSA,
THE DOG THAT CHANGED MY LIFE.

CONTENTS

PART THREE

OUR PURPOSE 195

PART FUR

DOGIST RESOURCES 249

INTRODUCTION

I owe my life to a dog. When I was two years old, my grandmother was babysitting me, and she decided we should go for a walk: me, her, and her six-year-old black Lab, Oreo. When we got outside, my grandmother realized she had forgotten her jacket, and she ducked back in the house. By the time she came outside again, I was gone. So was Oreo. My grandmother called my name, called Oreo's name, and looked everywhere. There was no trace of us.

She ran back inside to call my parents, who immediately called the police. Everyone was losing their minds, which were suddenly filled with the most terrifying visions: a fall into a well, a kidnapping, worse. The police started to look for me, but they couldn't find me either.

About twenty minutes later, a landscaper in the neighborhood saw a black Lab walking around the road. Next to the dog, closer to the curb, was a toddler: me. Whenever I tried to wander off the sidewalk into the street, Oreo herded me back, like a hairy guardrail on four legs.

There was no footage taken of this event, and my grandmother, understandably, clams up when the story is brought up, so I only have the story my parents often retell as proof that it happened. That, and the manufactured memory I've created over the years each time the story is retold. But I have a ton of proof that this kind of thing happens all the time. Go online and search for stories about dogs rescuing children. There's the one of a German Shepherd saving a kid from being attacked by another dog, a Boston Terrier in Connecticut that alerted parents when a toddler began turning blue, a Border Collie in Texas that somehow knew that a teenager in the family was having a stroke. One of my favorites is one of the simplest: a Bernese Mountain Dog sitting on the floor near a crawling baby, a flight of stairs on the other side of the dog. The Berner knows the stairs are a hazard and that the baby is too young to know any better. As the baby starts to wander near the staircase, the dog repositions itself to block the baby from getting anywhere near it. The whole video is under a minute, but it's hard to watch without tearing up a little bit.

Those moments should fill us with wonder. They should remind us of the power of technology to connect, not just to divide. But they should do more than that. They should encourage us to think more about dogs and the roles they have in our lives. They should answer any questions we might have about animal intelligence, or the bonds between dogs and humans. They should help us to understand why an otherwise perfectly sane person would exit the ordinary work world and devote himself to photographing dogs as they walk along city streets—and not only photograph them but ask about the way that they affect the lives of their owners, and then write a book about that amazing process. That otherwise sane person would go out into the world, not just the city streets around him but to Puerto Rico, to China, to a prison in upstate New York, on a cross-country drive with his recently unemployed brother, all in the service of understanding the ways that dogs make the lives of their people better in every way.

I am that otherwise perfectly sane person.

The Dogist—the blog I run on Instagram and other social media platforms where I post photographs of dogs that I encounter on the street—started in 2013, when I posted a picture of a Boxer I met in Vienna, Austria. In some sense, though, I've always been a Dogist.

As a child, I loved animals in general. As a very young kid, I mostly kept rodents: guinea pigs, mice, rats, and hamsters. My family branched out from there. We owned parakeets. My aunt had a potbellied pig. My mom always half-joked that she would love to have a pet chimpanzee, and I wouldn't put it past her. I grew up in a scientific household—both of my parents are physicians, as were both of my paternal grandparents. The pig-owning aunt was a veterinarian, and my maternal grandfather, Leon Weiss, was a pioneer in animal research and the founder of the Center for the Interaction of Animals and Society at the University of Pennsylvania.

In this world of animals, not all species were equal. Or rather: no other species was the equal of dogs. They were *the* pet, as important to the household as people. I grew up mostly around Labrador Retrievers like Oreo, though we also had Poodles, Doodles, Goldens, a Pug, and even a Brussels Griffon (they're a fairly rare toy breed, part of a broader Belgian companion breed called Smousje, which reads either like a *Star Wars* character or a typo). In this mix of breeds, Labs were held in the highest regard. Their names were Ruby and Snowy, Matilda and T-Paws, Rigby and Mr. Bigglesworth (named for the hairless cat in the *Austin Powers* movies—we called him Biggie), Babka, Bialy, Willy, Tuggy, Layla, Bailey, and Maggie. Ruby, a black Labrador Retriever, was "my" dog—she belonged to the family, but she and I had a special bond.

Dogs were a constant presence in the house, but they were even more so during summers. We spent the season on Cape Cod, in a town called Woods Hole, where we had a family compound with room not only for my parents and siblings but also aunts and uncles and cousins—and their pets. At any given point there were an average of five dogs living with us. Our kitchen had a comically large communal water dish in it, and you always had to watch where you stepped in the front yard, if you dared cross it. When the dogs escaped, we would always know where to find them—the closest beach. It was someone's private beach, but our family referred to it as "Dog Beach."

I was also a photography enthusiast, in part because my dad was. Most of my friends went to camp during the summer. I went to something called "Science School" (formally Children's School of Science), a four-week program where we collected ocean specimens and pinned insects. My earliest pre-Dogist moment must have been during my advanced photography class at Science School. We were tasked with submitting entries of our best work to the photo contest at the local fair. My first roll had boring images of flowers, buildings, and cars. But the last few frames were of a dog I had met. I went on to start a "company" with my cousin Aaron called S&R Studios, named for Snowy & Ruby. We were only ten or eleven years old, but we had business cards printed and made films. "Films" may be too grandiose a word. They were essentially short, shaky videos starring our dogs. Our magnum opus showed our portly Labs, Ruby and Matilda, walking around the yard as the *Cops* theme song, Inner Circle's "Bad Boys," played in the background. We thought it was hilarious.

Those first videos didn't make me a legendary dog filmmaker, a Steven Spielbark or Alfred Hitchwoof or any other terrible pun. But I stayed close to photography. If I couldn't be a rock musician (I tried) or a professional tennis player (also tried), that was at least possible. I admired the discipline and work ethic of Ansel Adams and the eye of Henri Cartier-Bresson. Most of all, I was fascinated by the concept of "the decisive moment"—the idea that you could capture a slice of time and space that would, when fixed as a photographic image, mean something more profound.

I remained an enthusiast but, after college, got a normal job. Then I lost that job. After losing it, I had a brainstorm. The early 2010s were a golden age for NYC street photography blogs. *Humans of New York* (created by Brandon Stanton) and *The Sartorialist* (created by Scott Schuman) were sensations, carried into the world by new social media platforms like Instagram, Facebook, and Tumblr. I thought it would be funny to create a spoof or spin-off of *The Sartorialist* that featured dogs posing like NYC's fashion-forward crowd, with the same simple caption style: location, name, a brief remark. If these people were so deserving of getting photographed for a popular blog, their dogs deserved it, too. I also knew that dogs were beloved, and not just by me—when I would post images of them on my Instagram, they got more likes and comments than almost anything else. I made a business card for my new project, just as I had for S&R Studios. I remember walking through Williamsburg in the fall of 2013 and coming upon a brindle Frenchie. I asked its owner if I could take its picture. "What's it for?" he asked.

"The Dogist," I said. It rolled off the tongue perfectly. A day later I made my first post. The sky was the limit. And that was where The Dogist went. The Dogist not only put me out in the street for years, meeting people and their dogs, but it brought me to college campuses and corporate boardrooms and countries around the world. It brought me to professional sports stadiums. It even brought me to the White House. What propelled me from place to place was a fundamental truth about dogs: people love them. That fundamental truth is actually a number of other truths rolled into one. People love them because they need them, and they need them because dogs are intimately connected to people's ideas about themselves. They make people better and stronger, at once more serious and sillier, in touch with their better natures. We love spending time with our dogs, and we sense that doing so is therapeutic, but we might not know exactly why.

This book explains and explores various versions of why. For starters, it looks at how our dogs help us understand our own identities—not only do they mirror us in fascinating ways, but the process of dog selection forces us to recognize certain aspects of ourselves. Second, it investigates the way that dogs teach us about relationships—not just our relationships with them but our relationships with other humans. And finally, it explores the ways in which dogs are creatures of purpose, and how the way they embody that purpose can help us to find our own purpose. In every facet of our lives, we would be wise to conduct ourselves with our dogs in mind. What I am laying out is a ground-up rethink of the way we engage with the world, a full advancement and enhancement, aided and abetted by our dogs. We can only be the people we are, but we can be better versions of those people if we let dogs into our lives.

Dogs can modify the way we move through the world. But they can also modify the world that we move through. If we watch our dogs closely, they can teach us how we can shift our human perspective for the better. As a species, we have not always gotten it right, and in recent years we have sometimes gotten it spectacularly wrong. We live in a time when opinion is the main currency, when facts have become questionable things, when each individual, having been granted a theoretical platform to be heard, has to then fight to be heard over the noise and against the tide of trolls. All these factors have bruised our sense of optimism and our willingness to extend ourselves into the world. We are more self-conscious than ever and at the same time more isolated. I sense this all the time, because my job involves venturing out into the street and connecting with other people, at least for a few minutes. When I approach another person on the street, I sense an initial resistance. If we were just two people at a party, or in a classroom, or at an airport, the resistance would probably win out. But because my attempt to connect with them is routed through their dog, they tend to stay in the moment. That's when I sense something other than resistance: I sense relief. People are hungry for engagement. They need it, even when they don't know that it is what they need. That's the first spark of a series of larger epiphanies. Once we recognize that our dogs inspire our love and empathy, our social instincts and our unselfconscious enjoyment of the world, we are more likely to venture down that path.

I mentioned how Oreo saved my life when I was a toddler. In the years since, I have encountered dogs that help save people from drowning, dogs that find people lost in forests or buried by avalanches, dogs that defend people from bears or mountain lions. But dogs save us in less dramatic yet more profound ways as well. Simply by being themselves, they can teach us not to be self-conscious and vain, help us to reset our priorities, and keep us away from certain kinds of error and confusion.

Over my decade as The Dogist, I have learned that no two dogs are exactly alike. This one likes chasing squirrels. That one has destroyed three comforters. The other one can reach speeds of more than forty miles per hour but prefers a speed of one mile per hour. At the same time, all dogs are the same: they increase and intensify the human capacity for love, joy, and honesty. I want this book to reflect the tone I have created at The Dogist: curious, friendly, unafraid to be silly, informative but not in a pedantic way. The tone should be inclusive because the message, too, is inclusive. We can get closer to living our best lives, but to get there we don't need some arcane spiritual system taught only at a retreat halfway up a mountain in an obscure part of Oregon or in a tent at a music festival. All we need are these adorable, furry creatures. In that spirit, I have punctuated each chapter with a quote from a dog owner I have met through my street encounters as The Dogist. They're not hard to find: I have marked them with an icon: 🐾. They offer a brief breather, a place to . . . paws.

A human life improved by a dog isn't just a theoretical concept. It's a real-life event that happens a million times a day, all over the world. I have a friend named Angus. He's smart and good-looking and has an interesting job selling rare vintage sports cars to high-end collectors. But he suffers from somewhat debilitating anxiety and depression, invisible to you, glaring to him. Over the years, he has tried a variety of treatments and cures: he's taken, alone or in combination, a buffet of drugs including Klonopin, Lexapro, Zoloft, Celexa, Paxil, and more. Each has its effects and side effects, and each has brought temporary relief, but a few months later he'll feel himself sliding back down.

He went through one of those bad patches recently: a breakup destabilized him, and his sense of isolation deepened. I kept in touch with him as much as I could without making him feel he was being monitored, and one day he texted me to hang out, grab some food, maybe have a beer. One of us said "bro-time," not completely ironically, and the other one didn't object. We met up at one of my favorite local bars, Tom & Jerry's on Elizabeth Street. The bar is named for the Christmas cocktail—eggnog with brandy or rum—rather than the cat-and-mouse team, but it does have an animal component, which is that it's an unofficially dog-friendly bar, which is a significant reason why it's one of my favorites. When I went to meet with Angus, I brought my dog, Elsa, along—she needed to get out of the house to pee anyway.

The three of us hung out, two of us talking about anything and everything. I complained about something minor related to my work, to take his mind off whatever was plaguing him. He was the one struggling with an overt emotional downturn, but the more we talked, the more the difference between our lives dissolved. It wasn't that I discovered that I had equal or even similar problems to his or that his problems went away: rather, both of us discovered that we were in the middle of this confusing, sometimes taxing midthirties existence. These kinds of hangs and talks were more common in my twenties, though we didn't have any real issues to talk through back then. As we got older, as the larger issues started to take shape, the bro-time was increasingly hard to come by. Life catches up to you. You get busier. You get older. You get a serious girlfriend or fiancée or wife. People start having kids. The balance shifts away. It was a therapeutic process for us: on the walk home with Elsa, I felt lighter, and I could tell Angus's spirits were lifted. The next morning Angus texted me to confirm they indeed were.

The first time went so well that we scheduled a second, and a third. The talks continued to be a tonic for both of us, but I also started to see that Angus wasn't getting this kind of thing—casual but intimate contact with someone he trusted and who supported him unconditionally—in the rest of his life. One day we met not in the bar but out for a walk with Elsa in the neighborhood. Before we did, I needed to move my car to the opposite side of the street for parking. "Here," I said to Angus, and handed him Elsa's leash. When I came back from moving my car, when I saw him with a dog, I could see that he also saw himself with one. He was looking down at Elsa with a smile on his face. There was a connection that had happened just through holding the leash.

But I wasn't about to give Elsa to Angus. I had another idea. The next time we met, I shared my thoughts. "Dude, you should get a dog," I said. He brightened until I said the next part: "A service dog." At that, Angus tilted his head strangely, like I had spoken a phrase in a foreign language. "Service dog?" he repeated. I understood why. The world of service dogs is exceedingly nebulous unless you've seen it up close. There's a sea of them out there, on the streets of cities, in suburban malls, many wearing vests that say "Service Dog" or "Emotional Support Dog" or just "ESA" on them. But the vast majority of those vests aren't issued by accredited organizations. Rather, they are purchased off the internet—they'll run you twenty bucks on Amazon. I am not advising that you buy one and not shaming you if you have bought one. I am just explaining that the proliferation of those store-bought vests muddies the waters. The dogs that walk around sporting them must improve their owners' moods, I am sure, but they are not necessarily doing the things that a specifically trained dog does. They are not staying completely silent and calm under the seat on flights and at restaurants. They have not learned to pee and poop on command. They are not restraining themselves from pulling toward that piece of pepperoni on the ground or that squirrel in the park. Those retail-vest dogs are certainly of service, but they are not truly service dogs.

I explained some of this to him. He absorbed it. But he had something else to say. "Me?" he asked. I understood that confusion, too. The accredited organizations that train and place service dogs typically focus on a few kinds of clients: people who are visually impaired, people who are physically impaired, people with medical alert needs, and retired veterans and first responders who often endure debilitating PTSD. Angus was just a *regular guy* suffering from a serious but invisible malady.

When I got done explaining this to Angus, his head wasn't tilted anymore. It was nodding, if tentatively. "Maybe I'll rescue a dog to become my service dog," he said. I've heard this idea before. While noble and certainly possible with experienced trainers, it adds a significant degree of variability in an already tricky equation. "Or I could get a puppy and train it."

"That's possible," I said, "but do you feel that you're up to the challenge of training? Do you have the knowledge, time, energy, and patience? Most likely, you'd mess it up. I mean, I'd mess it up. Most people would. The nuance of raising any dog is difficult, and a service dog is a thousand times harder." I suggested that he start looking at breeders who have had success with service dogs. If they had credibility in that world, he could investigate further.

In the weeks after I pitched Angus on a service dog, he was traveling for work, and we didn't check in as often. When we did talk, I circled around the dog idea. I didn't know where it was going. Like many friends who have come to me over the years and broached the subject, I expected he would become overwhelmed by the complexity of the decision and punt on it indefinitely. It's hard to commit to a dog, to take that step. There usually has to be some catalyst that pushes you over the line.

Then one day I got a call. "I'm at the airport. I'm going out to Iowa." He had found a breeder with a good reputation for training service dogs. They had several dogs that were somewhere between six months and a year and a half that they had put through their service dog training program. "Any advice?"

I did have one piece of advice. Even though people shine to the puppy that comes forward toward them, it's smart to keep an eye on the one in the back that seems a little more reserved. That's often the calmest dog. (This is probably something that my aunt, the vet, instilled in me.) He wasn't going to be meeting weaning puppies in the pen, but the same principle would apply to the six-month-and-older dogs he would meet.

"Okay," Angus said. He told me that the dog he had pictured in his mind was a black Lab. His color preference didn't surprise me. His job required a high level of aesthetic engagement. A Ferrari not only had to be red; it had to be the right red—Rosso Corsa.

I repeated my advice. "Don't worry about the color. Focus on the energy," I said.

Iowa was freezing. Angus's rental car wasn't a Ferrari but some run-of-the-mill sedan that couldn't handle the ice. I got texts about sliding around on the road and then I got a video of a chocolate Lab. "What do you think?" he asked me. I wanted to follow his lead, but in my mind the dog didn't quite have the right energy. "I don't know if that's the one," I said.

"Yeah," he wrote back. He agreed with me, but he was a bit discouraged. He didn't like seeing all the dogs in crates, even though nearly all service dogs are crate-trained—you need to be able to leave them alone for a while or load them up for travel without issue. Day one had been a bust, but I figured he'd at least learn something and get closer to finding his dog.

The next morning went by, and though I was curious about how it was going, I didn't have my hopes up. But then, just after two in the afternoon, Angus texted me: "I think I found the one." What followed was a picture and a video of an adorable yellow Lab named Opal. I watched the video of the dog and recognized the same relaxed vibe I had seen in service dogs over the years. "YES," I responded. Then I took off caps lock. "That is the energy. Great-looking dog. Waggy tail, little derpy, curious, adorable. Winner winner chicken dinner." He called me, and by the tone in his voice, I could tell the dog was already working its magic. I was happy that my friend's outlook had just gotten brighter (and personally happy about having another amazing dog in my circle). We stayed on the phone while I walked Elsa through Washington Square Park, pulling toward the tree with the squirrels.

Angus left Iowa. The breeder told him they would finish the dog, meaning that they would give Opal extra training for city readiness, after which one of their trainers would drive her to New York. When he got home, he called me. He sounded a little nervous. "Big step," he said.

"Angus," I said. "This dog will change your life."

I'm not sure why I said it. It's not the kind of thing I usually say. As I spoke, though, I knew I meant it, both in the ways that we had already discussed—it would furnish regular companionship and sand the edges off his depressive episodes—but in a million other ways too. The dog would get him out of his apartment to go for walks. It would serve as a social bridge into conversations with new people. It would help him dodge the perils of the modern world—cellphone addiction, the numbing divisiveness of social media (though he's still my only friend to have *actually* deleted his Instagram). It would force him to build a structure around mealtimes, playtimes, bedtimes. It would keep him out of his own head. Over time it might even let him wean off his medications, or introduce him to his future spouse, or help him to understand what having a child felt like. It was the only sentence that made sense at that moment. As I heard myself say it, I realized it was not only the perfect thing to say to Angus but the perfect title for this book.

There was a long pause. He was taking it all in. "I think you may be right," he said.

Angus waited for Opal to complete her training and make the journey from Iowa. One day she arrived, and things immediately began to change for him. He told me about how he had gone on a date that ended poorly. Instead of doing what he usually would do—mope about it and wonder if his medication dose was high enough—he happily said goodbye at the end of the night, no hard feelings, and went home to see Opal. Opal didn't ask him what happened, or why they didn't hit it off at dinner. She ran to the door, tail wagging, and rolled over for a belly rub the moment he set foot inside. His angst and scarcity mindset were starting to wash away.

Angus is one individual dealing with a specific set of emotional and psychological issues. But what he experienced in those first few days with Opal is a universal experience, a transformation that I have seen in people whether they are single guys in New York, female veterans suffering from PTSD, people serving prison sentences for violent crimes, or children with serious illnesses. Throughout my time as The Dogist—and throughout this book—I have met so many different people with diverse stories who are forging forward in life with the help of their dogs, and myriad kinds of dogs that are in their lives for many different and important reasons. I have a group of friends that I keep close, and their dog stories are meaningful to me. But they are just the tip of the iceberg. Dogs are the ultimate human connector; they are what help forge and preserve happiness, community, and meaning.

You know the famed French anthropologist Claude Lévi-Strauss? I do, sort of—I remember hearing about him back in college and becoming aware that he wasn't the guy who had made my jeans. Years later, I ran across a passage where Lévi-Strauss was discussing animals, and specifically the ways in which certain animals become symbolic to certain cultures. The anthropologists before him argued that animals acquired symbolic status when they became central to human survival, which meant when humans realized that animals could be eaten. Lévi-Strauss pushed back on that. He argued for a second cause of symbolism—the moment when animals acquired meaning to us. He put it more elegantly: that some animals were chosen as symbols "not because they are 'good to eat' but because they are 'good to think.'" Dogs are great to think. And the more you think about them, the more you want to keep thinking about them.

One final note: The special essence of dogs, and the way that they serve as bright bulbs in the fixtures of our lives, has had many chroniclers over the years. People have written about them, painted them, given lectures about them. Some of the most affecting works on this subject are photographs, and there is a group of photographers who have dedicated themselves to exploring the essence of dogs, which also means exploring the essential relationship between dogs and their people. I count myself among that group. But one of the earliest and best was Elliott Erwitt, the French-born, American-raised Jewish photographer. Erwitt met giants like Robert Capa and Edward Steichen while he was stationed in Europe in the 1950s, and then embarked on a groundbreaking career of his own. Erwitt photographed major international events, from Richard Nixon visiting the Soviet Union in 1959 and confronting Khrushchev during the Kitchen Debate to the funeral of John F. Kennedy in 1963. But he was also a supremely gifted photographer of everyday life. One of Erwitt's favorite subjects was dogs, and he returned to them time and again in book-length collections like *Son of Bitch, Dog Dogs,* and *Woof.* There are so many of Erwitt's dog photos that are not only personal favorites of mine but also direct inspirations for my own work, to the point where it's nearly impossible for me to pick just one. But if I had to choose, I'd go with *New York City,* 1946, which shows a sweater-wearing Chihuahua at street level next to the feet and shoes of a woman. More than any other photographer I know, he understood the relationship between dogs and people, and understood how to capture and convey that relationship through simple, beautiful images. I try for a little of the same energy, intelligence, and soul in my photos, and sometimes—as in a 2017 campaign I did for Neiman Marcus (a series with little dogs standing next to models in designer shoes)—I get close. Erwitt, the OG Dogist, died at ninety-five as I was working on this book. I dedicate it, at least in part, to him.

ME WITH RUBY

PART ONE

OUR IDENTITY

CHAPTER 1

WHAT IS A DOG?

I feel kind of awkward that the last part of the introduction included a quote from Lévi-Strauss. Well, not totally awkward, maybe, but I want to be careful. I'm not an academic or anything close to it, and I don't want this book to be academic either. It's a celebration of the joy that dogs bring into our lives, and more specifically of the way that they can help us have a better approach to our identity, our relationships, and our purpose. It's meant to attain and then maintain a kind of emotional altitude, so I don't want it to feel too weighty. In that spirit, I want to issue a Dogist Pledge. Every time I quote a high-end academic thinker or author, I'll try within a few paragraphs to quote a comedian of some sort. In this case, it'll be Groucho Marx, who popularized the quote "Outside of a dog, a book is a man's best friend. Inside of a dog, it's too dark to read." When I first heard that quote, I was younger, and I thought it was funny. I still think it's funny, but I also think that it's profoundly inaccurate. Books *are* great, sure. No argument there. You're in one now, and hopefully you're enjoying it. But as it turns out, you *can* read inside of a dog. I've been doing it for years, trying to look into dogs through their expressions and movements, to locate their essence and understand how it changes our essence. What I have learned is that it's not dark at all. It's almost all about light, the special radiance they possess that brightens the world.

What is a dog? It seems important to handle that question before we start talking about how and why dogs improve the lives of the humans around them. Ask a zoologist—or, if you can find one, a cynologist (someone who specializes in the care and training of dogs)—and you'll get an answer that starts off like this: "Oh, good question." (Cynologists are very polite.) "It's a common domesticated animal, *Canis familiaris*, sometimes referred to as *Canis lupus familiaris.*" Then they'll probably clear their throat, politely, to signal that if you want to know much more, you should probably read their peer-reviewed paper "What Is a Dog?"

Even that brief answer, though, contains much of the story. Why sometimes *Canis familiaris* and sometimes *Canis lupus familiaris*? To answer that question, we need to travel to the past. Ready? Okay—it's not now anymore. It's long ago, maybe twenty thousand years ago, prior to or perhaps just at the beginning of the Last Glacial Maximum, an ice age in which sheets of ice covered most of North America, northern Europe, and Asia. These sheets of ice accounted for much of the planet's available moisture, locking it in place and reducing it elsewhere, and this in turn lowered sea level, expanded deserts, and created harsh and isolated environments. That's the world that early humans had to live in, and they shared that harsh world with other animals, one of which was the wolf. Wolves back then were not exactly like modern wolves, but they were close cousins of the gray wolf, which we ended up calling *Canis lupus*. Back then, I'm not sure what anyone called them. There was no Latin yet, obviously. There was probably a specific grunt that these humans used to alert others to the presence of this four-legged, furry, sharp-toothed, hundred-pounds-and-change creature.

Remember, it wasn't an easy time to be alive. Various species were competing for the same resources. At some point, these wolves began to interact with early humans. It wasn't all the wolves. It was certain wolves, the ones that felt comfortable enough to come nearer and nearer to the early humans, to approach their camps. They weren't just comfortable. They were motivated. Humans had food, and wolves, like all animals, like food. And they weren't just motivated. They were amenable. Many wolves tried to approach encampments and score scraps of food, but the ones that approached while still behaving in wolflike ways were most likely driven off or killed. They scared people. They were considered a threat. The wolves that got near or even into an encampment and got food were the ones that acted friendlier, even affectionate. Making friends with humans not only meant food but also a less harsh and hazardous environment. It was a relationship that benefited the humans as well— a symbiosis. Humans got protection, and a relatively sophisticated version of it. These animals were four-legged ADT alarm systems that could smell a threat more than a mile away, hear more acutely, and detect movement better under poor visual conditions. (Dogs, and the wolves that preceded them, have a tapetum lucidum, a reflector system in the eye that gives them better night vision. That's why most dogs don't have red-eye in photos; rather, their eyes look lit-up because the tapetum bounces light back to the retina, similar to a deer in headlights.)

Fast-forward in time. Those protodogs that found their way into the company of humans didn't stay the same. They began to separate from the other wolves not just behaviorally but anatomically. When humans encountered animals with a particular trait variation that we found appealing, we took them in, fed them more, and provided the safety and stability for them to breed. Their teeth got shorter, their ears floppier, their faces rounder—all outward markers of their friendliness, or at the very least signs of difference that humans came to see as markers of friendliness. The main thing that separated them from what came before was not just their docility but a unique awareness of and responsiveness to the moods of humans. These new animals were (drumroll) dogs.

Or rather, they were a kind of dog. Today, we have more than many. So why don't all specimens of *Canis familiaris* resemble those early wolves-into-dogs? For the same reason that there is variation in any species: individual mutations and interbreeding. Those early dogs ramified over time into more and more types of dogs. Scholarship in this area is somewhat muddy, so no one knows for certain if there were seven ancient breeds of dog, or nine, or ten, or twelve, or sixteen. But everyone agrees that in the period following the conversion of wolves to dogs, different types of dogs began to appear on the earth.

How this happened was complex and confusing, and pushed forward by a mix of natural dog interbreeding and human intervention in the process. Again, I am not a dog academic. I do not have an advanced degree in dog. I am careful to stipulate this in part because there are people in my family who have advanced degrees—biologists, doctors, veterinarians—and in part because I want to claim my own space as a dog enthusiast, dog evangelist, and dog documentarian (dogumentarian?). What this means is that I read whatever I can about dogs eclectically and seize upon the parts of my reading that stick. One idea that has stuck is the idea that there are sixteen basal breeds at the trunk of the canine genetic tree. These are the ancient rivers of dogness, and every dog now includes distant flows from them.

So what are they? Well, according to one study, the sixteen basal breeds are the Afghan Hound, the Akita, the Alaskan Malamute, the American Eskimo Dog, the Basenji, the Canaan Dog, the Chow Chow, the Dingo, the Eurasier, the Finnish Spitz, the New Guinea singing dog, the Saluki, the Samoyed, the Shar-Pei, the Shiba Inu, and the Siberian Husky. What's amazing is that they are still around, and I have run into them on my Dogist rounds. (I actually haven't met a New Guinea singing dog yet, but they sound incredible, no pun intended.) I remember a Finnish Spitz named Fritz whose owner told me "he's a big pain in the ass is what he is." Fritz was only two at the time, so he may well have mellowed.

In thinking about these original breeds, the main thing to keep in mind is that dogs, from the moment they appeared, were partly a human invention. They coevolved with us because of us, and it's not an overstatement to say that they are a part of us. We can say for certain that there would have been no dogs without humans. But there might also have been no humanity without dogs. How we moved from those first post-wolves to a diverse, fascinating, and wonderful universe of workers, helpers, and companions is central to our development as well.

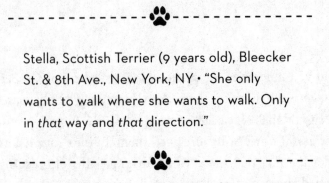

Stella, Scottish Terrier (9 years old), Bleecker St. & 8th Ave., New York, NY · "She only wants to walk where she wants to walk. Only in *that* way and *that* direction."

CHAPTER 2

BREEDING IS FUNDAMENTAL

D id you memorize the sixteen basal breeds? No? Go back and take another look at them, A to Z (actually it only goes A to S, which should make it easier).

How about now? Still can't pack them all into your head? Now consider the fact that the various forking paths of breeding have multiplied those sixteen basal breeds into two hundred modern breeds, and those are just the ones that are officially recognized by the American Kennel Club. There are people in the dog world who can rattle off the names of every single breed, believe it or not. Once, at an event, I talked to a man who claimed that he had met a woman who could recite them all in song form, the way that kids name all fifty states. "Can you show me who it is?" I asked. The man pointed kind of vaguely into a crowd of people, which wasn't any help at all, and later on I started to wonder if he had invented this breed savant. (If you are that woman, I apologize. @ me.)

Many things about breeds are hard to understand. Some have weird names (can you pronounce Xoloitzcuintli?). Some have weird backstories (the truffle-hunting Lagotto Romagnolo). What is easy to understand is that none of the breeds would have existed, or would continue to exist, without human intervention. You will never find a wild Pug. Humans domesticated the first dogs from wolves and then as time went on, invented more and more kinds of dogs. The modern dog world divides dogs into seven major groups, an organizational system that is not biological but rather functional— there are sporting dogs, working dogs, toy dogs, herding dogs, terriers, hounds, and even a non-sporting group that serves as a kind of catchall for dogs that don't fit easily into the other groups. The group system illustrates that all purebreds were originally created for a purpose, whether that purpose was hunting or pulling a sled or sitting in the perfumed lap of a noblewoman. Human ingenuity was applied in full, sometimes to the detriment of the nonhuman, as we will see, but it's still an amazing story of how one thing became many.

What's central to remember here is that from the very beginning, dogs evolved alongside people. They reflected changes in human habitats, human labor, human life. When humans started to hunt on horseback, they needed a dog that was a suitable companion for that activity, fast enough and focused enough to keep pace with the humans on horseback—the Foxhound. But what about the people who settled in a dense forest where horses were impractical and hunts had to be conducted on foot? The fleet hunting hound who could fly at those speeds might outrun a horseless hunter. The solution? Shorten up the legs to slow up the hunting dog—the Beagle. If you were a human who settled in a cold coastal climate, you might need a dog designed for beaches and shallow water. Maybe I could interest you in a dog with an oily coat for low temperatures, webbed feet for swimming, and a fat tail that can be used as a rudder in the water. Voilà! The Labrador Retriever. (That was the main kind of dog in my family growing up, specifically the English Labrador, which has a boxy head and a small, rounded "otter tail.") Water too cold even for a Lab? The Chesapeake Bay Retriever is your cold-plunge extraordinaire.

The result, over time, went in all directions at once: bigger dogs and smaller dogs, rounder snouts and sharper snouts, thinner coats and thicker coats, eyes and ears and tails of every shape. Think of how we buy our cars, how we take into account speed and size and handling and overall design. Dogs were diversified through a similar process, where each new form factor was also a function factor, and over the centuries, the early species that came out of the gray-wolf-in-encampment era became kaleidoscopically diverse, accommodating everything from tiny Chihuahuas to massive Great Danes. And even those two breeds can interbreed, though the mix (a Great Chihuahua, a Chihuadane, a Chidanedane?) has to be the offspring of a male Chihuahua and a female Great Dane because a female Chihuahua can't carry a half Great Dane to term. A crossbreed only achieved with the help of a stepladder.

Who sets up that stepladder? Again, people. People are the answer to any question about dog breeding. People made dogs to start with, diversified the idea of the species, and then developed and enforced breed standards. Out of a need for human order and classification, they started to define and clarify what made this kind of dog this kind of dog and that kind of dog that kind of dog. They formalized these ideas in dog shows, properly called "conformation shows." The first official dog show took place in Newcastle upon Tyne in the summer of 1859, and they grew into major global events. Crufts, in England, is the flagship event internationally, and America has three major shows: the National Dog Show, the AKC National Championship, and the Westminster Kennel Club (WKC) Dog Show. The WKC Dog Show has been elevated in recent years. While the National is in Philadelphia and the AKC moves around—it's been in Orlando and Long Beach—Westminster had a longtime home in Madison Square Garden in New York (though it was actually hosted in Tarrytown, New York, and the National Tennis Center in Queens during COVID but returned to Madison Square Garden in 2025). That gives it a regular TV presence, and it was also the setting of what is perhaps the most important dog show movie ever made, Christopher Guest's *Best in Show*.

I have worked the Westminster show as a photographer every year for the past ten years as The Dogist, and it's a largely joyful experience, a place to see dogs at their best, or at least their purebred best. I loved photographing Donald, a Bichon Frise whose owner both laughed and was dead serious as she told me that "his registered name is 'Grand Champion He's So Full of Himself.'" I loved seeing other owners care for their dogs with both intense personal love and intense professional rigor. The show is an almost perfect illustration of how human breeding has broadened the idea of "dog" while simultaneously narrowing the ideas of individual kinds of dogs. Every dog that is trotted out at Westminster must satisfy a very specific set of criteria as outlined by the American Kennel Club, and every dog that wins has to satisfy those standards at the highest level. That was true for Buddy Holly, the Petit Basset Griffon Vendéen who won Best in Show in 2023. It was true for Trumpet, the Bloodhound who won in 2022. It was true for Wasabi, the Pekingese, who won in 2021.

That kind of thinking goes beyond the show. Last summer, I overheard a conversation between a family, two parents and two little girls, who stopped to admire a woman's dog. "He's cute," one of the girls said. "Hi, puppy!"

There was a long pause before the woman spoke. "He's a champion," the woman said.

"That's his name?" the girl said. "Champion?"

"It's not his name," the woman said. "He's *earned* his championship. He's a show dog."

I am not relating this story to mock the woman. To participate in a dog show, let alone win it, her dog needed to embody the breed standards as articulated by the AKC, meaning that her Beagle needed to have a "fairly long" skull "slightly domed at occiput, with cranium broad and full," not to mention a "muzzle of medium length." And then there's the section on ears:

Ears set on moderately low, long, reaching when drawn out nearly, if not quite, to the end of the nose; fine in texture, fairly broad—

with almost entire absence of erectile power—setting close to the head, with the forward edge slightly inturning to the cheek—rounded at tip.

"Erectile power" doesn't mean what you might think it means, but this short paragraph still produces all kinds of performance anxiety if you are a dog owner (dogs, luckily, can't read). Creating dogs that exactly meet these standards can only happen with precision breeding. On the one hand, that illustrates human achievement—it requires focus and attention just like high-level gardening or high-level boatbuilding or high-level science. But it can also be problematic for the dogs, for reasons we'll get into a little later.

When I am out on the street doing Dogist work, I love encountering purebreds. They are beautiful animals. I have always felt this way. One of my favorite books as a kid was the dog encyclopedia, which lists all the breeds and their characteristics. Back then, I think there were nearly 200 breeds. Today, there are exactly 200. (Actually, that was yesterday. Today, another breed was officially recognized by American authorities, which brings the total to 201. It's the Lancashire Heeler, a relative of the Corgi that has been recognized by UK breeders since 2006 or so and was declared endangered. I have not yet run into a Lancashire Heeler, as far as I know. They are described as courageous and affectionate, and when happy, they look like they are smiling.)

The dog encyclopedia consumed me. To me, it was a combination of the Bible (I had reverence for the subject) and a shopping catalog ("What kind of dog do I want? Or for that matter, *dogs*—one of those, two of these, and sure, let's throw in a Pug for good measure!"). I liked the beauty of each individual breed and the differences between breeds, which extended not only to looks but to personalities. Terriers tended to be high-strung. Labradors and Golden Retrievers were laid-back. German Shepherds occupied the gorgeous-but-they-may-bite-you end of the spectrum.

As I got older, I developed a healthy skepticism. How could the book truly know how any individual Doberman would behave? As I got even older than that, the pendulum swung back a little bit: the facts out on the street support the idea of breed-specific personalities. Consider the Chow Chows. Chows were one of the most important dogs in ancient China. Medium-size (forty to eighty pounds), sturdy, with a thick double coat and a distinctive purple tongue, they were either originally bred there two thousand years ago or they were bred in Siberia in the centuries prior and drifted down to China through Mongolia. In China, they were used as work dogs, pulling sleds through swamps, and they were also companion dogs in the imperial court (they allegedly modeled for the lion statues outside Buddhist temples, though I have always thought that they looked more like little blue-tongued bears). The second of these responsibilities was a particularly good fit for their temperament. I have heard it described with all kinds of euphemisms. People have said that they have "discernment when it comes to strangers," or that they are "territorial," but the fact is that they are fiercely bonded to their owners and notoriously unfriendly to anyone else. In the modern world, they are a rare breed because despite their adorable fluffy-bear looks, they can also be a little bitey.

Some people aren't willing to onboard the baggage that comes with owning a Chow or a German Shepherd, and would rather bring a family friendly classic, floppy-eared retriever into their lives. Chows can still be a fantastic choice because they are so protective of their immediate family, including kids. It's just tricky to put them in environments where they encounter strangers regularly, which is why I'm always a little surprised when I see one in New York. I've seen Chows in the park in the summer, which is itself potentially problematic—their double coat insulates them so much that the hot summer weather can affect at least their mood and maybe their health. I remember running into a Chow in Tribeca. I'll withhold the dog's name to protect its privacy, but I can say that it had a human name. Let's call him Andy. The owner introduced Andy with a caveat: "This is a Chow—it doesn't like people." I went in with some overconfidence, like an NBA player on a hot shooting streak. My inner monologue was all about how the warning was directed at mere civilians, and how I would be the exception. *I'm The Dogist . . . I know how to speak dog . . . He'll see that I'm special and trustworthy . . . I mean, I may not be the Dog Whisperer, but I've done this ten thousand times . . . I'm an expert and I've NEVER been bitten before. I'm batting a thousand.*

My approach was strategic. I gave him some space and just stood there relaxed, talking to his owner to establish that one of his people was cool with me. I said his name and knelt down to see if he was ready to investigate me further. Finally, it came time to test that trust. I ruffled Andy's fur—or rather, Andy let me ruffle his fur. "Wow," the owner said, "you're the first person he let pet him like that." I was suffused with the glow of achievement, imagining some kind of magazine cover, "Dog Man Tames Chow," probably with gold lettering, which is the same thing I was imagining five seconds later when the dog turned and snapped at my hand. He was finished extending his goodwill.

Jack, Jack Russell Terrier (13 years old), Madison Square Park, New York, NY • "His name is 'One-Eyed Jack.' He ruptured his eye due to high blood pressure. We both have high blood pressure and take our medication together."

CHAPTER 3

DOGGELGANGERS

Breeds multiplied because people needed companions that specifically reflected their lives. Initially, this took the form of dogs designed to perform precise tasks, but it's persisted into the modern world of pets. Do you consider yourself an active person, the kind who likes to wake up at dawn and go on a hike? Get yourself an appropriately active breed, maybe a German Shorthaired Pointer. Are you more the homebody or shy type? Maybe try a Shih Tzu. For that matter, if you are a large Cape Cod family containing a future Dogist, consider an English Lab that loves to retrieve tennis balls out of the cold Atlantic Ocean and entertains all five kids in the house by begging for table scraps of the burgers your parents made lovingly but also definitely overcooked. (Our Labs were all overweight.)

But dogs aren't picked solely for functional reasons. My average workday involves donning my Dogist garb, grabbing my camera, and heading out into the street to stalk dogs and their people, and that means that I have seen thousands of dog-human pairings. Some of them are precise mirrors: the J.Crew couple with the Vizsla, the muscle-bound young guy in a sleeveless T-shirt leading around a giant Harlequin Great Dane, the woman in her late twenties with a Mini Labradoodle that has 4,372 Instagram followers (and is upset that the number is down slightly from the week before). In these cases, dogs are highly visible cues, signaling the essence of the human who accompanies them. This kind of visual matching is more prevalent now than ever, in large part because of the ways in which social media, and particularly Instagram dog culture, foregrounds aesthetics.

For proof that dogs visually reflect their owners, you don't have to believe me. Believe science. A 2009 study at Kwansei Gakuin University in Nishinomiya, Japan, asked people to match dogs and owners only from headshots. They were right 80 percent of the time. Even when some human facial features were obscured, the pairing was still apparent to participants more than 70 percent of the time. The author of this study, Sadahiko Nakajima, noted in his abstract that he was not breaking new ground so much as confirming the findings of existing studies:

> Previous studies conducted in the United States and Venezuela have demonstrated that people can correctly match portraits of unknown purebred dogs with their owners at statistically significant levels, suggesting that the popular belief in dog-owner physical resemblance is empirically valid.

And you don't even have to believe science. You can believe movies. In the male-bonding comedy *I Love You, Man*, Jason Segel's character coins a term for people who look like their dog: "bowsers," he calls them (as opposed to meowsers?), and the film then flashes to an especially egregious pairing, a woman with puffy white hair walking an equally puffy doggelganger. (If you go in the other direction, you can create instant comedy. Think of the scene in *True Lies* where Arnold Schwarzenegger walks a Chihuahua in the rain. It's layered comedy, of course—the size juxtaposition alone is comical, and Schwarzenegger is also playing a superspy camouflaged as the typical husband doing rainy-day dog-walk duty, so the low-key pet works as part of his cover story.)

Dog ownership is not always about finding a dog that's an aesthetic match. But it is fairly often about finding a dog that has a certain look. Some people like their dogs big, some like them small. Some like fluffy, some like sleek. Some want their dog to look similar to the dog they had growing up, or to look exactly the opposite. Now and again you'll find someone who has their heart absolutely set on a corded breed, like a Puli, a Bergamasco, or a Komondor—this last one is best known as the mop dog from the cover of Beck's *Odelay*. (Mark Zuckerberg has a Puli named Beast. A bit of trivia for when you meet him or another Puli owner: the plural for the breed is Pulik, not Pulis.)

Pairing people with the right dogs has always been a complex process, one that combines selecting from available breeds and developing new breeds. That process can be a vexed one. Take the Pug. Pugs first came to Europe from China in the 1700s. People liked the breed, which was a favorite of royals. Back then, though, the Pug had a different appearance than it does now. Its face was longer. Its legs were stronger. Its features were more evenly proportioned. Over time, it became clear to breeders that there was a demand for dogs with a more conspicuous puggishness. Chinese Pugs were crossbred with Dutch Smoushonds, Rat Terriers, and other breeds, and the resulting dogs started to look different from their ancestors. Their features got smushed, especially the snout. The eyes bugged out. The body got bigger, the legs smaller. The tail took on a unique curl, but at the expense of the straightness of the dog's spine. Because of the aesthetic desires of owners—you could even say "whims," if you were so inclined—Pug anatomy was distorted and distended. The consequences were serious for the breed. A narrow breeding line increases the incidence of genetic diseases, and today Pugs are prone to respiratory issues, skin infections, brain infections, and more.

While most breeds of dog have a life expectancy of eleven or twelve years, Pugs tend to shuffle off their very wrinkled mortal coils before the age of eight or nine. That might only seem like a few years in human terms, but it's the equivalent for a human of dying in your early sixties instead of your mideighties.

The dogs that are the end result of this process are indisputably treasured and loved. Out in the field, doing Dogist work, I have consistently heard from Pug owners that they are especially adaptable, and make for good travel companions. They even have success in agility competitions, though they aren't setting any land-speed records. And there's no denying their cuteness, whether it's Noodle or Baxter or Wilbur or the especially cute year-old Pug I ran into downtown named Morpheus. His affinities included hiding behind curtains and licking the genitals of other dogs ("You don't have to write that," his owner said, and I wrote that down too). But Pugs are also a conspicuous case of breeding with human ends in mind rather than canine ends. Similar problems afflict French Bulldogs, which can't give birth without Cesarean section and thus would be extinct within a generation if humans didn't keep producing them. While I was researching the hazards of breeding, I ran across an article on Encyclopædia Britannica's website about teacup dogs. Its argument was roughly the same, but its presentation was very . . . encyclopedic:

> The ofttimes incestuous genetic gymnastics required to produce these ever-more-portable companions, it turns out, have some rather nasty side effects. In order to achieve levels of diminution conducive to habitation in a handbag, unscrupulous breeders often resort to "backcrossing," or mating dogs to their immediate relatives, in the hopes of increasing the likelihood that the offspring will be equally tiny.

Ofttimes? Genetic gymnastics? But the point is taken.

While the history of dog breeding has been generally defined by a headlong rush toward refinement and conformation, there are also plenty of dog owners who are trying to reverse the course. Some advertising agencies have banned the use of Pugs and other brachycephalic breeds in their campaigns, under the theory that overexposure could promote irresponsible ownership practices—a supercute Pug in a commercial could kick off Pug fever, increasing demand without a corresponding awareness of risk. In the Pug world, specifically, there's something called the International Retro Pug Club, which is trying to reverse engineer Pugs back to their original form by breeding them with Parson Russell Terriers, Miniature Pinschers, Danish Farm Dogs, leggy Jack Russells, and others. These other breeds will produce in offspring an improved anatomy and a theoretically healthier genetic line—here, humans are no less interventionist, but they are determined to counter the historical trend toward the breed becoming an unhealthy caricature. A similar fate has befallen the English Bulldog, with some of its fanciers pushing the breed to look more like its healthier ancestor, the Olde English Bulldogge.

In addition, alternative dog shows are popping up across the world that reward not conformation to breed standards but rather health and longevity. Scruffts, an annual show that was started in 2000 by the UK Kennel Club as a kind of parody of Crufts, the nation's premier conformation show, awards trophies in categories like Child's Best Friend (a dog aged six months to twelve years handled by a child between the ages of six and sixteen) and Golden Oldie (dogs aged eight to twelve years). This show and others like it operate outside of the rigorous breed system—any dog is permitted to enter, not just pedigreed purebreds—though they do not seek to dismantle it so much as offer an alternative. Even Westminster has begun to allow All-American Breeds (i.e., mutts), to compete in their agility competitions, a welcome sign of evolution from an institution based on tradition. These dogs are changing human lives by awakening a sense of accountability to other beings, a sense of empathy with animals we all love, and in turn they are changing their own lives.

Lincoln, Labrador Retriever (7 years old), Nick's Fish House, Baltimore, MD · "He's afraid of lightning—he squeals and runs under the bed. He was named after the Great Emancipator, Abraham Lincoln. He grew up six blocks from the White House. His dog park friends were Jefferson, Washington, and Roosevelt."

CHAPTER 4

THE TAIL THAT WAGS THE HUMAN

J eff has been a friend of mine for more than a decade. When people ask me what he does for a living, I say that he's a computer genius turned artist. Is that a job description? It is for him. He was able to skip college and dive right into a career in coding. Jeff was in my apartment when I made the first Dogist post. A few years ago, he decided that he wanted to get a dog. This is not an uncommon occurrence among my group of friends, men of a certain age beginning to better understand how certain responsibilities can (should?) shape their lives. But this wasn't like my friend Angus, where the idea originated with me. Jeff thought of it all on his own and called me to see what I thought about it. Occupational hazard.

I typically start these consultations with broad thoughts and breed thoughts. Had he considered fostering a rescue dog? That's a major issue in the dog world, of course, and I didn't want to give it short shrift with Jeff. (I won't give it short shrift in the book either—we'll get to it in greater detail later.) Jeff cleared his throat. He was too polite to cut me off, but he had something to say. "I want a purebred," he said. "I'm sure of it."

"That's fine," I said. So long as a dog finds its way into a loving situation, I am largely neutral about how it happens, though I know that choices are made within a large, ever-changing system of dog supply and demand. (That's part of the "in greater detail" we'll get to later.) I started to run down a list of breeds that were popular in the city, among people with similar lifestyles to his.

He cleared his throat again. "I already know what kind of dog I want," he said. "I want a Basset Hound puppy."

"Well," I said. And then I said it again: "Well." I have learned a decent amount about Bassets over the years, and one of the things I have learned is that there are some very specific considerations that come with being a Basset owner. The issues begin with their singular anatomy. Bassets have big, long, drooping ears that hang down to the floor. This is a feature designed through breeding to aid the dog in tracking scents—the ears act like a big funnel, channeling all the little smells on the ground toward the Basset's highly sensitive nose. A Basset also has folds of extra skin on its face that cover its eyes when their nose is to the ground, further blocking out visual distractions. Their entire physique pushes them closer to the ground (long bodies and tails, but short, outward-facing legs) and even their name foregrounds this strategy: "basset" is derived from the French word "bas," meaning "low." The short legs also limit their speed, which is helpful for hunters trying to keep up on foot, which is additionally helpful because Bassets, as hounds, tend to follow their nose independently rather than listening to orders from humans the way a bird dog (for example, a Labrador Retriever) would. This can make them stubborn and harder to train, and that's not the only issue. With those huge ears and all those skin folds, you need to make sure they stay clean—they can be prone to ear and skin infections if not properly tended to—which leads to daily ear drops and skin wipe downs. They are also gluttons who will go to great lengths to find food, no matter how disruptive it is to the space around them.

That's just the initial maintenance. As they age, you have to be mindful of their long back and learn to support their long spine. You have to be wary of how they climb stairs and descend from the couch. And you have to brace for the inevitable back problems that will crop up. And then there are the rest of the issues: arthritis and hip and elbow dysplasia.

Jeff was a step ahead of me here. "That's why I want a female dog," he said. Female Bassets weigh about fifty-five pounds, while males can be sixty-five, too heavy to pick up and move around easily.

I conceded that point but was still reluctant to give my blessing. The headaches, I started to explain again . . .

"I hear you," he said. "But my mind is made up. My sister wanted a dog to go hiking with. I want a dog to sit on my couch and read with. Plus, they have such character." Here he was talking about the Basset's physiognomy, which can be exceptionally emotive. They communicate a kind of droopy sadness, or a droopy happiness, or a droopy droopiness. This is especially true of the European Bassets, which was the variety Jeff wanted. American Bassets' facial skin looks less droopy, essentially. The European breed is like a puddle of skin with a dog inside.

Jeff went on—it wasn't just that he wanted a Basset, but that he was already well on his way to getting one. During the first days of the COVID pandemic, getting a purebred wasn't easy. We have heard all about how new cars were backlogged: they weren't being built, so they weren't being delivered to lots. Getting a dog from a breeder was just as tough. All of a sudden, everyone wanted pets. American families were involuntarily, claustrophobically focused on the home, and the nature of the home was changing. Parents had to work in the same spaces where their kids played and went to school. Parents needed new routines to stay sane, and they also had to find replacements for the things that had previously filled up young lives—sports, band practice, jobs, visits from friends. A dog was often the solution. But increased demand outstripped the supply from breeders (who were already years behind in delivery times) and even shelters.

Jeff found a way around this problem. At the start of the pandemic, he had used his computer skills to utilize a website monitoring app that would alert him (and, more important, his mother) when vaccine appointments were available. He turned this same technology toward dog acquisition, changing the alert so that it monitored the website of his preferred Basset Hound breeder, Tait's Bassets. As soon as the site was updated—in other words, when there was a new litter—he was pinged. One day, he got out of the shower, saw an alert, and called the breeder right away. It was a litter of five, two females and three males, and he put down a deposit for one of the females.

"So you're not calling to consult me, really," I said.

"Not really," he said. "I wanted to know if you would take me to pick up the puppy." She was in Pennsylvania, five hours away. I had a car, and Jeff wasn't prepared to drive his Ducati motorcycle ten hours round trip, returning with a three-month-old puppy pooping and peeing in his backpack. (My friends also know they have a Dogist card in their back pocket, which Jeff chose to—wisely—play on a Basset puppy.)

"Sure," I said. The kennel was in a converted horse barn, where we were greeted by barking Bassets. Those were the adults. We found the puppies and then found Jeff's puppy. He had already seen pictures of her, but it was also love at first real-life sight. He had also already given her a name: Gertrude, Gertie for short, and even secured her Instagram handle: @badgirlgertie, which was a play on Rihanna's Instagram handle, @badgalriri. No fewer than a dozen of the women who frequented his local (dog-friendly) bar knew of Gertrude's imminent arrival.

When we left the breeder, I thought that he was right to do what he had done. He had found a being to love, a being who would love him. But within a few months, it was also clear that I was right about the rest of it. That first winter with Gertie was hard for Jeff. It was difficult to potty train her, and he discovered that it was in part because she had a persistent urinary tract infection—one of the other common complications of a Basset anatomy. She was having accidents in the house, and the vet prescribed a high dosage of antibiotics. It didn't work. More accidents. They gave her two more rounds over a month, and finally she was able to hold her urine. She also had cherry eye, a problem common to the breed that results from a prolapsed tear duct. Her eye surgery happened at the same time she was spayed.

Even a healthy, potty-trained Gertie ran him ragged, or so it seemed from how he described his life with her. "She has so much energy," Jeff said. "More than many other Bassets. But it's not general energy that you can direct toward anything. You have to like the quirks, stubbornness, shedding, and cleaning. When you walk her, she doesn't really walk so much as she goes out to explore. She's always sniffing. It's all about the floor or the sidewalk. If you pass a spot where a trash can has recently been, it's a five-minute stop while she reviews all the scents. She's incredibly stubborn about getting her way, so a slight alteration in plans, like her ball getting stuck under the couch, means this pained whining." Add to that the regular ear drops and wipes and the slobber that comes off a Basset like motion lines in a cartoon and the regular trips to the laundromat to fix up the various things that have been peed on or thrown up on or otherwise Basset-fouled. Add, too, the fact that she stays close to the ground means that she's constantly uncovering all that an urban ground supplies. "She is a detective of what's down there," he said. "Juul pods, syringes, baggies of coke." And add to that the specific physical limits that I had mentioned to him during our first calls. "You have to pick her up a certain way and be mindful of stairs," he said. "And even with care, it can really catch up to her. She's only three now, but I imagine that our future might involve an elevator building."

Jeff said these things over the first few years of his life with Gertie. But I noticed an absence of anything approaching real despair, anger, or consternation underneath his complaints. They were delivered matter-of-factly: *This is the dog that has come into my life, and now this is the life that contains this dog.* We were all maturing out of the shell of our twenties—the reluctant evolution to take on adult re-sponsibilities. Our friends were getting married, having kids. Making plans to just hang out the way we used to was getting to be impossible with all the more-pressing matters. If those other things weren't happening for you in your life, "Dude, you should get a dog!" was the recommendation because maybe it would catalyze the rest of those things. And even if it didn't, at least you would have something to busy yourself with while the rest of us became increasingly preoccupied.

More recently, I talked to him about how Gertie has changed him. "Oh," he said. "In many ways. She has made me feel okay about being home more in the evening. I have to go home first to take care of her before I go out and do something. It's like a speed brake on life." On top of that, his prediction came true—he has moved to an elevator building.

The change isn't just something he talks about. It's something I have noticed. I knew Jeff as a person who burrowed deep into his own preoccupations—not only was he a programming whiz, but he was a photography enthusiast. He built his own camera. He invented a photo app that produced slow-motion portraits. That person is still there, but now it's balanced by another dimension. He has a meaningful commitment that not only anchors him but forces him to set sail. "She's been great at helping me create a morning routine: I walk her, get coffee, get the newspaper at my doorstep when I get back. It keeps me outside my apartment and off my phone." Out in the neighborhood, Jeff lets Gertie take the lead. "When we are out walking, she clearly has more friends than me. Everyone looks at her. She's so photogenic, and she has a kind of bad-girl persona."

Gertie not only gives him motivation for circulating in the neighborhood during the day, but she structures his social life. "She's a great bar dog," he said. "Nobody doesn't like her. Everyone wants her attention and she isn't startled by crowds or noise." On Valentine's Day, Jeff had nothing to do, so he made a date with Gertie. "I put on *Homeward Bound,* the 1993 one with Michael J. Fox as the voice of the Bulldog and Don Ameche as the voice of the Golden Retriever. I was curious if she would watch it with me and she did!" Jeff liked the movie but had some concerns about the pacing. Gertie's review was not available at press time, though I know that she is a rabid fan of Ameche's work, especially late-career highlights like *Trading Places* and *Cocoon,* though she frequently asked Jeff to pause the movie to retrieve a fallen piece of popcorn.

Those are the short-term benefits. Long-term, Gertie has gotten Jeff thinking about the passage of time, truly and profoundly. Bassets have an average life expectancy of ten to twelve years. Jeff is already moving forward in his mind. "I'll be real depressed when she goes," he said. "I'll be what, forty-five?" His face overcast with this thought, he stood up and went to retrieve her ball from under the barstool that she's grown too big to fit beneath.

I remember once running into a fashionable couple walking a pair of Great Danes, Astrid and Klaus. They were a niece and an uncle— the dogs, not the owners. The owners were a pair of dog dads who were happy to share details about their pets' pasts. Astrid had contracted bloat when she was young and had almost died. She had recovered fully, though, and was now the dominant of the pair, lording her power over her uncle. And Klaus? "Klaus was in *Vogue,*" the man said. When he said it, I thought he meant "in vogue," and I was slightly confused. Great Danes are a medium-popular breed, maybe top twenty, but they don't compare to Bulldogs or Poodles. I eventually figured out what he meant, which was entirely plausible for two Harlequin Great Danes, cropped ears and all, being paraded down Prince Street in SoHo.

In America, different kinds of dogs have surged and receded in popularity over the decades. At the beginning of the twentieth century, Border Collies were the most popular national breed. Boston Terriers took over after that for a decade or so, with German Shepherds briefly popular (and then, in large part because of World

War II and the shift in our attitude toward Germany, less so). Cocker Spaniels, Poodles, and Beagles all had their times in the sun, and plenty of other breeds enjoyed stretches of popularity.

But human psychology is a strange thing, and sometimes prospective dog owners swing to the other end of the spectrum, where they value rarity and associate it with a kind of luxury. Breeds are converted to brands. At a Dogist event a few years ago about an hour outside the city, I met a couple who couldn't contain their excitement about the new addition coming soon to their family. It wasn't a baby. It was a puppy. And it was a very specific kind of puppy: a German Shorthaired Pointer, or GSP, a breed of hunting dog, energetic and versatile. GSPs are very willful—I remember someone referring to them as a "two-by-four" breed, meaning that you needed to train them with a two-by-four. Not actually, not seriously, but that was the spirit of the description. They are sturdy dogs, heavier than spaniels, and far more likely to run around your house or apartment knocking things over. When they come around to their training, they are great, but they require extra effort. The couple at this event had their heart set on being members of the GSP club. They wanted nothing less than that, and they wanted nothing more than that. After they were done breathlessly explaining their plan, they had a request: When their new puppy arrived, would I photograph it? Sure, I said.

For a little while, I got updates from the couple, all filled with the same level of extremely specific excitement. During the pandemic, the correspondence tapered off. The breeder supply chain had slowed, with some breeders shutting down entirely, and dogs were hard to come by. Six months went by when I didn't hear from them. Finally, they DM'd me. They had their dog. Could I come and take a photograph? They sent me a snapshot of him. He was a beautiful dog, like all dogs. I had done other similar assignments where I had to make minor requests of owners, like requesting haircuts so I could see a dog's eyes, but this dog looked camera-ready. We were good to go.

I got out to Grand Central early one morning and took a train out of town to meet the couple and their dog at a park near their house. I spotted them in the corner of a somewhat busy baseball field—no actual game in progress, but plenty of kids running around or playing catch with their dads. As I crossed the street, the man turned and saw me. He waved, and his wife straightened up and gave a half wave. Even from that distance, I could sense that something was wrong. "Hi," I said as I got within earshot. "Is this the new arrival?" They smiled a little too tightly. Their eyes had a little apprehension in them. When we started to take the first picture, I understood why. The dog that they had brought into their home and family, the dog that they had waited two years to acquire, was on edge and then some. It was clearly overwhelmed, even in a not-very-crowded suburban park, and it was seemingly trying to get away from everything, including me. This behavior wasn't altogether abnormal, especially for a puppy. I was another crazy new thing in its new world of craziness. But something else was at work too. This couple had imagined their perfect dog so specifically and for so long that they had preemptively created a high-pressure situation for their puppy, a narrow runway on which to land. New dog parents are often surprised to find themselves in the puppy-rearing deep end when their dog isn't as turnkey as they were expecting. When you try to curate a dog-human relationship in this way, fixating on a breed and expecting them to perfectly slot into your existing life, you may be barking up the wrong tree. Bringing a dog into your home, and into your life, isn't like hiring an interior decorator to match the couch and rug.

This account is not meant to diss this couple. Anyone who invites a new puppy into a loving home is doing Dog's work. And things didn't stay strained forever, you'll be happy to hear. Months after I showed up at the park to witness two people not quite understanding what—or who—they needed to be to give their dog a good life, I heard through a mutual acquaintance that the situation had improved. The couple had figured it out. Their dog had helped them to see that they were operating under a philosophy that was not fully productive, one focused on expectations, and it had also helped them to adjust it accordingly. They became flexible problem solvers rather than people at the mercy of inflexible presumptions. A dog's love, and a human's desire to engage in ways that protect and promote that love, is a powerful thing. It can smooth out rough patches. It can teach us lessons we didn't know we needed (or wanted) to learn. It can turn a tentative half wave into a full happy wave.

- - - - - - - - - - - - - - 🐾 - - - - - - - - - - - - - -

Hudson, Labrador Retriever (8 years old),
85th St. & Amsterdam Ave., New York, NY •
"She has a lot of energy. She walked thirteen
miles yesterday—we hike a lot."

- - - - - - - - - - - - - - 🐾 - - - - - - - - - - - - - -

CHAPTER 5

ORIGIN STORIES

Sometimes I learn about how dogs enter the lives of others while I am dog spotting on the street, searching for dogs to photograph. Sometimes I learn about it from my friends. And sometimes I learn about it from a female boxer in Puerto Rico. Not the dog kind of boxer. The human kind of boxer. A fighter. This particular boxer is named Chrissy Beckles, a petite blond British woman who can take and deliver a punch. (Her Instagram handle was once Chrissy Boom Boom.) These days, though, she is more about love than glove, as the founder and president of The Sato Project.

Puerto Rico is an island, and the types of dogs that exist there are determined in large part by that fact. People have to introduce breeds or else they aren't there in significant numbers. They can't just swim there from the mainland. As a result, Puerto Rico—like most islands—is home to a specific kind of island dog, locally called "satos." (In my early days as The Dogist, I was amused by the way New Yorkers debated pronunciation: "sah-to" or "say-to"? Tomato, tomahto.) Puerto Rico isn't the only place like this. Turks and Caicos has potcakes. Guam has boonies. Aruba has cunucus.

In all these places, the dogs are the result of generations of island breeding, and generally, these island dogs end up reflecting some combination of Chihuahua, Pit Bull, Labrador, Husky, German Shepherd: the usual suspects. The result is effectively a "super-mutt"— a hardy, medium-size brown dog that is perfectly suited for a life in warm climates, and likely as a stray. They tend to have shorter hair so that they don't overheat. They tend to be leaner so that whatever food they're able to scrape up or catch or beg for suffices; to be agile enough to avoid passing cars; and to be cute and people-friendly, too, which always helps. There are differences—satos have trademark "airplane ears" that jut out at ninety degrees, potcakes have more terrier-esque tulip ears, and boonies are more shepherd-like, thanks in part to the U.S. Army German Shepherd dogs left on the island to fend for themselves after the Second World War—but they are in all cases a combination of the dogs that survived, the opposite of pedigreed purebreds systematically bred by man. Darwinian dogs, if there were such a thing. Even though these dogs reflect animal nature, dogs are not purely nature without nurture. They are domesticated animals. And the fact that satos result from unregulated street breeding—they are often literally born in bushes or abandoned buildings—means that they multiply in unregulated numbers and become, over time, overpopulated. That's where Chrissy Beckles comes in.

Chrissy started boxing in young adulthood, after she encountered a prowler in her house in Manchester, England. That was in the nineties. She was working in advertising, but she wasn't entirely fulfilled (a situation I understand all too well). She ended up moving to the United States with her husband, Bobby, a stuntman, and she continued to box as a super featherweight.

That was in the late nineties. Around ten years later, Chrissy and Bobby were in Puerto Rico, where he was working on a film project. While they were there, she noticed the large population of street dogs. (You can't not notice them.) She also noticed that they weren't getting enough food or enough love. The couple got involved, first as adoptive parents, then through financial support, and finally through creating The Sato Project. The pugilistic tone remains: the organization has shirts emblazoned with their slogan, "We Fight So the Dogs of Puerto Rico Don't Have To." The project is a struggle in more than one way: Chrissy is so allergic to dogs that she puts Benadryl on her arms before she starts work each day. When you are dedicated to improving the lives of dogs, you learn to overcome obstacles.

The first time I met Chrissy was at a fundraiser for her organization. I remember thinking, "Why is there a boxing ring at this gala, and who are those two women fighting?" The various adoptable puppies in the room made the juxtaposition even stranger. Someone leaned in, pointed to one of the fighters, and got me up to speed. "That's Chrissy." I was as impressed as I was intimidated to meet her after her bout, but given her role as a savior of dogs, I wasn't surprised that she was a sweetheart when the gloves came off. After featuring a number of her adoptable dogs on the blog—and going to other Sato Project fundraisers that didn't involve Chrissy getting punched—I was invited down to Puerto Rico. Chrissy and her assistant and I patrolled the island in her Jeep, looking for stray dogs. We found several where she expected them to be: "Dead Dog Beach," a remote beach at the end of the island known to be the spot people slink off to dump their pets (and their guilt) and go home to live dogless lives. Within five minutes of arriving at the otherwise picturesque beach in Yabucoa, we found a pair of young puppies lying in the shade by an abandoned building. The first one was intrigued by us, and we scooped him up instantly, but the other one was shy, and despite Chrissy's expert puppy-talk, it disappeared into the dilapidated shack that had been ravaged by Hurricanes Irene and Maria. "Why don't we just go in?" I said (cavalier male instinct to be the hero).

"We can't," Chrissy said. "That building could collapse at any second. We can't have you in there."

"Oh," I said, sheepishly (cavalier male instinct to downplay mistake).

This was not Chrissy's first stray puppy. She quickly went to her backpack, i.e., her puppy wrangling kit, and opened a can of wet dog food. She left it close to the shack, but not *too* close. The puppy couldn't help himself. Within minutes he reemerged and crept up to the plate of irresistibly disgusting dog food. Chrissy gave me a wink, and, like a ninja, slowly closed in on Mr. Hungry while he gorged himself. I stood as still as a tree, so as not to spook him. Then, like a praying mantis, or a stalking cheetah, or a hawk (you choose which animal you want to imagine), Chrissy made her move and got him. We all breathed a sigh of relief. It had gone quickly. Sometimes it takes days to capture them. I got to hold Mr. Hungry on the car ride on the way to the vet to get them evaluated. They insisted I take a wee-wee pad (of which they had hundreds in the trunk) to put under/around him for the drive. "Just in case," they said. But it wasn't a wee-wee situation. All the contents of Mr. Hungry's stomach came out like a mystery meat purée volcano, mostly on the pad. The car smelled, uh, delightful. They told me it was a rite of passage. I may not have been thinking it in the moment, but that puppy puke baptism gave me a sense of purpose I hadn't felt before. I was rescuing dogs at the source. Right off the beach. The beginning of the supply chain. I had a hand in putting both of those puppies on the path to being spoiled by young Park Slope couples. They probably have their own Instagram accounts by now.

Chrissy and her rescue organization must come to terms with complex logistics and decision-making as they figure out how to move large numbers of dogs from place to place—specifically, from a place where there are an excess of dogs and/or a shortage of potential homes to a place where there are an excess of potential homes and/or a shortage of dogs. Once I was walking with a friend in New York, and we ran into the founder of a local rescue organization. My friend was either genuinely curious or great at pretending, but he stood at rapt attention while she explained the long and short of their mission. As we were leaving, my friend called them "virtuous puppy traffickers," and while I think it was a dark joke, there's some truth to it. And while each organization is slightly different in approach, I have noticed some common threads. Shelters tend to be started and managed by women, and there's a certain type of woman who is common in the industry—tough women, often excessively tattooed, who are hell-bent on saving dogs.

Still, the overpopulation (over-pup-ulation?) problem persists. The contributing factors aren't going away anytime soon. On top of all the chronic issues, there are acute ones, massive historical events that create temporary regional gluts of unhoused dogs. During the Camp Fire in Paradise, California, in 2018, for example, thousands of pets found themselves abruptly abandoned as families fled or were separated in the chaos. Some of them ran away at the first signs of fire and could not be found in time. People had to save themselves, and the days that followed the human evacuation brought pictures of the surviving dogs roaming what was left of the neighborhoods, often by where their house used to be. Usually all that was left standing was the chimney. I was invited by North Valley Animal Disaster Group (NVADG) to help document the destruction and to help reunite dogs with their families and find homes for the dogs that weren't otherwise claimed. The dogs were placed in a makeshift shelter at a local airfield, where they were given immediate medical care and food. Seeing this many lost and scared family pets was tragic, but the experience wasn't without some profound silver linings. While visiting the local pet food pantry (also makeshift), every person I spoke to shared the same sentiment: we lost everything, but we still have our dog, and that's everything to us.

Then there are even dogs that survive *un*-natural disasters. In 2020 I found myself on a Zoom call with Lucas Hixson, phoning in live from the Chernobyl exclusion zone (I make a point to try to personally visit and photograph the dogs of each of the projects I work on, but in this case I made an exception). After the nuclear plant meltdown disaster in 1986, the residents of Chernobyl were forced to flee and leave their dogs behind. The animals contended not only with abandonment but with radioactivity. Decades later, the descendants of those dogs still exist, with apparently more than three hundred living, seemingly happily, at the industrial disaster site. "They're not feral, but they are also not domestic," Lucas told me on Zoom as he introduced us to several of the dogs that had proved friendly enough to be given names and to be photographed. After raising some funds and getting the word out (and giving them a thorough exit interview with a Geiger counter), a handful of them were able to be transported to adoptive homes. Dogs are also displaced and abandoned during international conflicts. Anywhere people are losing their lives, dogs are losing their homes, and the world scrambles to figure out how to handle the aftermath. Canine tragedy, ironically, is often what makes people feel the inhumanity of war.

I am sometimes ruffled when I hear people say "we rescued our dog." Certainly, the dogs are "rescued" by people like Chrissy driving out to Dead Dog Beach. But once they make their way to New York, the term is a little misleading. Taking home that adorable four-month-old Beagle-mix puppy from the mobile adoption van in Columbus Circle over the weekend is certainly a wise, noble, and loving choice, one that frees up a direly needed kennel in a shelter. But you're not the sole savior. You're the one who timed it right and submitted a compelling application. Not all rescued dogs have it that easy. The more challenging cases—whether because of a dog's behavioral or health or cosmetic reasons—require additional consideration and additional love from prospective dog parents. These are the dogs that face potentially languishing in a cramped kennel for months if not years—the "long stays." These are the dogs, in my mind, that justify the sense of being truly "rescued" by their person, and these are the people who deserve the additional credit. You know who you are.

Each shelter has a different approach to finding their animals homes. Some foreground their puppies in their marketing to bring in families with kids who "want one," under the theory that once a family is in the door, it is likely to go home with a dog. Other shelters tell stories—true and sometimes maybe exaggerated—that foreground the urgency of a dog's plight. (I have heard from new dog owners more times than I can count that their dog was an hour away from being euthanized but was spared by their fortuitously timed adoption. This scenario certainly happens, but given the frequency with which I hear it, I sometimes raise a skeptical eyebrow.)

The Sato Project is one variation on this strategy. There are others. The Humane Society of Wichita County (it's in Texas, even though I would have guessed Kansas too) took in a one-year-old Dachshund-mix named Eddie in late 2023. At first, they wrote about him the way many shelters write about many dogs, explaining that he was shy and quiet, "a little nervous to be in the shelter," but ultimately a good companion. That didn't work. Weeks passed. The shelter changed direction, and instead of focusing on his cuteness or his neediness, the second post foregrounded the dog's orneriness. "Eddie is a 💩," the post said. "We want Eddie out of here because he scares our big dogs." The post worked wonders. Eddie was out of there within hours. The shelter's director, Cheryl Heineken, told *USA Today* that she had experimented with different kinds of sales techniques during her time at the shelter. When she had first arrived, puppies were flying out of the place, but older dogs were staying at the facility too long.

She tried to right the balance by letting the older dogs speak for themselves. "We would make cute little flyers like 'Oh, I won't chew on your flip-flops because I'm a grown [expletive] dog,'" she said. (It's not clear whether the flyer said "[expletive]" or included an actual expletive. Thanks, *USA Today*.) "Some people thought it was hilarious and we got quite a few shares on it, but then some people were like 'You shouldn't talk like that. You're supposed to be professional.'" But the profession is to move dogs through the system, to get them out of shelters and into homes. The automaker Subaru has even created a holiday, National Make a Dog's Day, which falls on October 22 each year. Through online and television ads, the company reminds Americans that "older and special needs shelter dogs wait the longest to find loving people," while showing them pictures of those dogs: a one-legged spaniel in a park, a shepherd with four prosthetic legs standing by a fence. The commercial can seem manipulative because it is, but the tugging of heartstrings can be a perfectly virtuous act if it results in adoptions. Big companies capitalize on the goodwill and warming sentiment of being proponents for dog rescue and using it in their advertising, and good on them. I've been the resident photographer behind the Puppy Bowl (you know, the one that airs the same day as the Super Bowl) for three years running. Picture me in a basement for three days photographing 120 puppies in a row. It sounds amazing, but it's work. Is the Puppy Bowl essentially a three-hour-long commercial for a slew of sponsors that you'll endure because there are rescue puppies running around "scoring touchdowns"? Yes. Does it give much-needed exposure to a bunch of rescue groups and sow the seeds of dog rescue with the general public? Also yes. Using profane humor, using adorable puppies as corporate shills, and excessively tugging at the heartstrings can all be perfectly virtuous strategies if they result in adoptions.

Shelters and rescue organizations alike are in a strange position. They are a reactive industry. All of them are actively working to stop the need for them to exist. If they could magically remake the world so that there were no unwanted dogs, they would gladly dissolve. But of course, that's not reality, or even close to it. As long as people keep being, well, people, millions of dogs along with other pets will find themselves unwanted. We spoke earlier about how natural disasters can abruptly unhouse large numbers of dogs. Economic and social disasters function similarly. Much of 2023 was a stressful time for families. Inflation upended many people's financial security, and that affected their ability to care for their pets, especially on the heels of the pandemic, which brought more dogs into homes and protected tenants with anti-eviction measures. Even when employees were asked to return to the office, their dogs were not invited, and the prospect of hiring a dog walker five days a week was an expensive one. Many of these dogs were also deprived of proper socialization or developed separation anxiety during that time, requiring owners to hire professional trainers. When circumstances changed, the COVID adoption pendulum swung back the other way, and dogs ended up being surrendered at a higher rate. This strained shelters even more. Some animal welfare organizations tried to help people keep their pets at home by giving struggling owners assistance with everything from food to medical care. This helped matters, but it didn't eliminate the issues entirely. What resulted was a dog economy even more strained, where questions of responsible care—and the consequences—became even sharper. The business card that I hand to every dog owner I meet has a slogan on the back: "The story of dogs." That's my mission in every photo shoot, every essay, every book. One thing I think we can all agree on is that all dogs are beautiful animals and deserve to be given their time in front of the camera. In the first press coverage I got back in 2013, in the *Huffington Post*, I was quoted saying, "All dogs deserve recognition," and I have always stood by that. But dogs also deserve to be treated like family. Dogs can change our lives, which is awesome, and they deserve the fundamental respect and kindness we extend to kin. Failure to provide that reflects human flaws—selfishness, shortsightedness, ignorance about options. We should work hard to do our best by our dogs.

----------------- 🐾 -----------------

Hudson, Pembroke Welsh Corgi
(4 months old), Washington Square Park,
New York, NY • "The only time he barks is
if you tell him no."

----------------- 🐾 -----------------

CHAPTER 6

GIMME SHELTERS

Over the summer, I spent a cloudy day doing Dogist walks in Brooklyn. In Park Slope, I ran into a friendly dog named Abu. The first thing I learned about him was that he was extremely photogenic. I don't know if he was aware of his handsomeness, exactly, but he was a natural. The second thing I learned was that he was a possessive humper. As the owner explained to me, Abu didn't like it when men came around and told jokes that made her laugh: when that happened, he went right for her leg. The third thing I learned about Abu was that he was a man of mystery. His owner didn't know exactly what kind of dog he was—he was a mixed-breed, black around the face and head and black and white along his body, probably at least part Border Collie. I couldn't even get a precise age, which is something else I like to post for the dogs I feature. "He's from a shelter in Miami," his owner told me. "My friend found him when he was going to college there ten years ago."

There would have been a time in my youth when this last piece of information—or lack thereof—would have surprised me. This was back before The Sato Project, back before I was The Dogist, back when I was just a shy kid in the Philly suburbs. As I have said, my family was a Lab family, but more than that, we were a purebred-Lab-from-a-breeder family. We had a relationship with one specific breeder, Dickendall Labrador Retrievers, and each time we were in a position to acquire a new dog, we got back in touch with them. My aunt Alice, the veterinarian, recommended the breed and the breeder, and we deferred to her in these matters. Even though Dickendall was in Texas, they had a reputation for the highest quality dogs, to the point where my mother was willing to drive out to a small airport and meet the new arrival, which had been transported to us by plane. This wasn't uncommon back then. In fact, this kind of thing was typical not just of my family but of most of the families we knew. It didn't matter if they went for Labs or Pugs or Poodles or Westies—the default process involved a visit to a breeder. In the two decades since, the culture around dogs has shifted, to the point where breeders are less and less commonly at the center of dog stories.

One of the first contemporary moves into crossbreeding involved a Labrador, in fact. Since the mid-1950s, dog owners had experimented with mating Labradors and Poodles together. In the 1980s, an Australian breeder named Wally Conron tried to increase the popularity of the mix under the theory that it would solve a very specific problem. The gentle intelligence of the Lab, which made them ideal as guide dogs, could be combined with the coat of the Poodle, which shed significantly less. The result would be guide dogs for people with allergies. Conron believed that this was a market waiting to be supplied, and he brought his Labradoodle to the Royal Guide Dog Association of Australia. They showed some interest, and the cross took off. The dogs were perceived as perfect family dogs, medium-size and friendly and hypoallergenic. In recent years, their popularity has increased further, helped along by the fact that they were often seen in the company of celebrities: Tiger Woods, Miley Cyrus, Taylor Swift, Henry Winkler. And they were cute to boot! Though the dogs had plenty of fans, Conron was not one. He has consistently expressed regret for promoting the crossbreed, in large part because the process resulted in the familiar breeding problems—health issues, temperament issues. His most famous quote, "I opened a Pandora's box and released a Frankenstein monster," is a kind of mixed mythological metaphor, but it gets to some of the inescapable truths of breeding and crossbreeding.

Conron's circumspection seems almost quaint now. In the wake of the success of the Labradoodle, other doodles followed, including the Goldendoodle (a hybrid of a Poodle and a Golden Retriever), Bernedoodles (Bernese Mountain Dogs + Poodles), and Sheepadoodles (a hybrid of Old English Sheepdogs + Poodles), to name a few. And there were other designer breeds as well: Puggles (Pugs + Beagles), Pomskies (Pomeranians + Huskies), Frenchtons (French Bulldog + Boston Terrier), and the interestingly named Sharp Eagles (Shar-Pei + Beagle). This last one makes you wonder if they'll ever breed giant flying predatory dogs. Squirrels, watch out.

Designer crossbreeds are one thing. Then there are the dogs that are nonspecific mixes. Before The Dogist, I would have used the term "mutt" to talk about these dogs. The terminology has evolved: mongrels, mixed-breed. My sense of things has evolved also. A dog that's not a purebred doesn't feel like the absence of a conforming identity anymore. It feels like the presence of an individual identity. If I am heading out for the day with my camera, I still wonder if I'll encounter a beautiful Golden Retriever or a rare Otterhound (I have yet to ever see one in the wild, outside of a dog show). But I also wonder if I'll run across a dog that is quite literally like no other, one whose bloodline has jumbled together so many breeds that I'm looking at a print run of one. A piece unique. Both possibilities excite me equally. My increasing appreciation, I am sure, is related in some way to my feelings about coming to New York as a young adult. I grew up in the suburbs, where homogeneity and predictability were easier to achieve. When I first arrived in the city, there was a noticeable change, an overwhelming and thrilling amount of action and interaction, interchange and change. The diversity and energy of dogs matched the diversity and energy of the place. Embracing difference, change, and unpredictability is just as much a human virtue as appreciating the beauty of careful planning.

This was a lesson I had to learn. When I started out as The Dogist, even as the site was hitting its stride, I found myself dogless. More to the point, I found myself self-consciously dogless. I was The Dogist. That was more than a job. It was an identity. Because of that, any dog I owned had to be . . . well, I hesitate to use the word "perfect," but that's the word that kept surfacing in my brain. It had to embody and project the best qualities of dogness. What if someone saw me out walking with a dog that seemed depressed, or pulled too hard, or wasn't well-behaved? What if I had a dog that barked too much or lunged at ghosts that only it could see? What if my dog was not aesthetically interesting enough? When I was out photographing dogs, I would think about what it would be like to have that dog in my life and, more often than not, decide that it wasn't quite right for me. I would look at dogs in the street and mentally cross them out, like Seinfeld picking a girlfriend. I was paralyzed. And maybe, I rationalized, it was somehow cool not to have a dog. Lots of rock stars didn't have partners, at least not long-term ones. I enjoyed the autonomy of being unattached, the freedom of a long leash—or none at all. It was lonely but fun. Single and dogless in NYC (note to self: future book title), I knew my dog days would come, but having everyone else's dogs—"dogs by proxy," as I called it—scratched the itch enough. Or so it seemed.

During the pandemic, I fled the city with my best friend for my family's summerhouse on Cape Cod. We made it to Cape Cod in a straight shot, stopping only for gas and toilet paper (one roll per customer). It was freezing cold. At the house, we bunkered in to deal with the upended world. I was trying to keep my work as The Dogist moving forward despite the fact that everything had changed. I went out around town with my camera once, but I could barely find any dogs out walking, and when I did, their owners crossed the street upon seeing an oncoming person. It was like I was a zombie. It was like everyone was. There was a local dog park that proved more fruitful, as dogs could approach me while owners stayed at the opposite corner. As long as I stayed masked and didn't touch their dogs, we were cool. Dogs weren't known to harbor the virus. When the well of local dogs started to run dry, I revisited old photos from my early Dogist days that new audience members might not have seen—"throwbacks," I called them. We also posted submissions from first responders and started something called The Dogist Olympics, funny contests where fans would submit pictures and videos for Most Extreme Head Tilt and Longest Dog. It was a great change of pace that brought some levity to an otherwise depressing time for everyone. But soon enough, I felt the restlessness seep in. It was like the movie *Groundhog Day,* but you couldn't talk to anyone or their dogs. My friend was good at making breakfast, but soon enough avocado toast and eggs got stale. My creative juices were waning and I realized it was entirely because I had lost access to dogs. I needed to do something about it other than sit like an idiot with my idiot friend (a term of endearment in our relationship) in the cold and suffer through a series of gray day after gray day after gray day.

One day, I broke. I needed access to a dog, and the path was clear: it was time to foster a rescue dog. This was something I had done very short-term in the past (maybe a weekend) but had never fully committed to. I knew there was a run on rescue dogs at the time too (probably even more so than toilet paper). As Jeff's Gertie-quest proved, the pandemic made everyone simultaneously feel the fragility of life, enough that the fuck-it-I'm-getting-a-dog sentiment swelled. Many people came out of the woodwork to see if I could pull a Dogist string for them to help them get a dog. Once or twice I did. Pulling my own string was a little easier—with my nearly four million followers (at the time) and a verified IG badge, I figured I would have enough cachet to get a dog to foster. I entered "dog rescue" into Google Maps and started down the list of results. I sent out some emails and DMs from my Dogist account, and one of the places got back to me pretty quickly—Sandy Paws Rescue, headquartered on Martha's Vineyard, across the sound. "This sounds great," she replied. "Could you fill out the foster paperwork on our website?" I got the sense that this was just a necessary formality. I knew it was happening. I was quickly approved and received an email. "How about Elsa?" it said, and the question was followed by a picture of a little girl petting a white dog. "Sure!" I said. I wasn't about to push my luck by asking to see their larger roster of dogs. This, after all, was *just* a foster dog.

All I had was a name: Elsa. A few days later a Toyota Camry appeared outside the house, and out stepped the Sandy Paws adoption coordinator, wearing a dog-hair-covered black sweatshirt—I would be able to tell you more about what she looked like except that she was wearing a mask, like everyone was that year. She opened the back door of the sedan, and inside was a crate with two or three adorable mixed-breed puppies and a medium-size skinny white dog. That was Elsa. The woman unceremoniously handed me the leash, ticked through a bunch of fostering details, none of which I retained, and went on her way to deliver the puppies to their foster parents. Elsa was a bit scared, but my friend and I led her into the house, feeling two things at once: *What have I gotten myself into now?* and *Who would entrust me with this incredible responsibility?* Elsa sniffed around the house excitedly, and then within minutes lay down for her first belly rub. An auspicious start.

She was a Husky-mix who had grown up in Texas. I announced Elsa on The Dogist, and that she was "available" for adoption, just like any of the hundreds of adoptable dogs I had featured over the years. But in my heart, I knew this wasn't the same. I shared some more pictures of her, but nothing about her availability. In my typical way at the time (it was similar to how I approached dating), I looked for reasons why now was not the time. Why she wasn't the one. Anything that would let me cop out of taking on real responsibility. Peter Pan Syndrome in a nutshell. But Elsa was infallible.

Sweet, good mannered, nondestructive, not vocal, and (mostly) housebroken. The fact that she was a gorgeous dog, too, didn't help.

The only issue we had was that she had a strong desire to go outside and explore—she was a flight risk. She liked me and my friend, but she was not fully bonded with us yet and had zero name recall. I reinforced all the exits with chicken wire, and when my parents came up to visit, I made a point to stress the importance of closing all doors behind them. This system worked until it didn't. My dad left the side door open while moving in some things. I saw the opening and so did Elsa, and we were off to the races. I don't think I've ever run as fast or as far for such a long duration in my life, not to mention that the lockdown had put me in the worst shape of my life. I vividly remember seeing Elsa bolt down the street in full gallop with her white tail tucked behind her for maximum aerodynamics. She was peaking and I was in a full panic, with complete tunnel vision. I knew the consequences if anything were to happen to her would be awful, not just for her, not just for my audience, but for me personally. I was beginning to love her. After darting through multiple people's backyards yelling her name at the top of my lungs, I lost sight of her. I felt like I had just majorly screwed the pooch. I called Ashley, the founder of Sandy Paws. She calmed me down and told me to keep calling for Elsa. This wasn't Ashley's first rodeo. As predicted, Elsa reappeared and I could tell that she was starting to lose steam. I gave up running and just walked toward her, and eventually I got close enough to make a lunge for her collar. I got a hand under it. I had outrun a Husky, or at least kept up. I could taste the iron in my lungs. I called my friend and he met us with a leash. My dad didn't leave the door open again.

Before that chase I had been in a state of running from everything, of avoiding anything lasting in my life. It took a crisis in the form of a Husky at full sprint to make me realize I *did* care for her more than I had been willing to admit. (That or trauma bonding. It isn't a fond memory, but at the very least it was the inspiration for her Instagram account name: @ChasingElsa.) I signed Elsa's adoption papers very shortly thereafter. I became what so many people in dog rescue refer to as a "foster-fail" (maybe technically correct, but a strange term for a success story). I had found my dog and Elsa had found her person.

Takashi, Akita (5 years old), Central Park, New York, NY • "He's my fourth Akita—I couldn't go back to any other dog after I got my first Akita. They're just themselves. He's quite exuberant, and he's a lot of fun. He doesn't steal food, but he'll steal mittens and gloves."

CHAPTER 7

TOO MANY DOGS?

Elsa's arrival reiterated the central argument of my life, which is that a dog can help you understand yourself and your needs better. It can clarify matters of human identity, both practically and psychologically. In part, this is because that's what dogs have always done, what they were designed to do. But it's not a one-way street. Both Gertie and Elsa ended up safe in loving homes, but the Gertie process and the Elsa process illuminate different ends of the spectrum, different parts of the larger systems that unite people and dogs. Remember when Jeff first called me and told me that he was thinking of getting a dog? My impulse at the time was to push him toward fostering to adopt. But Jeff had an idea in mind, which involved a breeder.

Again, I didn't mind. If a dog finds a loving home, I am on board with whatever process brought said dog into said home. And breeders are a major part of the large and complex economy that brings dogs into the lives and families of humans. At the most basic level, they are supposed to breed healthy dogs with other healthy dogs and offer healthy puppies to responsible people. There are guardrails that ensure that reputable breeders will carry out their mission correctly. A reputable breeder won't overbreed their dogs (veterinarians generally recommend one litter per female dog per year once she's two years old, and no more than three to four litters in her lifetime), or overburden their infrastructure (they won't whelp more than two to three litters per year, lest they divide their attention). Before placing a dog with a new owner, these breeders engage in a more extensive vetting process, both when it comes to the health scores of the dogs and the identity of their prospective owners. A proper breeder will never let one of their dogs end up in a shelter should their family not be able to care for their dog anymore—they usually make families sign contracts to that effect. Many will even make you agree not to breed your dog so as to control the population of dogs, to maintain the integrity of their breed, and perhaps to eliminate competition on the market and in the dog show ring. All of this happens because they understand that their core mission, to pair great dogs with great people who have an affinity for preserving their chosen breed, has a second goal, which is to make sure that their dogs don't end up abandoned in a shelter.

But not all breeders are reputable. Some, in fact, are the exact opposite. The country is littered with backyard breeders trying to turn the desire for dogs into dollars. And then there are puppy mills, breeders who capitalize on the demand for certain breeds through commercializing dog breeding. Bad breeders allow for quick transactions—a good rule of thumb (paw?) is that any breeder that lets you show up within a week and slap down your credit card is a bad bet. These breeders will often choose a trending breed, often have five or more concurrent litters on the ground at once, and have slick websites. They prey on the impulsive prospective dog owners who want to get a dog "next weekend," so they always have dogs ready to sell. There is a spectrum, of course, but the worst breeders treat their dogs with neglect, and are possibly abusive, breeding female dogs excessively like little cash cows. That's not to say these dogs are "bad dogs" or completely unhealthy—many live long, well-loved lives. But the risks for these dogs are higher. Veterinarians and dog trainers alike can often identify a puppy-mill dog, noticing congenital health problems and unpredictable temperaments. Poorly bred dogs not only tend to be more difficult in terms of health and behavioral issues, but the owners who impulsively acquire them often just as impulsively relinquish these dogs once the kids lose interest or they grow out of their puppy cuteness into a dog with all its adult dog needs. Maybe it's cooped up and won't stop barking, or maybe it chewed the couch. People will often surrender it to their local city shelter, citing "lifestyle change," and move on with their lives. Or worse, they will abandon the dog to fend for itself on the side of the road. This may speak more to the bleakest parts of human nature, but irresponsible breeding certainly enables and makes these types of outcomes more likely.

This vicious cycle strains a system that is already overburdened. This is the second, darker half of the equation. Any stray dog, roaming the street or living in an abandoned building, faces immense challenges. If it negotiates that gauntlet—if it avoids starvation and exposure to the elements, not to mention getting a disease or getting hit by a car—it is eventually wrangled by local animal control and placed in a municipal shelter. Or at least that's the way the system is designed to work. Local governments all have personnel to that end: animal control officers, though in old movies and cartoons they are called dogcatchers.

Going to a shelter is unavoidable for many of these dogs, but it's a stressful and possibly tragic outcome. Why? Because shelters are temporary and imperfect solutions. Generally, there are three categories within the realm of "unwanted dogs" (an oxymoronic term if you ask me): open-admission shelters, limited-admission shelters, and foster rescue groups. Open-admission shelters have to accept all dogs that people bring in for any reason. Nicely referred to as animal care centers—and not so nicely referred to as "kill shelters" or "the pound"—these are the places where people surrender their dogs and police drop off dogs they encounter in the field. Limited-admission shelters work with city shelters to pull dogs into their own facilities, especially the ones that show good potential as a pet in a home. And foster rescue groups work with both city and local shelters to transport dogs and have their volunteers foster dogs, usually in their own homes, while they're waiting for their "forever homes." Each group's goal is to find dogs homes, though it's not always that easy. Dogs that don't get adopted from open-admission municipal shelters after a certain length of time will often be euthanized, unfortunately. The dog shelter world as currently constructed doesn't have the resources or the space to keep all its dogs forever, even doubled or tripled up in kennels or stacked in crates in the hallways, not to mention that the quality of life for those dogs is terrible. Dogs, social beings, don't like living in cages. It can drive them crazy, literally. Reputable breeders know this and want to avoid it at all costs.

Add to that the fact that negative conditions are self-amplifying. Dogs loose on the street, or those who come from bad breeders, are often not spayed or neutered. This, too, is a vexing issue. Some people find forced sterilization to be a ghoulish practice. On the other hand, dogs that are not spayed or neutered will make more and more dogs at an unchecked rate, which will lead to more crowded shelters and then more euthanized dogs. The goal is to prevent dogs from being born to die. As a result, spaying and neutering are critical, to the point where dog-welfare organizations hold events called "spay-athons," where vets donate their time and perform hundreds upon hundreds of procedures for free. This removes at least two barriers: the top-of-mind one, where people might not be thinking about spaying or neutering, and the expense of the procedure. Widespread spaying and neutering legitimately mitigate the stray population. My personal story here is not about a dog at all but a guinea pig. When I was a kid, I got one from Petco and took it home. Great. A new pet. I felt the same way the next day, and the day after that, all the way up until the morning a week later when I went to feed my guinea pig and saw about ten tiny new ones in the pen. I had bought a pregnant pet without knowing. I gave one to each of my siblings and gave the rest back to Petco. No one wants to be an unwitting breeder. Imagine not a litter of guinea pigs appearing in your house but a litter of dogs. (Coincidentally, baby guinea pigs and baby dogs are both called pups.)

When I'm out as The Dogist, I sometimes encounter a dog that has not been neutered. There's no easy way of telling if a female dog is spayed, though it's now common practice for vets to give dogs a small green tattoo on their belly to indicate that they have been through the procedure. Elsa has one that we joke she got in Cabo. Male dogs are easier: just look for the balls (or the absence thereof). I have learned over time that there are a few possible reasons for male dogs to persist unfixed. The owner, usually a man, may have skipped the procedure because he feels that it would rob the dog of its masculinity, which really means that he feels that it would rob him of his masculinity. (I leave the question of whether dogs even have masculinity to other canine theorists.) Alternatively, and more rationally, there are cases where an owner has elected to delay a dog's spay or neuter until they've reached a certain age, often with their vet's advice, to facilitate hormonal growth and development. I defer to the vets on that one. Lastly, there are show dogs, which are required by breed standards to have their reproductive systems intact, both to demonstrate their overall health (dogs with an undescended testicle are ineligible) and in part so that they can become sires or dams. Bloodlines matter to pedigree show dog breeders and owners. Owners who have a clear goal for their dog's health or dog show prospects not only have their dog in mind, but the chance of them allowing their dogs to create unwanted litters is also drastically lower.

Even with that, the sight of a recently spayed or neutered dog can warm the heart. Back in February 2016, I was out on Third Avenue and ran into an adorable Dachshund puppy. I think she was six months or so. Her name was Florence. She had, around her neck, a pink inflatable balloon collar, known in the dog world as "the donut." Her owner explained to me that she had it because she had just been spayed. The post with Florence did especially well that summer, and I think part of the reason is that people remembered taking their own dogs for the procedure, and how they felt pained but also protective and ultimately virtuous. The cute quote he gave me ("She sleeps in bed with my girlfriend and me and insists on sleeping in the middle. I usually wake up spooning her instead of my girlfriend.") didn't hurt.

Though the web of factors that produces unwanted dogs is complex, the result is simple: too many dogs. They often come from the American South, where culturally it seems dogs are viewed as more fungible or expendable, like livestock, and each year produces a surplus of hound dogs during the hunting season, which are then often set loose in the woods once the season is over. A rescue expert I worked with alluded to the phenomenon of some lower-income populations viewing dogs as a luxury that (as we have seen) alleviates depression, at least temporarily, but without a corresponding plan for the dogs' well-being. Pop culture can also contribute to overpopulation, whether it's people acquiring the same kinds of dogs as their favorite celebrities or buying breeds they see in shows or movies. And then there is the stubborn cultural belief that certain breeds are more troublesome and are thus passed over at shelters. Pit Bulls are the dogs most mentioned in this vein, and in my experience are the dogs most likely to languish for months, if not years, in the shelter system as long stays. German Shepherds can also be tough to place due to their shedding, health issues, need for consistent exercise, and potentially territorial temperament.

On the street, I have seen thousands of dogs that have come to owners through shelters, which means that I have encountered plenty of these disproportionately sheltered breeds. I remember one Pit-mix in particular, Mr. Vinny, who I ran across in Union Square in February 2023. I typically select my subjects by looking primarily at their face. Mr. Vinny had a typically cute Pit Bull face, but it was his butt that caught my eye. Particularly, it was his tail, which was completely absent. Not even a stump. I had to get to the bottom of Mr. Vinny's bottom. As it turns out, Mr. Vinny was found neglected in a crate with rubber bands tied around his tail. Whoever did that to him was likely attempting a DIY crop of his tail to avoid the expense and inconvenience of hiring a professional. After the dog was collected off the street (I assume by police) and rehoused, the owner's sister, a vet, had to amputate what was left of his probably infected tail stump.

Mr. Vinny was obsessed with water. "He's been in every body of water from coast to coast," his owner told me. "They're running out of rivers for him." Mr. Vinny didn't have a tail to wag, but he definitely got a happy ending. I have also seen large hound dogs in New York City. They only got there through shelters—there are no Treeing Walker Coonhound breeders in the city, no one looking for a dog that will systematically hunt squirrels in Central Park and then bay loudly when they're left alone in their one-bedroom apartment afterward. These dogs come from the South, where chasing varmints up a tree is totally a thing. I met Fester, a hound-mix, also in Union Square, where his owner told me he was a counter-surfer and once "got a good batch of scones." The scones were in New York; Fester had come from Biloxi, Mississippi, as a rescue. Biloxi is a Gulf Coast city best known for its casinos. The owner had taken a gamble on Fester and won.

As many Mr. Vinnys and Festers as there are on the streets of New York and other American cities, there are places in the world where dog overpopulation isn't really a thing. Switzerland, for example, has very few extra dogs. This is the result of the way Swiss culture treats dogs as signs of cultural pride (think of all the famous Swiss breeds—Bernese Mountain Dogs, Saint Bernards, Greater Swiss Mountain Dogs, Entlebucher Mountain Dogs, White Swiss Shepherds, and so on). In order to get a dog from a rescue or a breeder, applicants have to undergo an in-depth background interview and complete ten hours of "dog school." And it's very difficult to become a recognized breeder accepted by any of the Swiss breed clubs.

When I visited there, I saw it firsthand: there is virtually no back-yard breeding, and while there are certainly mixes and rescue dogs in general, each of the rescued dogs I met came from elsewhere. Spain was a common point of origin. Dog overpopulation isn't a thing in Switzerland because they treat the problem at the source: human idiocy. While I was there, I got an overwhelming sense that the Swiss just love following the rules. We accidentally drove our car into the small ski village of Zermatt and parked it in a garage. When we told the hotel concierge we had done that, she looked like she'd seen a ghost (cars aren't allowed in Zermatt without a special permit). In the same vein, breeding dogs unethically for profit would likely go against Swiss cultural expectations. Moreover, Switzerland, like many other European countries, has a controversial "dangerous breed ban," which means that any individuals interested in breeding dogs as a symbol of power or aggression—the dogs that are unfortunately extremely common in the U.S. shelter system—are discouraged from doing so before they even start.

As you might expect, meticulous breeding comes with its controversial practices. If a breeder has a litter of Rhodesian Ridgebacks that are born without the breed's telltale ridge, they may well be euthanized (this has created a subset of individuals interested in specifically owning/saving Ridgeless Rhodesian Ridgebacks). Australian Shepherd and Great Dane breeders will often euthanize dogs born "double merle," as they're usually deaf and blind and prone to more health conditions. Puppies are often culled if their litter size is deemed too large for the mother to properly wean them with her milk supply. These practices do seem inhumane in the extreme (and I leave it to you to form your own opinions on these matters), but it is part of a larger sensibility that strives to preserve the health of the breed over time, and to prevent dog surpluses that can lead to even more widespread euthanasia.

A few years back, I shared a set of images of some guys pushing a stroller of three Frenchie puppies down Madison Avenue on the Upper East Side. As a set of photographs, it was internet gold: adorable, surprising, good composition. But the reality of the situation was that these guys were basically breeders advertising their dogs to Upper East Side passersby. I didn't notice it at the time, but one of their shirts even carried their business name. And so, despite the popularity of the post—it had more than 150,000 likes—it was also highly controversial in some ways, with a comment section filled with people criticizing my decision to feature the Frenchies-for-sale stroller brigade. They said I should know better.

The second the critiques began to mount, I did what I always do in a situation like this. I sat down and thought about which of Pandora's boxes I had opened. On the one hand, it seemed like I should stick to my decision to post the photos, which was guided primarily by their visual and narrative appeal. It's impossible to vet every backstory, and not really the job of the site. On the other hand, there was the chorus of boos and hisses from the internet jury—my audience. I tried to get past the angry language and hostile emojis and locate their actual argument, which had to do with the feeling that this type of post ran directly counter to the central point of my site, which involved promoting ethical ways for dogs of various types to reach their prospective human owners. I asked myself a key question: "Have any of the responsible breeders I've met marketed their dogs by parading down Madison Avenue with a bassinet of their latest litter?" Definitely not. So what was the post doing?

A post like this, people said (the calm, articulate ones struck the deepest nerve), instead encouraged people to go about getting a dog in the same way you'd go about getting a fake Gucci bag from a sidewalk street vendor. The fact that it was a trendy breed, a trio of Frenchies, advanced their argument further. These guys were harping on people's naivete by appealing to their lowest instincts, to impulsivity and instant gratification. Those dogs may very well have great, long lives. But they say relationships usually end the way they start, and if someone decided to care for another being while ogling the various window displays along one of Manhattan's premier shopping streets, I wouldn't be surprised if the same impulsivity caused them to treat their dog like last season's fashion. And did those guys with their breeding company's name emblazoned on their shirts have their dogs' health and well-being in mind, or were they just eyeing a quick buck? That's a rhetorical question.

That was a watershed moment, too, in recognizing that the popularity of my platform had created a different kind of responsibility for me. Understanding how I affect the world I am documenting is a complex issue in some ways. In this case, though, it was simple enough, and I took the post down.

--------------- 🐾 ---------------

Arlo, mix (9 years old), Hudson St. &
Charles St., New York, NY • "His full name
is Arlo Guthrie Marshmallow. He's a rescue
from Georgia—we got him at eight weeks.
He's a sweetie pie. He's been getting seizures,
so he's on drugs for it. He loves other animals.
I rescued an eastern red bat here in New
York—I found her on Hudson Street and
named her My Little Baby. She's currently on
her way to a sanctuary in South Carolina."

--------------- 🐾 ---------------

CHAPTER 8

TO THE RESCUE

One cold fall day, midweek, I left my Greenwich Village apartment to catch a flight to Dallas, where I was scheduled to shadow Whitney Fang. That sounds kind of scary but is not: Whitney is a very nice woman in her early thirties who is the cofounder of Hearts & Bones Rescue (HBR), a nonprofit that has, since its founding in 2017, devoted itself to solving—or at least helping to solve—the dog overpopulation crisis in the American South. Before I became The Dogist, when I was still just a Dogist, I had no idea of the scope of the problem, and the fact that many if not most of the rescued dogs that end up in New York City come from the South, from Georgia and Tennessee, from the Carolinas and Louisiana. Texas was the hottest hot spot: maps that track the population of discarded dogs get the reddest in Texas, where there are "unwanted surpluses" of hound dogs, Huskies, Pitties, Chihuahuas, and everything in between. It's a cold way to talk about living beings as unwanted surpluses, even though those are the facts in reality.

I had talked to Whitney on Zoom a few times before I traveled to Dallas, and she had explained her organization's vision and mission.

Hearts & Bones was a "transport-based rescue," which meant that they had people on the ground in both the source and destination areas—in this case Dallas and New York City. This gave them access to both ends of the process: while many rescue organizations facilitate relocation, HBR was the rare soup-to-nuts operation, with their own transport vans and local foster networks in both cities. "When you come," Whitney said, "we'll tag dogs at DAS." By "we," she meant herself and her coworker Alicia. I'd be there watching and learning. By "tag," she meant "select for transport north to be adopted." By "DAS," she meant Dallas Animal Services, Dallas's primary city-run shelter. I flew in, slept, woke up, and drove to the DAS parking lot by 9 A.M. Whitney was waiting. We shook hands and she motioned toward a man with a Husky on a leash. He was standing in front of a small door with a big sign that said INTAKE. "The first of many today," she said in a hushed voice. I nodded like I understood.

But I didn't. Not until we went in through the main entrance and started to walk the kennels. What I saw were dogs on top of dogs on top of dogs. Every kennel was occupied, most by more than one dog. Many kennels had to be made into "half-kennels" to accommodate all the animals. Many of them were puppies, the kinds of dogs that would be adopted in a heartbeat if they were in a New York shelter; Whitney and Alicia told me that of the 500 dogs that had been added in the previous week, more than 150 of them were younger than six months. And that was just the first wing. For an hour, Whitney led me through the labyrinth of DAS, eight rooms of five rows of twenty-some kennels side by side, each with a sad face looking out. It was visually dizzying, but that was only one of the three senses being assaulted. My ears had to deal with the cacophony of barking—if you were stuck in a 2' × 5' cage for most of the day, you'd probably be barking, too, and this was an unconducted symphony of hundreds of prisoners. And my nose had to deal with—not to put too fine a point on it—the dog shit. The smell was like a wave that never receded, though I knew from experiences in prior years that it could have been worse. Many of the dogs in the shelter were "owner surrenders," meaning they had previously lived in a home, were house-broken, and were used to being let outside to go. They were reluctant to poop inside because of their previous lifestyle. The noise and the smell were overwhelming at first, but after a few minutes the desensitization set in (like it always does when I visit a shelter). That was good in one sense, but bad in another sense. What respite did these dogs have? They were allowed outside to a small artificial-turf yard once or twice a day to run around and get some air. It was better than nothing, but it was also close to nothing.

While we walked around, Whitney pointed out this cute dog or that one—I could tell she was making mental notes in her head. There were no shortage of cute ones: two Husky-mix puppies (littermates) scratching at the Plexiglas window in a humorous but also tragic way, a sweet-looking shepherd-mix who kept his back to the wall (if you stopped to say hi, he'd put his ears back and timidly approach the kennel door as if he knew to temper his expectations about his prospects for a new home). When I felt my heart start to connect in any way, I took a moment to give that dog a few extra moments of love, but I knew I had to press on to focus on the task at hand—selecting thirty or so of the most eligible dogs to go on the next transport north.

Eventually, we worked our way around to the highly taboo topic of euthanasia. Some shelters will advertise themselves as "no-kill" shelters. This suggests that the problem lies with the philosophy of the place, that some are designed to be kill shelters (and that's what they're commonly referred to as). This is not a fair term. No organization happily chooses death as an outcome for any animal. No person choosing to embark on a career working with animals does so for the euthanasia. The reality is that there are two types of shelters—open and limited admissions. Limited-admission organizations decide which dogs they accept into their facility or program. Open-admission organizations are not allowed to turn any dogs away. DAS is one of the latter, unable by law to turn away a single dog, regardless of the person's reason. And yet, these organizations, though hopefully large enough to accommodate their area's supply of unwanted pets, inevitably reach capacity—a lack of space to put all the dogs and cats and guinea pigs and rabbits and birds and reptiles that families discard or that the police or animal control bring in. That in turn creates population issues, or rather overpopulation issues, which in turn leads to the euthanizing of dogs—"space-based euthanasia."

At DAS, they use a more clinical term: it's called the "pre-lab list," which is essentially an algorithmically generated list of dogs that are scheduled to be euthanized by a certain date based on the factors of their intake and adoptability, among other things. Dogs that arrive as strays get about a five-day hold, after which they are considered unwanted. Dogs surrendered by their owners get the unwanted tag automatically. Could you imagine being a family pet for a decade and then being dropped off at the shelter because you may have a medical issue or maybe stopped being as entertaining? It's not a fate that any dog wants, especially if that dog happens to be in a city shelter that is already at capacity. In truth, even the so-called no-kill shelters euthanize dogs, albeit at a far lower rate. The no-kill designation means a 90 percent live-release rate, as euthanasia in some cases poses a less tricky moral dilemma—for example, for dogs with critically serious health or temperament problems.

The day I was there, DAS did what it always did, which was everything in their power to adopt out as many dogs as possible into homes. I saw many young couples and families with kids there browsing the kennels, seeing if one struck their fancy. I admired them choosing to adopt and taking the time to physically come to visit the shelter, a not very glamorous place, instead of just browsing for dogs online. It made me happy, but I also had my fingers crossed they would make a choice that would stick. One particularly high-spirited volunteer told us his strategy for getting dogs noticed: unique names. One was Bonquiqui. Another was Kerrica. It seemed to work—all of his specially named dogs had been promoted to the most coveted list in the system, "on hold." If you've ever walked into a shelter, you'll probably notice a narrow variety of names that shelter staff enter on the intake form. This is usually the result of (understandably) not feeling particularly creative after a long day of creating adoption profiles for fifty dogs (or a hundred), many of which look the same and many of which the shelter workers have likely not met yet. In a sea of Cocos and Bellas and Lunas, having a distinctive name can make all the difference in the world.

City shelters use many strategies to get dogs adopted: discounted or waived adoption fees, local adoption events, marketing for awareness, etc. One of the most powerful methods of saving dogs is by working with rescue groups like Hearts & Bones. Whitney and Alicia are often at DAS and other area shelters every day of the week. While I was there, they celebrated their five thousandth rescued dog, an impressive milestone. And they have their own algorithm that got them there. "New Yorkers *love* fluffies," she said. Whitney got into more detailed and market-based specs. "We're looking for dogs that we think will thrive in the Northeast, specifically in a New York City apartment. Chill, nondestructive, and dog- and people-friendly." In the three days that I was there, we tagged about fifteen dogs, several of which had been on the pre-lab list, and moved them to the on-hold list. Each drag and drop through the app on their phones felt like a mini celebration. They were saved. Two of the dogs we pulled from their kennels to "take for a spin" stood out—Moonlight and Snugzz. Both had been surrendered by their owners. Both fit Hearts & Bones' criteria for success. Moonlight leaned toward Alicia's sensibilities: seven years old, demure and fluffy. Snugzz was more Whitney's style: an adorable Cattle Dog–mix puppy who had been adopted and quickly returned for some reason. I got great images of both of them to feature on The Dogist. When I posted the reels from the visit, the comments reinforced the painful truth of my visit. One woman from Dallas wrote that as soon as she saw where I was, she knew where things were going: "They are simply overwhelmed as are the rescues," she wrote. "Too many animals not getting fixed for whatever sad reason. Thank you for shining the light no matter how grim." She wasn't wrong. Another woman chimed in: "Adopting is the best thing ever!" She's wasn't wrong either. All the dogs we tagged made it to NYC and were adopted in the days and weeks that followed, Moonlight and Snugzz included.

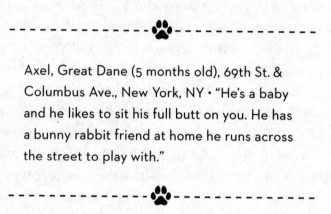

Axel, Great Dane (5 months old), 69th St. & Columbus Ave., New York, NY · "He's a baby and he likes to sit his full butt on you. He has a bunny rabbit friend at home he runs across the street to play with."

CHAPTER 9

EVERY DOG TELLS A STORY

'll say it again, at the risk of being repetitive. You can rescue a dog or get one from a breeder. It's entirely up to you. If you really want the adorable Goldendoodle puppy, follow your heart. After a decade of seeing dogs with their people, I have thoughts about how these decisions reflect your identity and your priorities, but they are dependent on time and place, on the individual situation of each animal and human. I'm not—brace for incoming pun—dogmatic about what people choose to do to bring dogs into their lives. What I am, though, is interested in what our choices tell us about ourselves.

One summer, in New York, I was breaking in a new Dogist videographer, a young man who would shadow me, taking behind-the-scenes footage of the dog photo shoots: he'd film me approaching dog owners, chatting with them, crouching down and making absurd noises to get a dog's attention. We had been out and about in Jersey City and had good luck finding a bunch of interesting subjects: a sato named Umi, a Dalmatian named Homer, a Chinese Crested named Jack. Our second outing, in Manhattan, was supposed to be in Central Park, but weather kept us closer to my home base in the Village. We met on Waverly Place and went west from there, and after about four blocks we came upon our first dog of the day. The first dog of the day I wanted to photograph, I mean—I let several dogs go by, terriers and doodles and one Dachshund, all great, but without that little extra bit of unique character that would compel me to cue my videographer and tell him we were going in. The dog west of Waverly caught my attention. It looked Lab-ish but was clearly a mix. I gave my videographer the sign and we crossed the street. As we approached the dog, I noticed some scarring around its nose and muzzle.

The owner sensed me coming and turned. "May I take a picture of your dog, quickly?" I asked.

"Sure," he said.

The dog's name was Lunchbox. A great name, I thought, and an original one, too, which I appreciate more and more as The Dogist rounds into its second decade. I have heard more dog names than probably any person on earth, so when I hear a new and charming one, I am tickled. (As it turns out, it wasn't *entirely* original. When I went back through my archives, I found another Lunchbox from Astor Place a few years earlier. So, a rare edition of two.) The owner laid out Lunchbox's backstory. It was a heartwarming one. Lunchbox had been rescued from Texas. Due to his scarring and missing teeth, they figured he had been locked in a cage and been trying to escape. He had suffered some form of abuse and neglect. He was transported to Seattle, where he had been adopted. At first, Lunchbox had been scared of other dogs, a sign of improper socialization, but with his new owner, he learned to love other dogs and play with them in the park. "He's just so chill," the man said. The owner was straightforward and kind. The dog sat and smiled proudly for the camera. It was a successful Dogist encounter.

When I was done with Lunchbox, I turned and ran right into my next subject, a woman who had been standing on the corner watching my session with Lunchbox. That happens sometimes. People who are Dogist fans will see me doing my thing from afar and position themselves so that they can "spontaneously run into" me. Lucky for them, I like meeting dogs. The woman had a Bernedoodle by her side, a breed I often pass up because they're so common. But it had been a while since I'd featured a Bernedoodle and I'm not the type of person to deny a person's dog their fifteen minutes in the spotlight because of breedism. I obliged her enthusiasm. As it turned out, the woman was very nice, and her dog, Rigatoni, was sweet and well-groomed. She demonstrated that she could deadlift him. Not something I was expecting, though Rigatoni's calm demeanor suggested this was a feat of strength she had been demonstrating since he was a puppy. The rest of the day's haul included a terrier-mix that belonged to a woman who spoke very softly, almost to the point where I was worried my microphones wouldn't pick her up, and a bulldog (French) whose owner smoked through our talk (also very French).

A few days went by and I posted those West Village interactions. The first dog that went up was Lunchbox. And when he went up, he went up and up. My posts on Instagram at the time would usually peak in the high five figures. A decent number of dogs snuck into low sixes. Lunchbox got there in a matter of hours, and his engagement showed no sign of slowing. It was even more viral on TikTok, where the usual play count was 150,000 to 250,000. Lunchbox? People watched his video 14 *million* times.

I have had other posts go viral, of course. Otherwise I wouldn't be here. But this was the first big blowup in a while, so I submitted it to another level of analysis. Why had the post gone crazy?

In part it was because Lunchbox was the prototypical rescue dog—an abused and abandoned mutt from humble origins now walking contentedly through the West Village. Everyone loves an underdog story, and Lunchbox was the underdoggiest dog imaginable, a rescue organization's dream. But there was something else. Lunchbox's owner had been candid with me not only about the dog's past but about the way that he, as a human, had processed that past. "It took me a while to get over that . . . that someone abused him," he said. This wasn't just an emotional confession but a narrative one.

When you bring an adult dog into your life, it changes the story, or rather it changes the fact that it is just *your* story. More specifically, you are entering a story that is already in progress. When you pick up a young puppy from a breeder, you not only get the cutest version—and let's not understate the value of cuteness—but you get a version that begins, give or take, with you. Puppies, generally, are tabula rasa, purely impressionable, and you're the one who is about to make the impressions. Some people like that feeling. It speaks to a kind of benign egotism: this is *my* dog and has always been *my* dog.

Those thoughts have to shift when you adopt an older dog. Those dogs are not blank slates. They have been marked by other people and other experiences. Their personalities have been formed in some way, shaped, and the best you can do is attempt to re-form and reshape them, if necessary. This requires at least a basic understanding of what they experienced before coming to you. It's like being an adult and dating other adults with complex histories of their own versus, if you'll pardon the expression, puppy love. Adult men and women have their own pasts, scars both visible or invisible. Every adult relationship is in some sense a reaction to what came before.

I went through a version of it with my own dog, Elsa. When I got her, the shelter told me that she had been tied to a tree in Texas. I took this with a grain of salt, but even so, I found myself thinking about it. What kind of tree? Was it because she had tried to escape? Did they even care enough to put out food or water for her? Being a double-coated Husky in Texas, she was already at risk of overheating: Did she bark for help? Did she have anything to play with? I invented scenes and then tried to inhabit them emotionally. How did Elsa feel before I met her? I can't say that it made me love her more than I would have loved a puppy I drove home from a breeder. I would have loved that dog with my whole heart too. But my head would have entered into the equation differently. With Elsa, my feelings for her are reinforced by earlier circumstances that I cannot quite know but that I continually imagine. I refuse to stop imagining them, in fact. It takes me outside myself, exposes a broader root structure.

This process can sometimes result in a kind of defensiveness. Sometimes when I'm out doing Dogist work, I encounter owners with nervous dogs. That's fine. Dogs have a right to be nervous. It's my job to try to put them at ease as best I can. Recently I was uptown in New York and ran into a woman with a jumpy shepherd, which isn't a breed but maybe should be one. Jumpy Shepherd. She wanted him to be photographed but had trouble calming him down, and at some point she turned to me in frustration. "He's a rescue," she said. This was true, no doubt, and it may have been a completely valid explanation for his angst—shepherds are a temperamentally sensitive breed to start, and any rehomed dogs can take a while to adjust— but it also felt like hands being thrown up. *It's not me. He's a rescue. I'm doing the best I can.*

When it comes to a rescued dog's past life, it can be hard to recover precise information. The ways animals end up at shelters are numerous and nuanced. Were they captured as a stray by animal control? Seized by police in a hoarding or animal abuse case? Did the kids lose interest in them? Did they bite someone? Maybe their owner died. Dogs can't communicate these details to us, and in a way, the details don't matter. What matters is that we know there is a story before the story we are fashioning. (While a dog may still be carrying traces of the past, what matters to a dog most is the present. The future matters, too, but I don't know if dogs can truly conceive of it.)

Again, pasts play differently for different dogs. Newborn puppies are blank slates, or as close to blank slates as possible. Their mother and her caretaker make the very first impressions, but when they come to a home, their owners get to fill in the rest of their world: here's your house, here's your family, here's your food dish, your toys, your bed. It's an opportunity to write a life starting on page one of a fresh notebook. When you get an older dog, you must pick up writing where someone else has left off, and you may not know how to feel about where they left off—the dog's prior narrative may come with some good habits, but also some bad ones that need adjusting. (I'm picturing a scene from one of my favorite movies, *Turner & Hooch*—Tom Hanks plays a cop who has taken possession of a dog from a crime scene investigation after its owner was killed, and he has to tell this big drooling French Mastiff which things in the house are his and which are *not* his. Chaos ensues.)

Bringing a dog with a past into your home means understanding and accepting that past before you and your dog can fully inhabit the present. This is a form of empathy. It requires new dog owners to move outside their own minds and think about the thoughts and feelings of another being, the struggles they have undergone and the ways in which they have overcome them. It is a particularly important form of empathy, in that it concerns the happiness (and unhappiness) of a being that is both a source of and a recipient of love. The process, undertaken together, has ups and downs, progress and setbacks. But the result is something beautiful: two beings doing their best to write a successful future.

Human pasts are also a factor in this equation. Just as a dog can have experiences that frame and complicate the situation before coming to a human, people can have experiences before coming to a dog that do the same.

Adam is one of my best friends. I met him soon after I started college at Boston University, and we hit it off immediately. Right away, I noticed that he had a facial scar, a somewhat noticeable line on the left side of his nose. I didn't ask about it, though, because that seemed rude. What if he didn't want to draw attention to it? One day, he asked me if I was curious how he had gotten it. "Yes," I said, trying not to sound too enthusiastic.

"Well," he said, touching the scar, "this is a story with a dog in it." Now I was even more interested. The story took place when Adam was in high school, spending time at the house of a friend of his whose family had a chocolate Lab.

"Oh," I said. "We have Labs." I didn't yet have all the language around dog intelligence and personality, but I was imagining a story with one of my dogs in it, Ruby or Snowy, dogs I knew to be intelligent but not *too* intelligent, kind and calm and affectionate, broadly successful across all the smart-dog categories.

"Yes," he said. Then there was a pause. He touched the scar again and went on with his story. He had slept over at his friend's house on a Friday night, watched movies, ordered pizza. The dog hung out, played a little, ate a few pieces of popcorn, fell asleep downstairs with them in the basement. Now it was Saturday, and everyone was in the kitchen, eating breakfast. Adam was taking a slice of toast, maybe some bacon, and the dog trotted up and hung out around the edge of the table. Nothing about the story had surprised me up to that point. People eat meals, and dogs come closer where there's food. That's how we domesticated gray wolves in the first place.

From there, though, the story took a turn. "I think maybe I was looking at the dog," Adam said, "and then at some point he was looking back at me."

"Uh-oh," I said. I was thinking about what I knew about staring, which is that some dogs don't like it at all. They can perceive it as a threat, especially if they are unsure of a person or their intentions.

"Uh-oh is right," he said. Adam didn't know dogs well enough to sense the tension in the Lab's body language. He leaned in closer to the dog, and in an instant the dog snapped. Teeth went into skin and by the time the dog had all four of its paws back on the ground, a chunk of Adam's nose was hanging off and blood was everywhere. His friend's parents drove him to the emergency room, where doctors managed to save his nose but left a scar as a souvenir of the experience.

I tell this story not to make people afraid of the average family dog (though Adam later learned that that dog had bitten someone before), but to reiterate that dogs are living beings, constantly responding to their environment. Adam's attack confirms that breed tendencies are only that. All dogs bite. The United States Postal Service has a podcast, a sentence I never thought I'd write. It's called *Mailin' It!*, which I think is a takeoff of the Netflix show *Nailed It!* but also not a takeoff. They had a special episode of the podcast devoted to their National Dog Bite Awareness Campaign, an annual initiative that the postal service has conducted since 1980 (a year that included two particularly problematic attacks in California, one that resulted in death). Linda DeCarlo, senior director of occupational safety and health for the USPS, outlined some of the recommendations: equip carriers with pepper spray, teach them not to wear earbuds or headphones so that they are aware, and so on. She touched on rural areas with feral dogs and urban neighborhoods where dogs are accustomed to guarding a home and consequently may be more aggressive. The 2024 campaign had a slogan, "Don't let your dog bite the hand that serves you," and a kickoff event in the Philadelphia area, my hometown, though I didn't know about it before it happened.

It's not only postal employees who should be conscious and careful around dogs. But sometimes dog owners paper over problematic behaviors. I see it all the time. People get Labradors or Golden Retrievers because the dogs have such a stellar reputation when it comes to temperament and personality. The process of acquiring the dog produces in their mind a kind of advertisement: "See me with my nice dog." Much of the time, that's the case, and everyone is happy to agree. But when the dog isn't like that for one reason or another, owners retreat into denial. *Oh, that barking and baring of teeth that you are seeing? It's a fluke.*

Once I was out taking Dogist photos and ran into a woman with a Lab. I stopped and engaged. After a few seconds, though, the dog snapped at my videographer, who managed to avoid what would have certainly been at least a moderate bite. The woman waved us off. "Oh, sorry," she said, "he's being a little crazy." (That denial extends to all breeds, actually. In the early years as The Dogist, I ran into a guy with a Pit Bull named Piney. The dog was troubled, and at times had been an overtly bad actor. The guy was clear that he was dedicated to dealing with the dog and working through its issues. The day after I posted the photos, I stepped out of the shower to see my phone going crazy. Piney's human had been Ira Glass, public radio icon, and Glass had used one of the photos I had taken to illustrate a feature about Piney. The response to the radio piece was mixed, and an early lesson for me in how charged conversations around dogs could get. Some people supported Glass's desire to stick with Piney; others felt that he was irresponsibly keeping a dangerous animal in circulation.)

Adam's scars were not only of the physical variety. He remained terrified of dogs. His cynophobia—that's the word, not often used—wasn't irrational, but it was still hindering. Humans should not be afraid of dogs. Humans should explore bonds with dogs. Failing to do that can shrink your life and limit your happiness.

I can report with some relief that Adam's story has a happy ending. During the first months of the COVID pandemic, as I have said, I went up to Cape Cod with a friend of mine who had just broken off a long engagement. That was Adam. Elsa soon joined the household as a foster and then a permanent pet. Even though Adam was deeply skittish around dogs, he knew he would be in close quarters with us, so he tentatively extended a hand to Elsa's paw. She regarded it with her specialties: an affectionate lick on the hand, her piercing blue eyes staring into your soul, and a full upside-down roll over for a belly rub. Magically, his fear began to fade. Within two weeks he was rocking her in his arms (all paws off the ground), his eyes closed, with Daniel Caesar's "We Find Love" playing on the speakers. He had unlocked a chamber of his heart he had thought was closed forever.

When he returned to his city and his life post-quarantine, it was with a new outlook. He met a woman and got married. He got two dogs of his own, Chihuahuas, and designed a custom hat for himself that says "Chihuahua Papa." I can't say with 100 percent certainty that his dogs, Lil Red and Abbi, made him happier. That would be presumptuous. But coming around to dogs definitely reinstated some part of his humanity that had been held in suspension. It cleared the channel and repaired the circuit. It increased both empathy and emotion. Just as my friend Jeff's sense of his own responsibility to others had been remade when he brought Gertie into his life, Adam's life broadened and brightened when he became a Chihuahua Papa.

Every interaction between a person and their dog tells you not just something about the dog but about the person. Both ends of the leash are illuminated. When I first started The Dogist, I was not as tuned in to this dynamic. The first idea of the site was to parody street-fashion sites like *The Sartorialist*. I admired the project, but at its core it took vanity so seriously, which I found incredibly funny. Imagining dogs *wanted* to have their picture taken and admired by an online audience was hilarious to me, not to mention a poke at human vanity. But to achieve that, I needed photos that made it seem as though they understood that I was the photographer and that they were the subject. To do that, I had to think like a dog. *SQUIRREL!*

For starters, that meant that I had to get down to the dog's level: the "Dog Zone," I called it. When I went out for a session, I took my camera, dog treats, and a squeaky tennis ball (the "glowing orb of delight," I called it). I even wore kneepads under my pants so I could drop down quickly to dog level over and over without pain. I went through lots of pants and shoes. But it was more than just getting the right angle. In order to truly break the fourth wall and get to the punch line of the project (dogs having their pictures taken the way that people do), I needed direct eye contact from them. That's not easy in animal photography. You can't tell them to "say cheese" and have them look right over (although most dogs probably know the word "cheese" and would look over, but you get my point). Here, I used the tools I had stuffed in my cargo pants pockets, and then some. I'd make the glowing orb of delight squeak and quickly move it above the lens to direct their gaze. I'd hold a treat out for the dog to sniff and then bring it back to the camera. I'd make my by-now-trademark array of bizarre noises: my crying-puppy whimper, my grumbling goat, the noise that's basically a fart sound, along with other clicks and grunts. I have to credit all the owners and trainers I encountered over the years for helping me to develop this repertoire of sounds.

It worked to get the attention of the dogs. It worked in other ways too. Keeping the image at dog level also meant that the dogs weren't eclipsed by people, which was vital for the photographs to work. Imagine a photo of almost anything: a banana or a piece of avocado toast or a tree branch with a pretty bird on it. Looks nice, right? Now put a person in the frame. Your attention will be drawn away from the object, no matter how striking it is. It's not your fault. As humans, we are hardwired to pay attention to other humans. They are the things that we find most interesting, most attractive, the things that reward our attention the most. If I was going to really direct viewer attention to the dogs, I would have to eliminate the people, at least for a minute.

Interestingly, that had a second effect, which was that I struggled to emphasize the relationships between dogs and their people. I was getting amazing quotes where people detailed their dogs' behavior, or described their personalities, or recounted various kinds of anecdotes (hilarious, heartbreaking, sometimes both). But the people weren't the center. The dogs were. Partly I didn't want the people to enter into the frame because that would just bring the pictures back to what social media was already littered with—people trying to pose a certain way. Why couldn't this just be for dogs? I would include people's lower halves so as to let viewers glean something about them—their gender, their shoes, their posture. But I refused to photograph beyond the Dog Zone. As the site grew, I realized that

I needed a way of better conveying the dog-human relationship. The captions spoke to it, but visitors to the site couldn't really *see* it. I needed some way of not only presenting dogs-as-dogs but of telling the stories about how they affected human lives—how they added to them, improved them, annoyed them, changed them, sometimes even saved them. The dog-human relationship, I realized, was just as real and powerful as any human-human relationship.

And so, around 2021, I started adding posts that were not just static photo sets but included behind-the-scenes footage that showed the process of my approaching the owners with their dogs on the street. I was resistant at first. It would require a second person to follow me and shoot video of my photo sessions. I had always thought of myself as a kind of Batman. Did I really need a Robin? (And how much does a Robin charge per hour?) Plus, it would mean editing not just photographs but video and sound. An entirely new format I wasn't accustomed to. I came up with every excuse to avoid having to change. Not to mention, *people* would be in the videos (an explicit violation of Dog Zoning). This was when Instagram was heavily favoring the short-form video format so as to keep up with TikTok. It was also a time when engagement on my posts was the lowest it had ever been. Did people not think my dog photos were enough anymore? Were dogs still cool? I began to question my future. But sometimes you have to hit rock bottom to get to the top. I stopped fighting Instagram's algorithm. If you can't beat 'em, join 'em. And so I let people, both myself and the dog owners, into The Dogist, and I realized I should've been doing that all along.

This new approach worked instantly. I had been so focused on the dogs that I forgot that relationships require two parties. My mission was still "the story of dogs," but dogs couldn't be the only characters in this story. People coming to The Dogist still got to see the adorable dogs and all the excited expressions they make, but also their equally excited people rubbing their dogs' bellies, ruffling their fur, and squeezing them like a tube of toothpaste. They also got to hear these people express their excitement: the audio on the footage was intimate and emotional and created even more connection. The funny, sentimental, or poignant comments, previously only printed in captions, were now spoken testimonials. Their words came alive.

When I look back across a decade as The Dogist, I see how this change in my content reflects a change in me. I came to see that not everything has to be a joke. Dogs posing for the camera like people is funny, but there's even more humor in the way humans act and talk about their dogs. Not to mention the sincere, sad, and beautifully sappy moments. I've cried more times in the last two years than I did in the previous eight. (Shit, am I crying right now?) What was illuminated, in post after post, was that dogs need us just as much as we need them. And I knew that the dogs would approve of this shift. If they were my social media consultants and I asked them if their humans should be in their Dogist posts with them, I know exactly what they would say: "How could they not?" (followed closely by "Are you going to finish your sandwich?").

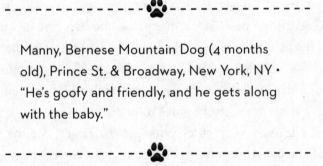

Manny, Bernese Mountain Dog (4 months old), Prince St. & Broadway, New York, NY · "He's goofy and friendly, and he gets along with the baby."

CHAPTER 10

WORKING HAND
IN PAW

My family had many dogs when I was growing up, as you may recall, but we didn't consider most of them to be particularly gifted in the intelligence department. Ruby could do "sit" and "down," Matilda knew "sit" sometimes, and the rest of our dogs weren't much further ahead. However, we had one dog that we all thought was smart. Maggie was a black Lab-mix my grandmother rescued from a local shelter. She was extremely wiggly and energetic, without a huge amount of focus. To our admiration and astonishment, she learned very quickly to "get the paper" for my grandmother. The paper was always delivered at the top of the hill above some steps, so this was not just a charming trick but an actual, necessary service for my aging grandmother. Each day my grandmother would fling the door open, say "Maggie, get the paper!" and Maggie would bolt out, ascend the stairs, and find it, rain, snow, or sunshine. Other dogs may have been gifted in other ways, but I'll always remember and thank Maggie for the service she performed for my grandmother. Good girl.

I mentioned earlier that I loved reading books about dog breeds when I was young. I liked the orderliness of them, the way they took the huge, chaotic world of dogs and organized it into breeds.

I liked books about how dogs operated, books that delved into their behavior and their psychology. (One of those books noted that a dog's brain is roughly the size of a tangerine—ever since then I like to say that Elsa is "using her tangerine" to make decisions.) I also liked general-facts books that reduced the complexity of the world into orderly lists of rankings: *The World Almanac*, say, where you could find a rundown of the world's longest bridges, or of all the Wimbledon champions from Spencer Gore in 1877 to Pete Sampras. (This was back in the '90s—now it would run right up through Roger Federer's eight titles and Carlos Alcaraz's two.)

And then, sometime after that, I ran across a book that combined these two themes. The book, *The Intelligence of Dogs*, was written by Stanley Coren, a canine researcher at the University of British Columbia. Coren was not the first to study the topic, of course. There was a famous 1976 study in which a test was administered to a hundred dogs of varying breeds to measure a range of skills, some of which were connected to memory, some of which dealt with an animal's ability to solve simple problems or navigate obstacles. Coren took up the thread of that study and did more work himself, including sending out surveys to kennel clubs. The results, a mix of hard science and anecdotal opinion, were collated and analyzed.

The brainiest dog, according to Coren's book, was the Border Collie. And here we were thinking you should call Lassie, a Collie (ranked all the way down at number 16), when you fell into a well. *Lassie* was created in 1954, before Coren's study, so we'll cut them a break, but I would like to go on the record as saying some Border Collie missed out on the role of a lifetime. Okay, so the study concluded that Border Collies were brilliant (slow clap), but I didn't have a Border Collie. I scanned the list, eager to see how my dog stacked up. Was Ruby a canine Einstein or a four-legged Lloyd Christmas? Second place went to the Poodles (show-offs), and third place went to German Shepherds. Labs had to be next, right? They weren't. Golden Retrievers were, then Doberman Pinschers, then Shetland Sheepdogs. Finally, Labs popped up in seventh place. Hey, top ten ain't so bad. They edged out the eighth-ranked dog, the Papillon, by a nose.

From there, the list went down through breeds like the Schipperke (number 15) and the Cocker Spaniel (number 20), the Samoyed (number 33) and the Siberian Husky (number 45), the Italian Greyhound (number 60) and the Shih Tzu (number 70). It arrived eventually at the bottom five: the Borzoi, the Chow Chow, the bulldog, the Basenji, and the poor, simpleminded Afghan Hound, dead last among ranked breeds. All the beauty, and none of the brains, according to the rankings. (Luckily, due to the Afghan's illiteracy, they were also not able to read the book, so they were spared the embarrassment.) I wouldn't want to hurt the feelings of any Afghan or Afghan fancier, though I wonder if they would corroborate this study. When I met Togo and Sudan, two- and three-year-old Afghan Hounds respectively, in SoHo in 2018, their owner described Togo as "daffy" and Sudan as "aloof." The owner of Clark, a three-year-old Afghan show dog, told me they were bred to hunt gazelles in the desert. Have you ever seen a Border Collie hunt gazelles? I think not.

It was fun to memorize that list and to pretend that when I saw dogs on the street, they were competing in some kind of Canine Battle of Wits: Boxer (rank: 48) beats Pug (rank: 57). But even back then, I understood that Coren's framework was limited. Though his book identified three broad categories of dog intelligence— instinctive intelligence, adaptive intelligence, and working and obedience intelligence—his ranking system focused mostly on the third of these categories. His rankings were based on a narrow metric: a dog's ability to respond to a human command and to learn new commands. The "brightest dogs" executed first commands more than 95 percent of the time and required fewer than five repetitions of a new command to understand it. By contrast, the dogs at the bottom understood first commands only 20 percent of the time and sometimes needed more than a hundred repetitions to learn a new command. That's a big difference when it comes to understanding commands, but how fully does that account for what a brain (even a dog brain) does? Narrow though it may have been, Coren's framework was also influential. At least for a while, other authors fell comfortably into the idea that a dog's intelligence was defined largely by its ability to perform tasks put to it by humans.

About a decade after Coren, a Hungarian scientist named Vilmos Csányi published a book called *If Dogs Could Talk: Exploring the Canine Mind.* Csányi reiterated some of Coren's conclusions. Border Collies were still smart. In fact, his book included a portrait of a Border Collie named Rico who could identify hundreds of individual objects when asked by people to do so. Rico was so smart, in fact, that Csányi's colleagues at Eötvös Loránd University in Budapest began a Genius Dog Challenge, which sought to find other canine savants like Rico. They didn't find very many, and concluded that was because savants are exceptional. Using him to draw broader conclusions even about other Border Collies was tricky, just as it would be to draw conclusions about the people working at the froyo store in your town from observations of Nobel Prize winners.

I have never met Rico, unfortunately, but I have met a different dog (over Zoom) that could "talk": Bunny the Sheepadoodle. Based up in Tacoma, Washington, Bunny became famous on TikTok for seemingly articulating complex thoughts through buttons that spoke preprogrammed words. By "complex," I don't mean Shakespearean prose, but simple-grammar sentences: "go" and "outside" or "go" "store" "now." This type of comprehension involving action and time and place was always thought to be out of the grasp of dogs. I was dubious at first, expecting Bunny to be the latest example of the old phenomenon where the animal is responding to a cue from a nearby human—in this case, Bunny's human mom, Alexis. (This is known as the Clever Hans Phenomenon. Clever Hans was a horse, not a dog, who performed in early-twentieth-century Germany, and the list of abilities claimed by his trainer, Wilhelm von Osten, included basic arithmetic, fractions, telling time, understanding a printed calendar, identifying musical notes—oh, and reading, understanding, and even *spelling* German words. He expressed himself by tapping his hoof a certain number of times. A skeptical psychologist, Oskar Pfungst, proved that Hans was not actually cogitating but rather following Osten's body-language cues. It wasn't fraud, exactly, but the horse's sensitivity to its human questioner—as the horse approached the right answer, the questioner would tense up or look more intently or otherwise send out a signal that the horse picked up on.)

Bunny did as advertised, which was impressive, but didn't necessarily disprove the Clever Hans theory. But then I thought about it. Don't *all* our dogs communicate that kind of thing ten times a day in their own way? My dog, Elsa, doesn't have preprogrammed speech buttons that say "poop," "now," "take," "me," "outside," "idiot." But that doesn't mean she can't communicate the exact same thing perfectly well with a paw to my abdomen while I try to watch one more episode of *It's Always Sunny in Philadelphia*. Maybe she thinks that show is making me dumber. Bunny is currently part of a study called TheyCanTalk, conducted by the Comparative Cognition Lab at the University of California, San Diego.

Csányi's book also constructs an interesting bridge between canine and human intelligence, in the sense that he encourages us to understand our dogs' minds in the context of their coevolution with humans. In other words, certain canine abilities have developed because dogs have been bred as human helpers, and sometimes almost as extensions of their owners. So while certain kinds of dogs might not ace Coren's tests, they are brilliant working hand-in-paw with humans. They excel in specific situations that require specific kinds of behaviors.

In recent years, studies have moved further in that direction, redefining certain personality traits as types of intelligence. The result is a whole new palette of colors in the dog intelligence rainbow.

Depending on where you look, you'll find different lists of dog personalities and types of intelligence, but a few crop up again and again.

- There's *biddability*, which refers to a dog's willingness to perform a task asked of it by its owner. Literally, it means a dog's ability to do your bidding. Think of a hunter who just shot a duck and saw it fall into a lake. The hunter isn't about to change out of his brush gear, don a bathing suit and snorkel, and fish the duck out of the muck himself. That's why he brought . . . (drumroll, please) his Labrador Retriever (or Nova Scotia Duck Tolling Retriever if that drives the point home better). His dog has no qualms about jumping into the freezing water, getting covered in mud, grabbing a duck with its mouth (pond water must not taste great), and swimming back to drop it (unchewed) by your feet. In fact, he *lives* for it, and will do it as many times as you let him (apologies to any duck enthusiasts). Biddability is a measure of a dog's ability to do what you essentially can't (or maybe don't want to) do yourself, and effectively. Retrievers, to me, are the classic example, but other examples of dogs with biddability are search and rescue dogs, explosives detection dogs, and herding dogs. (Biddability is similar but not identical to another trait, *trainability*, which refers to a dog's ability to learn new skills and is more closely aligned with the traditional Coren-derived measurements.)

- There's *softness*, which refers to a dog's sensitivity to feedback from an owner, whether a word or a gesture. These dogs can be communicated with efficiently and effectively. (They are susceptible to both negative and positive feedback, though most recent thought around dog training advises rewarding good behavior rather than punishing bad behavior. No more rolled-up newspapers.) And then there's *persistence*, which refers to dogs that have a strong sense of mission and will keep on task no matter what else happens.

- There's *bombproofness*, which is a fancy way of saying that a dog is especially cool, calm, and collected, unable to be rattled no matter what's being thrown its way. A bombproof dog is the guide dog (for a visually impaired person) who doesn't make their handler walk around the subway grate because it feels weird on their paws. A bombproof dog is the family Lab who lets the toddler pull and fiddle with its ears and tail (hopefully not too hard) without much reaction. A hunting dog that doesn't freak out when you fire a rifle or shotgun is bombproof (the dog that does is referred to as "gun-shy").

- Finally, there are *galoopy* dogs. This quality is defined as a talent for goofy, carefree playfulness. ("Galoopy" seems to be the current term of preference, though I like to say "derpy," and some people, including a professional service dog trainer I just interviewed, call it "goofy.") These are the clowns of the dog world. They get into the same space as you and refuse to get out of that space until you are smiling or laughing. They force you to be happy. Those kinds of dogs pop up all the time during my Dogist work, and the breed that comes to mind (and I have a feeling you may be thinking the same) is Golden Retriever. When I approach them, it's like activating a small tornado of fur. Except instead of flipping your car and taking out power lines, this tornado suffocates you with love and attention. Their butts wiggle back and forth like a trailer behind a truck that's careening out of control. I will never forget a trip I took to the Scottish Highlands for the Guisachan Gathering, the world's largest convention of Golden Retrievers. The event is held there because that's where the breed was developed back in 1868, when a man named Sir Dudley Marjoribanks, later Lord Tweedmouth, bred a retriever with a Tweed Water Spaniel, thus creating a new breed that would become one of the world's favorites. I flew to Scotland by myself, rented a car (and had to figure out how to drive a stick with my left hand), and drove out into what seemed like the middle of nowhere. If I ran out of gas, who would ever find me? Then I crested a hill and noticed a sudden and very conspicuous rise in the number of Golden Retrievers in my surroundings. Hordes of them were headed up the hill to Lord Tweedmouth's estate, where they would gather in the hundreds. Three hundred and sixty-one, to be exact. I don't remember them all, to be honest, though I do remember one of them was named Playboy, which I thought was a fitting name for a Golden. I documented the event and discovered some of the secrets of Guisachan, including how they were able to get all the dogs to pose for "the picture" in a field without a single person in the frame—each owner brought a stake to tether their dog's leash to the ground. I also learned that owners standing a hundred feet away could instantly zero in on their dog, even amid hundreds of other dogs that might, to the untrained eye, look identical. Guisachan is a singular event, but the number of pictures I have in my archives of Golden Retrievers "derping out" may astonish you (or make you incredibly happy, or both). Still, how is this a form of intelligence? Well, dogs with this trait are incredibly charming. You may even be smiling after reading that description. Dogs that can make us feel this way survive and thrive better than dogs that don't. They put our guards down and our endorphins up. It may seem like a silly personality trait (figuratively and literally), but it's something far more profound, a canine version of Richard Dawkins's *The Selfish Gene*.

I have met more than fifty thousand dogs through my Dogist work, and I have seen all these traits. Even if you've only met a hundred, or a dozen, you have probably run across them all too. There are independent-minded dogs, shy dogs, don't-go-anywhere-without-me dogs. And then there are the dogs with unchecked persistence. I had a childhood friend who had a big house, or bigger than mine at least. He also had a full-size Skee-Ball machine in his basement, if you can believe it. Probably my favorite boardwalk game, and I was good at it. I remember seeing it and thinking, *Why didn't you tell me you have a Skee-Ball machine? We could've been playing it this whole time!*

"Uhh, I don't think we should turn it on," my friend said.

"Why?" I asked. "Is it broken?"

He paused. "No," he said. He went around to the back of the machine to plug it into the wall, and I eagerly got into position to play Skee-Ball for the next thirty minutes without needing a pocketful of quarters. But when the Skee-Ball theme music started playing, I started to hear a rumble in the background.

A look of resignation washed over my friend's face.

"He's coming," he said.

"Who's coming?" I said.

He couldn't even get another word out before his Standard Poodle, previously peaceful, came barreling down the stairs at top speed and got on top of the Skee-Ball machine with an excitement far beyond my own. Nothing had deterred him from getting into the basement, and it was clear that nothing would convince him to get off the machine. I didn't get to throw one ball, and the game was over.

"Yeah," he said. "It's annoying." He unplugged the machine.

I never went back to his house again. That dog was persistent, and if persistence is a form of intelligence, he was too smart for his own good—and for mine.

When you think about the variety of complex situations that dogs find themselves in, you start to see the benefit of understanding intelligence as a complex combination of all these types of behaviors—a dog tasked to work with law enforcement officers, for example, needs to display biddable, trainable, and bombproof qualities. Dog intelligence is so situational, in fact, that behaviors that might at first seem problematic can reveal themselves as brilliant. Think of guide dogs for the visually impaired, which should be bombproof to a high degree. But there are even more specific traits that work to their advantage. Imagine a situation where the owner is standing at the crosswalk and has pressed the button to cross the street. After a few seconds, a buzz or a beep sounds, indicating that it's safe to cross. But what if, just at that moment, the dog sees an eighteen-wheeler that decided to gun it late through the yellow light? The owner, having heard the all clear from the crosswalk box, might start moving forward, and command his dog to do the same. But the dog, being aware of the oncoming truck, resists. A dog like this knows when not to follow its owner's orders. It can think on its own and make good decisions. That quality, which is called intelligent disobedience, is in this case a lifesaver. It is commonly understood in the working service dog industry that guide dogs possess something special that other service dogs do not.

Restoring nuance to considerations of canine intelligence also allows us to assess our own mental processes in a more sophisticated way. Imagine if we looked at human intelligence not simply in terms of cognitive speed and power but with an eye toward the full set of abilities, behaviors, and instincts that affect our movement through the world. I once knew someone who was incredibly smart and articulate. He went to an Ivy League school and read voraciously. But one day when I was wandering with him through the West Village, I noticed something odd. Every time we came to an intersection, he would look back at me like a lost puppy. "Which way?" he said. "Straight," I replied. This continued to happen, block after block. He couldn't make any decision for himself, even something as trivial as going left or right (it wasn't that he didn't know the area). In dog terms, he had a high degree of training but a low degree of adaptive intelligence.

Frieda, Samoyed (6 years old), 11th St. &
2nd Ave., New York, NY · "She swallowed a
piece of rubber and had to be hospitalized.
That's why she's muzzled—she eats stuff, she
doesn't bite. She once ate some ibuprofen
when I was in college. She's used to it at this
point."

CHAPTER 11

EMOTIONAL RESCUE

I have probably spent more time looking at different dog faces than anyone else ever (though I'll concede that you may have spent more time looking at *your* dog's face than anyone ever). With each of the more than fifty thousand dogs I've met, I take about fifty photographs over the five-minute period I'm with them. And while the owner and passersby are witness to a funny and playful interaction, what I see through the viewfinder and later in the editing suite is a whole story unto itself. Tongue out, tail wagging. Both ears back. Both ears up. One ear down, the other tucked back. Head tilt. Mouth pursed, eyes widened. Stance broadened. (Cookie comes out.) Back to smile and tail wag.

Think about a dog's face. I know what a joyful experience this can be. It's almost sacred. So I'll give you a moment to stay in it. Okay, fine, two moments. Let's now focus on the anatomy of that face, and specifically the eyes. Dog eyes are front-facing, symmetrically spaced on either side of the snout, and situated beneath a large forehead. In this regard, they look sort of like babies, and it's one of the reasons that we like them so much—dogs, I mean, though babies too. It's also why they are so easy to draw as cute cartoon abstractions.

These features not only make dogs easy to draw, they also make them powerful emotional communicators. I remember being a child and decoding when one of my dogs was sad (avoiding eye contact, tucked-back ears, tail tucked too). There is also something called a "dog grimace" that means, more or less, *I'm sorry*. (The lips are pulled back to expose teeth, eyes closed.) There's a famous internet video of an owner interrogating his dogs over who chewed up a bag of "kitty cat" treats. The first suspect is an old Golden Retriever, Macy, who looks back impassively: *Not me*. Then the camera pans to Denver, a yellow Lab, who is wearing a textbook expression of the dog grimace and, not coincidentally, licking his lips. He's the culprit, filled with shame and cat treats.

I have a friend with two sons, and while the older of them is emotionally articulate—he's aware of his own emotions and able to describe the emotions of others—his younger son has always had more difficulty in that department. When he was five or so, the family got a dog, and the younger kid bonded with it immediately. A few months later, he started doing what my friend described as "dog theater." He would interpret the dog's emotions at first: "Winston is sad" or "Winston is happy." Soon enough, that progressed to imitations. If he felt sad, he would do the classic sad-puppy face, pulling up his inner eyebrows to make his eyes larger. If he felt happy, he wouldn't necessarily smile, but he would open his mouth a bit and raise his eyebrows. "It made a big difference," my friend said. "He went from being emotionally blocked to having this whole range of emotions he could portray. All of them were taken from the dog." I liked hearing this because it reminded me of me. I gravitated toward dogs because they made me feel comfortable expressing myself, which in turn made me better able to engage with other people. If there was a dog, I would do my "canine ventriloquism," inventing funny monologues in what I thought (and everyone else in the room believed) was the dog's true inner voice. "I'm gonna bite you . . . later," said in the voice of something akin to a Russian Bond girl. Everyone would laugh and I would feel more like myself. Dogs can make humans more human. After a while, my friend said, his son started figuring out ways to express his emotions on his own. "That's great," he said. "But in a way we missed those dog imitations."

What we learn from dogs goes beyond their capacity for emotional expression. When I photograph dogs, I am trying to get them to look at the camera. But they don't know what a camera is (and they never will). When they appear to be looking into the lens, they are really trying to forge a relationship with the human behind the lens (albeit a very strange noise-making human who appears to have three eyes). But beyond the photographic techniques, there's a deeper dimension to the emotional state of dogs. Dogs are generally eager and energetic, unselfconscious and resilient, curious and trusting. They can be mischievous. They can be possessive, especially around food. I personally believe they're capable of many of the same emotions we possess: happiness, sadness, jealousy, anger, confusion, restlessness. Some experts may disagree with some of those, but I know many of you are nodding in agreement (and might actually feel as though I left out a few). But what dogs are not—what they *cannot* be—is vain the way that people can be vain, or spiteful the way that people can be spiteful, or disingenuous, or putting on a front to impress a colleague, or engaging in flattery.

A guy I know likes to text me passages from books that mention dogs. Recently he found a passage in a Dennis Lehane thriller where two guys are discussing a third guy's devious nature. It's hard for the two guys to say exactly what this other guy is like, but they can say what he isn't like: a dog. No matter what dogs are, whether they're loyal or mean or friendly, they are never less than sincere: "All of it, good and bad, comes from the heart." That's exactly right. In the dog world, desires travel along a straight line. They are felt and then they are acted upon. Dogs aren't burdened by egos that (pardon the pun) muzzle their feelings. If a dog feels love, it'll walk over and lick your face. If a dog feels loyalty, it'll walk over and sit right on top of you. If a dog is hungry, it'll knock at its bowl or beg for a piece of your dinner. If a dog wants to go outside, it'll stand near the door, or paw at it, or turn to whatever tactics it's learned to get you off your phone and get you to put your shoes on. This directness is refreshing in a world where too much human behavior is calculated. Dogs are candid by definition (though I may make it seem otherwise through my photography, every photo of a dog ever taken is a candid).

Not only are dogs straightforward, but people are straightforward about their dogs, often to the point of being TMI-level excessive. In a decade of being The Dogist, I have heard so much about people's dogs, and while it isn't always flattering, it's always delivered with love. When dogs look ridiculous, their owners whip out their phones to document and share it with their entire contact list. When a dog farts, their humans call them out in front of everyone (though dogs are often the scapegoats for human farts—a fact that proves my point even more). Love liberates honesty when it comes to the way people talk about their dogs. So why doesn't that extend to the way people talk about their children, say? Can you imagine a human being saying candidly that their young son stinks, or that their young daughter is clumsy, or that their newborn baby is passing through an awkward phase that makes him look like a Muppet? It would be satisfying to hear confessions like that from others—and probably to say them ourselves—but repression prevents us from speaking freely. Lest we offend someone, we typically hold these discussions behind one another's backs, which isn't healthy either. And it's even harder to turn the focus toward ourselves. We use mental gymnastics to come up with all types of excuses to avoid facing our true selves. The alternative threatens our fragile human egos. But what if we cast off this burden? What if we embraced our own truth the way we embrace our dogs' truths?

I have run into a few Dogist dogs that demonstrate this principle powerfully. The first was Rowdy, a thirteen-year-old Lab I met in

Oregon (I don't usually hop on a plane to visit an individual dog, but Rowdy was an exception). Rowdy was your typical-looking black Lab, until about the age of seven, when his owner started to notice the fur around his face changing. What developed was a case of extremely pronounced vitiligo, the skin condition that results in uneven patches of pigmentation. His toenails even turned white. Strangely, he developed strikingly symmetrical patches around his eyes that made him look like . . . well, opinions varied. His owner went through the growing list of all the things Rowdy's internet fans likened him to. An orca or a panda were popular comparisons. Some people said Spider-Man. Some people said he looked like he was Deadpool, or that he was in KISS.

Around the same time that I met Rowdy, I went to San Francisco and made my rounds at various dog hot spots in the city: Golden Gate Park, Duboce Park, Mission Dolores Park, and Crissy Field. Upon arriving at one of the reservoirs in McLaren Park, I noticed dozens of dogs playing, fetching sticks and balls out of the water. After a few minutes, I noticed something else, something peculiar. A yellow Lab went to fetch a stick (not the peculiar part), and when it turned around to head back to shore, I saw that it had no eyes. I grabbed for my camera like a Planet Earth photographer who has just seen a snow leopard. He headed toward a human on the beach, and I did too.

"Is that your dog?" I asked excitedly.

"Yeah, that's Cheeto."

Cheeto dropped the stick by his person's foot and immediately spun around to go for another retrieve.

"How does he know where you're throwing it?" I asked, perplexed.

"He can hear where it splashes."

The stick hit the water and Cheeto locked in on it like a laser-guided fur missile.

I was some combination of impressed and amazed. An eyeless retriever, retrieving.

Cheeto had been blind since birth with a condition called detached retinas and had a double enucleation at the age of one. (Enucleation means to have an eye removed. It's a rare procedure, but it can be necessary if a dog has eye tumors or cancer or suffers from intense pain from elevated ocular pressure.) But as I learned at the reservoir, his lack of vision did not interfere with his doggedness—or more specifically, his Cheeto-ness. If watching Cheeto with his owner was inspiring, watching him around the other dogs was even more so. The other dogs didn't notice his condition at all. It wasn't as if a few of them went off to the side to have a hushed, judgmental conversation about how the dog with no eyes was making them feel uncomfortable. It was just another day at the park. They had balls to chase.

Rosie, Australian Shepherd-mix, Brooklyn Heights Promenade, Brooklyn, NY • "She's a rescue from Texas and she's terrified of squeakers. It's bad—if someone does it in the park she'll bolt into the street."

CHAPTER 12

A DOG IS A NICER PERSON

In the last section, I mentioned this friend I know who sends me dog-themed passages from books. Some of them are too obvious: *Old Yeller, The Call of the Wild.* Others are too obscure. Recently, he texted to tell me that he had found something interesting in Graham Greene's *Travels with My Aunt.* I didn't know the book, and I told him so. He wrote back and told me that it was a comic novel from the late sixties about an English guy who goes to his mother's funeral and meets an eccentric aunt. I still wasn't sold. He called me to make the case.

Early in the book, he said, there's a scene with a guy in a hospital. He wants his dogs to visit him there, but the hospital objects. To get around their rules, the guy tells the nurses that his dogs are a married couple who were married in a dog church. This absurd lie somehow makes them respectable enough in the eyes of the nurses, and they are allowed in as visitors.

When the guy gets released from the hospital, he goes about making his crazy scheme a reality, and actually founds a dog church. In the course of developing the church, one of the characters in the book reads through the Bible to find references to dogs. What she finds disappoints her. Dogs aren't mentioned very often, and when they are, the mentions tend to be negative—dogs are considered dirty creatures, and dogliness is the furthest thing from godliness. In the book of Revelation, Jesus counts them among other disreputable figures: "Without are dogs and sorcerers and whoremongers and murderers and idolaters, and whosoever loveth or maketh a lie." As it turns out, the New Testament isn't alone in this view. The Old Testament also emphasizes the uncleanliness and the viciousness of dogs. (This seems plausible for the time. Space was limited. Hygiene was iffy—dog groomers were *very* few and far between. The dogs in these ancient cities may have carried diseases and were probably treated poorly and responded in kind: a vicious cycle. There wasn't a fully formed tradition of canine-human bonds, at least from a pet-owning perspective.)

The character in the book thinks that this view needs to be significantly adjusted, and I agree. If you look at other faiths and traditions, the picture brightens. Ancient civilizations buried dogs with people to serve as guides in the afterlife. Hindus believe dogs are sacred, that they guard heaven and that gods could appear in canine form. And while the teachings of the Buddha do not specifically mention dogs, Buddhism holds that all beings can come to embody principles of enlightenment. Contemporary Christian and Jewish institutions have also softened. Every October 1, in honor of St. Francis of Assisi, the patron saint of pets and animals, there's a Blessing of the Animals at the Cathedral Church of St. John the Divine, among other churches, in New York City. You can bring your pet, whether turtle or bird or camel (yes, there was one) or Boxer or Pomeranian or Lhasa Apso, to be blessed by a priest. If your pet is too big, you can bring a photo. If your pet is deceased, they'll bless its ashes.

Travels with My Aunt suggests that dogs may already be blessed. As one of the nurses says, "You can't tell me that dogs haven't got souls." I agree. If we believe that we have souls—and we appear, on the basis of all the religions we've made, to believe that deeply—then dogs have them too. And theirs can help ours: they can refine them, enlarge them, improve them. Dogs can connect the dots in our being. They can fill in the missing pieces. They can allow us to *human* better. Dogs are creatures not just of nature but of our better nature.

Andy Rooney, a famous curmudgeon, loved dogs. They made him think better of people. "The average dog is a nicer person than the average person," he said. Even the Grinch, kind of the Andy Rooney of children's literature, had a dog, Max, who kept his heart from freezing completely. See: I am keeping my Dogist Pledge. After each highbrow reference (Graham Greene) comes a pop culture reference (in this case, two!).

Encounters with these four-legged nicer people elevate everyday human experience. Over the past several months I have watched my site's traffic move steadily upward. Posts that used to average sixty thousand likes are consistently drawing three times that, and the half-million-like posts are turning into million-like posts. It's not lost on me that this increase in traffic is occurring at a time when the world is in flux and in crisis, both nationally and internationally.

To me, the greater engagement I'm seeing is directly connected to the greater unease in the world, and the discomfort people increasingly feel as they wake up to it. Everyone knows that business booms for defense contractors during periods of conflict. A bad time is a good time to be Raytheon. But business also booms for enterprises that are trying to dissipate the growing clouds of doom. That's where The Dogist comes in. The pictures of dogs I share, the quotes I collect from their owners, the videos that show the dogs and owners interacting, are specifically designed as a source of joy. Over the years I have come to feel that The Dogist is an antidote to the rest of the internet. From my perspective, 90 percent of what the average person sees in their social media feed makes them feel envious, depressed, angry, poor, or all of the above. Dogs fill your cup. They get you in touch with your inner child. They let you be you because they are being just themselves. They make you laugh and guffaw and get goose bumps.

I thought about that the other day when I was clicking around trying to find something to watch on YouTube and I happened to stumble across an episode of *Between Two Ferns with Zach Galifianakis,* the fake talk show. It's cringe comedy in the extreme: Galifianakis spends most of his time embarrassing both his guests and himself with insulting questions, pratfalls, and generally idiotic behavior. Natalie Portman was the guest for this particular episode, and Galifianakis was doing his schtick, complimenting her intelligence in a way that somehow insulted it, creepily asking for her phone number, making inappropriate comments about her body. Though Portman, like every other guest, was certainly in on the joke, she acted horrified. But she was not the only guest. She had come to the show with her dog, a Yorkie named Whiz (great dog name). Early on in the interview, she let him loose and he wandered around the set, eventually coming into the foreground and rolling onto his back. As the show got more and more awkward, Whiz just sat there, a little bundle of unconditional joy. Every time the camera panned to Whiz, the tone of the show lightened and lifted. Whiz killed the cringe. No one could compete with him, even Zach Galifianakis. Everyone was giving an impressive performance, but Whiz's was the most impressive, because it wasn't a performance at all. (It's one of the best dog talk show appearances, though some people prefer Amanda Seyfried's Australian Shepherd, Finn, who hijacked her David Letterman interview, balanced a hamburger on his head in an impromptu Stupid Pet Trick, and then sat in the chair next to her, staring attentively at Letterman.)

The ways in which dogs locate and nourish our better nature can play out in the shadow of the news, or on a TV show. But they are most rewarding when they happen right in front of us. That's what I experience every time I go out to shoot photos for The Dogist, every time I meet a dog. It might be the two-year-old German Shepherd named Lady who wouldn't relinquish the blue ball in her mouth—her most prized possession. It could be Davey, the Husky/Chihuahua–mix (Huskyhuahua? Chihusky?), that will howl with you if you start him off. Or it could be the eleven-year-old Norfolk Terrier, Arthur the Great, who I thought I had seen before (I was right—I had taken pictures of him with his grandmother Freya). Arthur sat on my foot as a way of showing that he liked me, or maybe even remembered me: "He has a crazy memory," his owner said, and while I waited for him to get off my foot (I did not rush him), we also discussed the difference between Norfolk and Norwich Terriers: Norwich ears go up, like a witch's hat, and Norfolks' flop down. Arthur eventually let me have my foot back, but before I left, I asked his mom a last question: "What would life be like without a dog?" She paused. "I hope I never know," she said.

When I started this book, I had a theory about how it would work—or rather, how I would work. I figured that I would think about the book while I was out doing Dogist photo shoots, encountering dogs like Lady and Davey and Arthur and taking mental notes. Then I would come home and write for hours straight. It ended up not quite happening in the way I had imagined. Sam, my fiancée, works from home, and my dog, Elsa (who also works from home), created a loving but real distraction.

Over the months, I tried a few times to do my writing in coffee shops. Sometimes it worked like a charm, but those chairs are never very comfortable. One day, I wasn't sure what to write about. I had my outline open, but there were too many options, all of which seemed important.

I got another cortado and waited for inspiration to hit. While time passed—I knew that it was passing because I began to see morning-walk dogs coming back around for evening walks—a man came into the place. He was older than me and well-dressed. Trailing slightly behind him, on a leash, was a smallish Boxer-mix. The dog had lots of energy. He was in a coffee shop, but he didn't need any coffee. The man ordered an espresso, sat down, and slid his laptop out of his backpack. Within seconds he was typing away quickly and confidently, to the point where I became a little envious. His dog patrolled around the table, sniffing what it could. It came over to me and accepted a head pat. Eventually it curled up underneath his table. I didn't even think of photographing it. It was a writing day.

More time passed. The door to the shop opened again, this time for a mom and two kids, a boy of about six and a girl of about four. The boy had thick glasses with thick frames, and he immediately started walking around the place, both curious and curiously. He was very intense, looked a little downcast, and refused to make eye contact with anyone. I noticed that he was tapping his fingers together, index finger to thumb, over and over again. While his mom and sister went to the counter to order, he wandered toward the corner where I was sitting, which was also the corner where the other guy was sitting. He noticed the dog curled up on the floor, and all of a sudden everything about him changed: his expression, his bearing, everything. "Is this your dog?" he said.

"Yes," the guy said.

"What's his name?"

"Miller," the guy said.

The kid immediately sat down in the empty chair at the guy's table. "Your dog is named Miller," he repeated. He bent down to pet Miller. He still hadn't looked directly at the guy, but he got his nose right up against the dog's nose. "This dog is . . ." he said. "This dog is . . ." He rubbed the dog's muzzle and its chest, and the dog nuzzled the boy's hand.

By now the mom was done ordering. She came over to collect the kid and apologize to the man for the intrusion.

"Oh," the guy said. "No problem."

"Mom," the kid said. "Miller likes when I pet him."

"You don't know this dog," the mom said.

"I just love this dog so much," the kid said. "I love Miller."

"Okay," the mom said. "Well, tell him that and then say goodbye."

"Bye, Miller," the kid said. "Have a great day." He straightened up.

"I love you," he said to the dog. There was joy on his face. That didn't surprise me. But when I looked at Miller's owner, there was joy on his face, too, which surprised me a little. Before the boy had come in, it had been a normal coffee shop environment: work, alienation, boredom, tension. We were all at the mercy of our technology, Modern Humans, passive and disengaged. But when the boy came in and walked over to the dog, a switch had been thrown, and a current had gone through the room.

The mom and kids left. The guy went back to typing. Now I wasn't as envious of him. Now I had something to type too.

- - - - - - - - - - - - - - - 🐾 - - - - - - - - - - - - - - -

Lily, Husky-mix (4.5 years old), 5th St. &
5th Ave., Brooklyn, NY • "One time I cooked
chicken cutlets and I left them on the counter.
I thought she was asleep, so I turned my back,
and when I looked up, she was eating a whole
chicken cutlet on the couch. There was an oil
stain for three years."

- - - - - - - - - - - - - - - 🐾 - - - - - - - - - - - - - -

PART TWO

OUR RELATION- SHIPS

CHAPTER 13

THE (DOGIST) SOCIAL NETWORK

I was a relatively shy kid. It wasn't that I wasn't social at all. I was good at sports, so I had a bunch of friends whom I played with at recess. We liked touch football and wallball. But I wasn't great at being social outside a structured activity. I was never the guy with the big personality in the room. Moving through the world felt awkward, and I was often self-conscious about it. A textbook introvert. Maybe that's a common affliction for adolescent boys, though at the time it felt like it was happening to me more—and more severely— than it was happening to the average person.

In those days, my black Lab Ruby was my best friend. She was always there to listen to me, to keep me company, and to make me laugh at a moment's notice. Back in my shyest days, I used Ruby as a kind of unofficial emotional support dog. But it was more than that. I designed a kind of vaudeville act with her, along with our other dog Matilda (Matilda was considered my siblings' dog). I remember making my siblings, Henry and Isabel, laugh by voicing Ruby and Matilda while they interacted with them, narrating what I figured they would be saying. "Henryyy, if you lub me you gib me chicken."

Or: "Don't leave me, Henry, don't leave me!" Canine ventriloquism sustained me for years. I was good at throwing my voice. (I also did a great Dr. Evil impersonation.) Mostly I was just trying to be funny, but I think it gave me a form of expression that not only let me hold court as a shy person but was something people looked forward to my doing. By voicing my dogs, I was freed from my self-consciousness. I could say things I'd never say in my own voice. Like a dog, I could just be myself. It wasn't like I was saying anything controversial, there's just something so funny to us about a dog's ability to just *say* exactly what they mean. Humor is ultimately a form of truth, anyway. I also threw in some lisps and infantile speech to make people giggle even more (in my head, all dogs have speech impediments). Each dog had their own tone and speaking personality. I'm fairly confident the majority of people who grew up around dogs practice some version of this. For me, humor was my superpower as a kid, and dogs were my favorite muse.

Ruby (along with my other dogs) elevated me in the private setting of my family. She made me feel loved, confident, and funny. But she didn't just help me when I was in the house. She helped me get out of it. Dogs need walks, and their humans have to take them on those walks. It's one of the baseline responsibilities of having a dog, and it has measurable benefits for both parties. (There's a study conducted by the University of Minnesota that shows that dogs are good for your health and especially your heart. Dog owners had an 11 percent lower risk of death overall and a 15 percent lower risk of heart disease. When I saw that study, it didn't surprise me at all, though I didn't read the dogs' effect as some kind of mystical benefit. I just figured that the people who had dogs had to walk them, and that reduced the sedentary habits that harm overall health.)

The ritual of the dog walk has therapeutic benefits that extend to the mind as well as the body. I remember taking Ruby for walks in the neighborhood. Sometimes we would run into other people walking their dogs. We would exchange a nod or a hello, an acknowledgment that we were members of the same club—Dog Walkers Anonymous, perhaps? But even when I wasn't courageous or comfortable enough to say hello to other people, Ruby had a way of breaking the ice. Let's say I was sixteen, in high school, out for a walk, and my head was chock-full of teenage thoughts. Teens always think that everyone is looking at them and judging them, especially when they're fresh from a growth spurt and preoccupied with things like *Does my crush like me*, and *Does my voice sound weird*, and *How many times will I have to repeat my uncommon name to new people*, and *Should I listen to that pretty girl who told me to grow my hair out*, and whatever else.

I would get lost in my thoughts, but not entirely lost, because I had the luxury of being distracted by what was on the other end of the leash: Ruby. I needed to make sure that she was still attached to it, for starters, and that she wasn't getting herself into trouble, eating a weird mushroom or rolling in something gross. But then there were the various people we'd encounter in the neighborhood: There was the goth-looking guy in his late twenties who walked his family's Rottweiler-mix named Roxy (I never knew the guy's name). Or maybe it was the art teacher who taught at a different school, which was great because I would've hated to live near one of my own teachers and run into them outside class anyway. She had a little white dog with tear stains. Or maybe it was the older couple who knew me when I was a little kid and recognized me, even though I had no memory of ever going over to their house. They were on their fourth Golden Retriever. My shyness made me want to go right past them, to avert my gaze, not from rudeness but from a general awkwardness. But Ruby didn't agree. These people were walking their own dogs, and Ruby wanted to say hello to Roxy, or Coco, or Luke. Ruby's sociability, which generally consisted of trotting up to the other dogs and sniffing their butts, maybe a bark or two, created a perfect opportunity for the humans to engage in some low-key small talk. *Hey, how's it going? . . . Oh, you teach art? Cool . . . Did your mom get that note I left under your door about the barbecue next week?* My self-consciousness wouldn't necessarily go away, but with Ruby's help, it would be temporarily defeated.

Having Ruby with me when I walked around my neighborhood as a kid was like a dry run for my later life as The Dogist. Photography wasn't part of the equation, but much of the rest of it was in place. Over the years, I have met more than fifty thousand dogs, which means that I have met slightly fewer than fifty thousand people (some people have multiple dogs, of course, and shelters house hundreds). It's an unfathomable number, one that the young canine ventriloquist would never believe. There are some key differences, of course. When I go out as The Dogist, I don't have a dog by my side. Instead, I have a mission to identify and photograph dogs by other people's sides. But the principle is the same. When I see someone with a dog, I go in like I'm Steve Irwin (RIP) and I have just spotted a rare crocodile. The first thing I say is "Excuse me, may I take a photo of your dog?" This phrase emerged from a distillation process over the last decade, but since the integration of Instagram Reels and TikTok, it has come to be a kind of trademark, one that amuses people. Sometimes I add the word "quickly." Sometimes not. While I want people to know that I intend to let them get on their merry way after a minute or two—or five—I don't want them to think I'm just taking an iPhone snapshot. (Nine times out of ten, that opener phrase works and it's game on. The one time per outing I get turned down, I generally attribute to someone being too busy or worried that it's a solicitation of some kind.)

Lucky for me, dog people are generally kind, thoughtful people, and asking for a photo of their pet while they're out for a routine walk is usually the perfect opportunity (if they're on a phone call, or jogging, or in the middle of eating, I try not to interrupt). Once I get a yes, the rest is pretty smooth sailing. A point of connection is established in the form of the four-legged creature at the end of their leash—and more than that, a point of agreement. I have stopped them because I believe that their dog is awesome, and they have received me in that same spirit. The clumsy set of questions, doubts, self-doubts, and concerns that can often crop up in an initial encounter are nowhere to be found. In that state, the two of us move more quickly to a relaxed and open discussion. If I ran into someone without a dog and we struck up a conversation, it would be harder to get comfortable, and the empty small talk would last longer. Our guards would be up. They would be thinking, *What does this guy want from me?* and I would be thinking, *Am I being weird?* But when a dog is involved, everyone feels like they can trust people a bit more.

Conversations that take place in the presence of dogs include another interesting phenomenon. Most of the time, I don't look directly at the dog's owner, and he or she does not look directly at me. We are focused on the dog, the expressiveness of its face, its habits, its overall adorableness. Conversation is reflected through their beloved pet, which means that neither of us feels put on the spot. There are human analogs. A friend of mine once told me that he was having trouble communicating with his teenage son. A therapist recommended that in approaching him for a discussion, it was advisable not to sit opposite him, with maximum eye contact, but to sit on the same side of the table or talk to him while driving. It seems counterintuitive. Wouldn't you want the maximum levels of intimacy? The therapist explained that the main goal was to decrease any sense of confrontation and in turn decrease self-consciousness. Dogs are a living, breathing same side of the table. They simultaneously disarm us and supply us with common cause. (In fact, whenever I approach someone, I always approach from the *dog side,* to communicate clearly that the dog is the focal point, the thing that will assist the conversation to exist and then to continue.)

I have experienced thousands of dog-assisted conversations in the last decade, and all have been proof of this canine unification capacity. I have spoken to people in their nineties and people in their teens. I have spoken to people of all races and stepped over language barriers. (I know one phrase in Mandarin Chinese: "Nǐ de xiǎo gǒu jiào shénme," which translates to "What is your small dog's name?"

I used this phrase when I visited China in 2014.) And dogs can even break down political differences—no easy task in present-day America. About a year ago, I was in the city and saw a handsome German Shepherd. When I first spot a dog, I get a type of tunnel vision, where everything around me disappears except the dog. After I asked the German Shepherd's owner for a picture, I looked up and noticed that he was very proudly wearing a Trump shirt. This wouldn't necessarily faze me, but in an overtly liberal city like NYC, he was clearly trying to get a rise out of people, and I tend to avoid politics when it comes to The Dogist. In this case, though, avoiding the man or his politics wasn't my first thought. Photographing his handsome German Shepherd was. As I took pictures, we chatted about his dog, who was named Max. I think my sincere interest in the dog made the owner comfortable, and also step back politically. Maybe Max was all he needed to feel seen. It made me feel for a moment as if I were in some pre-divisive version of America, where the default wasn't to be driven apart from one another but rather to be drawn together.

I got another reminder of the social power of dogs in late 2023. On the weekend before Halloween, to be precise. My fiancée, Sam, and I went to a Halloween party. Everyone wore costumes. I was dressed as Forrest Gump—specifically runner Gump, with a full beard, shorts, and Nike Cortez sneakers. She was dressed as Tom Cruise, circa *Risky Business*. People circulated and struck up conversations from behind the anonymity of their masks and outfits. We spoke briefly to one couple dressed as Beauty and the Beast, but in reverse—he was Beauty and she was the Beast. The conversation was nothing, really. We talked about whether LA's bagels could compete with NYC's (some can). It was light and superficial, but also genuinely friendly. Sam did her *Risky Business* sock slide down the hallway. The Beast laughed. We moved on.

About ten minutes later, I looked over at Sam. She had a completely dumbfounded look on her face. "What's up?"

She continued to stare across the room, fixated on something. It was the Beast, who had just recently taken her mask off to get some fresh air.

Sam motioned me down so I could hear her (I'm a foot taller than her).

"Do you know who that is?!"

"No," I said. Sam looked like she was about to cry.

"She's one of my heroes . . . I've been to three of her concerts."

For the next ten minutes or so, Sam stood there paralyzed, trying to simultaneously avoid and not avoid eye contact with her. People probably thought she was acting out the scene from the movie where Joel found out the crystal egg was missing from his parents' mantelpiece.

"You have to talk to her," I said.

When I saw that the Beast was about to leave, I tapped her shoulder and pointed her toward Sam, who instantly poured out all the thoughts that had been welling up over the last twenty minutes. And all that nervousness was for nothing. They got along like peas and carrots, as Forrest would say. Sisterly, even.

The next morning, I was thinking of the party in dog terms—occupational hazard. I've always loved Halloween and Halloween parties, but couldn't really articulate why. Then it dawned on me: on Halloween, we can all be as free as dogs. Donning a costumed alter-ego allows us to check our own egos at the door. Only after the Beast reassumed her human form did Sam's ego return. It was like when the lights come on at the end of a middle school dance. Do we really need to dress as beasts to feel comfortable enough to discuss bagels? In lieu of having a little beast with you (a dog), it seems the answer is yes. Without the costume-enabled bagel banter, neither person would've likely felt comfortable connecting if Sam had been star-struck off the bat. They each had to meet each other's inner dog first, free from ego. Halloween parties are metaphorical dog parks—places where you can run in and sniff anyone's proverbial butt without fear of judgment (and yes, I do know there are things called furry conventions where people dress as animal characters, but we won't go there). Helped along by her inner dog, Sam could approach the Beast without crippling awkwardness, or for that matter any awkwardness at all. People were drawn to each other simply because they were in the same space. They proceeded as social creatures. "We were all dogs at the dog park," I said to Sam.

"What are you talking about?" she said. "Does Elsa want to go to the park again?" Yes, and I think we should join her.

Dog cultures are not the same everywhere in the world, of course. I have logged thousands and thousands of miles as The Dogist, and wherever I have gone, I have paid special attention to how dogs are treated and what they mean. Sometimes the treatment is the same as in the United States but better. I have been to Ireland, where dogs are both revered and put to work—I did a series of photographs of working Border Collies herding sheep there. I have been to Switzerland, where the dog culture is strong but conservative, with a very regimented system of dog breeding and general behavioral expectations about them (I visited an actual museum dedicated to their most famous Swiss breed, the Saint Bernard). I have been to rural China, where Communist ideology makes it hard for people to prioritize care for a dog when their available resources barely cover the costs of their human needs. China also has a dog meat trade, unthinkable to Western sensibilities. I'll never forget the gut-wrenching feeling I got after making eye contact with one of the dogs in a dirty, cramped cage at an outdoor meat market, awaiting its demise. It haunts me, sometimes, to this day. But as The Dogist, I make an effort to focus on the positive instead of wallowing in the darkness. While there, in Guilin, we stayed at an Airbnb owned by an Australian couple. And on their porch, greeting all their visitors, was Dorji, a dog that looked just like the dog I had locked eyes with at the market. Dorji wasn't their "pet" per se, but he was given safe haven, food, and the occasional bath on their front porch. Dorji was lucky, at least for the time being, and his happy existence in an area where many like him were rounded up to experience a form of hell gave me some hope.

Since that visit, I have worked with several organizations that try to save dogs destined for that fate and transport them Stateside, where they're placed in loving homes. I even fostered one, named Bella, once. (Historically, dogs have been farmed for meat in other places too: Vietnam, Indonesia, Korea. I have not been to Korea, but a colleague of mine has told me that the Korean dog meat industry differed from the Chinese industry primarily in its optics. Korea has historically concealed the practice until the animals are slaughtered, at which time they look like any other animal hanging in a butcher shop. He also said that as South Korea has become more Western, the practice has declined. It is now frowned upon and will be illegal by 2027.) In India, the huge numbers of street dogs not only reinforce the idea that dogs are dirty, unruly creatures, but they create generations of children whose first canine encounters are angry barks or actual bites. Fear of dogs is widespread there and persists in many Indian American communities. This may be changing. According to a recent article in *The Times of India,* there are various large-scale attempts to raise awareness of the benefits of dogs. They have started to have a positive effect on pet adoption rates. I have felt it firsthand, a bit: The Dogist audience in India has steadily increased over the years. There are also places I haven't been whose dog cultures fascinate me. I'd love to spend some time in Japan photographing dogs and getting a sense of their unique canine culture, or go to Nepal for Kukur Tihar, a festival that celebrates the divinity of dogs.

For the most part, though, dogs are a universal currency—they mean the same thing in more places than they mean different things. In the summer of 2023, Sam and I took a trip to Greece. We were coming out of the constrictions of COVID, and there was no better place to do it—beautiful old buildings, beautifully clear water, delicious food. The people, too, were stunning, like they had descended from the gods that I had always assumed were mythical. While I was there, I tried to take dog photos that also incorporated the area's natural beauty. In the picturesque downtown area of Antiparos, I met Lily and Lita. They were both from the same small village in Crete, and though they were a combination of many different breeds, they were primarily Kokoni, a Greek native breed that has only recently been officially recognized. On Faros beach on the south side of Sifnos, I met a little white terrier-mix named May. May had been abused as a puppy and, her owner said, "was not very open to people," which is why it surprised her that she sat for me and gave me a few exceptionally cute moments. I was also delighted that, despite being on the opposite side of the earth from NYC, her parents were avid Dogist fans. Near the Platis Gialos beach in Sifnos, I met a two-year-old Golden Retriever named Simba, who was both exceptionally friendly and exceptionally hungry. "His favorite food is all of my food," his owner said.

Then, in the middle of our trip, we had a cloudless day when we chartered a speedboat with our friends—some we were well acquainted with, some we had just met for the first time—and ended up dropping anchor in what seemed like the middle of nowhere and sort of was, in the sense that it was a tiny cove near a beach on Polyaigos, an uninhabited island near Kimolos. The name means "many goats" because—if you care to venture a wild guess—many goats live there. This piece of information had not been communicated beforehand, or was lost in translation from our mostly Greek-speaking captain. I strapped on my mask and snorkel (yes, my personal snorkel I brought from NYC), put my iPhone in a custom watertight case (also brought from NYC), and hopped off the boat to start swimming into the little rocky beach with everyone else. We all made it to the beach, and I took some photos of everyone in this magically remote and untouched place. Then, out of nowhere, two goats appeared, having surreptitiously descended from the cliffs to see what we were up to (and probably if we had any food). I snapped into action with my iPhone, with everyone suggesting I had just captured my inaugural post as The Goatist. I giggled to myself, my inner voice saying, *I just can't escape from photographing four-legged crea-*

tures, even after flying across the world to make some attempt at a vacation. But then, while still in the midst of the impromptu goat photo shoot, one of my friends said, "Oh my god, Elias, turn around." I turned, and through the intensity of the afternoon sun in the background, I made out a figure approaching on a paddleboard. Well, two figures. I squinted my eyes to make out the silhouette of a beautiful young woman in a bikini accompanied by her dog.

I looked over to Sam, who gave me a look I recognized (*Duty calls, I know, but I'm watching you*), and then I approached them while they made their way in to shore. "Hi, there! May I take a photo of your dog? I photograph dogs around the world." I added a bit of extra explanation given the circumstances. "Sure!" she said, in an Italian accent. I snapped into action with my iPhone-in-a-bag beach rig and started making trademark noises toward her dog, Forza, a Border Collie. I can only imagine the goats found this to be amusing as well, but my attention had been diverted from them entirely.

"Are you The Dogist?" she asked.

My friends collectively said, "Ahh!" I was flattered to have found an international fan, though I also had the same feeling the goats elicited—an inability to stop working and just lie on the beach with my friends. Dogs (and I guess the occasional goat) are just that great.

Forza was two years old, and she was an agility dog. It's a particular distinction. She wasn't just an agile dog. I had met plenty of those. She was an agility dog, which meant that she was an athlete who competed in events that are best described as canine track and field. Dog agility courses require dogs to run off leash alongside their handler, who gives them verbal and gestural cues, through everything from high jumps to tunnels to weave poles. The dog that goes through the course the fastest, with the least number of errors, wins. Border Collies are almost always the best—this type of agility requires a high degree of athleticism and a particular type of canine intelligence.

I threw the dog's ball to photograph some water retrievals, and I asked the young woman what her plans were for Forza. "I'm still working on it," she said. "I would like her to end up on a search and rescue team or something." She described Forza's personality as "really dynamic when it comes to work, but when it comes to socializing, she's not really fond of it." I snapped a few more shots but felt the glare of her boyfriend, who had swum in after them. I thanked them and returned to my friends, who had been watching the whole thing like a captive audience. "And it's a write-off!" one of them said. I laughed, put my mask back on, and returned to the boat.

George Elliot, Great Pyrenees (7 years old), Washington Square Park, New York, NY · "She had to interview with the board of our building before we moved in. When she got there, she went around the table and gave each of them a paw. They liked her more than us. Dogs are really better than us."

CHAPTER 14

PUPPY LOVE

A dog can bring people into contact. It can bring people into conversation. But a dog can also bring people together. I mean *together* together: into sustained romantic relationships. When I am out as The Dogist, I regularly encounter couples who are not only walking with dogs but who have origin stories that center around their dogs. Sometimes they volunteer their stories. Sometimes I ask.

I remember speaking to a woman named Leigh D'Angelo, the CEO and cofounder of an app called Dig, a dating app that specifically targeted dog lovers. Over the course of our talk, Leigh addressed the entire swath of issues related to dogs, dating, and dating with dogs. Do your dog preferences make you less likely to meet certain kinds of people? How severely does your dog lifestyle restrict your dating options? How many long-term relationships grow directly from dog-aided dates? What if the people like each other but the dogs aren't compatible? The discussion with Leigh was fascinating. At that time, her site was still not letting visitors search by breed. "We don't want breedists," she said. She did want to collect dog-adjacent pickup lines, and she posted a number of them. ("I've always been a cat person, but for you, I'd be willing to go to the bark side" was one, but I can't imagine that it was one of the best ones. I was briefly tempted to use it, if only to see how quickly it would clear out a room.)

What I discovered pretty quickly, both from Leigh and in my own research, was that the serendipitous dog encounter that average people might think of first—man or woman out with his or her dog strikes up a conversation with man or woman out with his or her dog, cue romantic spark—is relatively rare, more wishful thinking than the norm. I'm sure many of you are shaking your head right now—full credit to your four-legged wingman/wingwoman. Once while I was out at brunch I overheard a woman say that her dog had helped her get together with three guys over the course of a winter, but the way she told the story, it seemed like she might have had the same winter even without the dog. But a human meet-cute with dogs getting tangled in a street leash tornado and the man catching the woman as she trips into his arms? That's more a Hollywood contrivance than anything. Maybe a lost episode of *Sex and the City* where Carrie fosters a dog. (As I was pressing the period on the end of that sentence, an ad came on TV for a new romantic comedy about two young people, both dog owners, who meet not-cute. They don't like each other very much at first. He's bossy and she's defensive, or maybe it's the other way around. Their dogs, on the other hand, like each other. They really like each other: her dog impregnates his. Cut to: veterinarian. "You're going to be grandparents," he says. Cut to: laughing, fumbling, kissing. This movie, whose title, *Puppy Love*, might well have been generated by AI, is exactly the kind of thing that doesn't happen in real life.)

Still, thinking about the ways that dogs behave can help us better understand and manage our romantic relationships. I like to start with the sniff. You know what I mean. It's the first thing that happens when two dogs meet. They unselfconsciously walk right up to each other and sniff butts. I wish there was a euphemistic way to say this. *They query the space around the top of the hind legs? They investigate* the other side of the other? *They make each other's ass-quaintance?* There isn't. When kids see dogs doing this, they giggle. Why would they not? Parents sometimes try to explain it away as the dogs' way of saying hello. "They're just getting to know each other, dear."

In truth, though, the sniff is less a conversational process than a research project. Each dog is scanning the other one for a variety of factors that can be communicated via scent. Dogs are good at smelling, somewhere between ten and a hundred thousand times better than humans, so a dog sniff produces a comprehensive dossier. A dog can determine if the other dog is sick or well, friendly or hostile, and even whether or not it is a good prospective mate. Humans, of course, don't do this. It would be considered rude, not to mention that our greatly diminished olfactory powers would bring us only a fraction of this information. But there are versions of it that have been re-created in a controlled environment that are eye- (and nose-) opening. Take the famous T-shirt study, in which single women were asked to smell a series of T-shirts worn by different men and then rate those men, sight unseen. The women tended to be most attracted to the shirts worn by men with different histo-compatibility genes, which means that they were picking men who were, as potential procreative partners, more likely to maintain ge-netic variation, improve species-wide immunity, and limit inbreed-ing. In other words, they were emphasizing the best practices of sexual selection.

In our everyday human life, of course, we don't roll that way. We have put a billion layers between ourselves and this natural process. The way we select our partners—through setups arranged by mutual friends, by internet stalking, or by swiping right—brings a number of other distracting factors into play: the college the person went to, or the designer jacket they are wearing, or the quality of their profile picture. This is not to say that those things are inherently bad rea-sons for picking a mate, only that nature has time-tried ways of de-livering us more sophisticated and layered information about prospective mates. Again, I'm not recommending that on your next first date you skip the hug and go in for a booty sniff. Definitely do *not* do that. I'm just saying that we should all be aware that even the most fundamental choices we make, like who we take as our partners, are at once more complex and more simple than we realize, and that at least some of our human confusion arises from the fact that we are not in touch with our more primal instincts. And as it happens, seeing a person with a dog does arouse some fundamental instinct. This is something that Leigh mentioned in our conversation, and something that I have felt for a long time. When you see a person with a dog, you understand immediately that you are seeing someone with the capacity to love. That's a great start.

As The Dogist, I don't generally take requests. On shoot days (my favorite days), I set out roaming the streets of New York (or whatever other city I happen to be in), looking for dogs I think will make for good Dogist posts. Generally that means something that stands out to me. When it comes to solicitations I receive by email, while I personally find fan mail fun, and while I enjoy looking at pictures of people's dogs that they've submitted, I generally have to leave it at that. There are, of course, always exceptions, when an email is telling me the beginning of a story that I feel needs to be told more fully.

A few years ago, I started to see certain kinds of requests pop up more frequently in my inbox. The messages came from men, mostly, and they would usually start by telling me that their girlfriends (sometimes boyfriends) loved The Dogist, and that they've always wanted to get their dog featured on the site. The guy writing the letter would explain that he and his partner had met a few years ago (or months ago), and that things were going great, to the point that marriage was on the horizon. Their dog was an integral part of their life. Could I work with them and their dog and somehow help them pop the question? At first, I wasn't quite sure how to respond to those requests. I wasn't sure exactly how I could help. Did they want me to come to their house and take pictures of the drop-to-the-knee-and-present-the-ring moment? If that was what they wanted, maybe a wedding photographer would be better.

What broke me was an email that was specific in its appeal. In fact, it was *Mission: Impawsible*–level specific. There was a man named Corey, a woman named Jordan, and something that Jordan had said to Corey more than once: that it was her dream to have her dog, Oakley, featured on The Dogist. The dream took root inside Corey, and one day he emailed me with a proposal for a proposal. He wanted me to photograph their dog on the bench in Central Park near Fifty-Ninth Street where he had first asked Jordan out. But the photograph wouldn't just be of the dog: it would be of the dog with a handwritten sign around its neck that asked Jordan to marry him. I was already leaning toward yes, but when I found out that Oakley was a Chinese Crested Powderpuff, a dog that had previously eluded me, it was a done deal. (The Chinese Crested Powderpuff is one of two kinds of Chinese Crested Dog—a rare breed originally employed as a ratter on ships. Some of them are hairless. Others have hair bursting out all over. Oakley had hair bursting out all over.)

I met up with Corey and photographed Oakley on their special bench with a "Jordan, will you marry our roommate?" sign on his neck. We then moved on to phase two of Corey's plan, which was to post the picture on a Saturday at the exact time when he and Jordan would be out walking in the park, Oakley-free. I made sure to have Oakley's proposal post go up right on the dot. Corey, out on the path near the bench, asked Jordan to check The Dogist Instagram. She did. She saw Oakley posted, and made a noise, something like the one you'd make if your kid got into their dream college. Then she looked closer at the sign around his neck. She made a second, similar noise and then looked up from the phone to find Corey, but he was gone—or rather, he had dropped out of sight, taking a knee so that he could complete the proposal. She had regained her composure enough by then to say yes. That triggered phase three: their friends, who had been waiting and watching from nearby, brought Oakley to them, and I popped out from behind a tree (okay, maybe not from an actual tree, but I like that visual better) to take pictures of the happy trio. I quickly raced home to upload and post the follow-up to Oakley-Corey's proposal, since my audience was waiting with bated breath for her answer. I remember everyone being really excited and happy for them in the comments section. Everyone loves love.

A year or so later I got another request from a guy who wanted me to meet him and his girlfriend in Bryant Park. We would play it like a random meeting—I would approach them like I approached any potential subjects, come up calmly with my boilerplate question: "Excuse me, may I take a photo of your dog?" Then I would continue on through the usual questions. What's the dog's name? What's its breed? How old? What's he like? Can he have a treat? Then I would notice that there was something hanging from the dog's collar, which turned out to be an engagement ring. "Oh, what's this?" I would say, and I would say it again if the girlfriend didn't hear me the first time. Eventually, she'd notice, and then the boyfriend would get down on a knee, and everyone would hug: man to woman, woman to man, everyone to dog. As I had with Corey, Jordan, and Oakley, I would document the moment. That one went off like a charm too.

I am still cool toward requests, on average, but if the request involves a marriage proposal, I'm more likely to thaw. Every time I get a new request like this, I spend a little time thinking about the motivation of the participants. I was a psychology major, after all. The canine motivation seems pretty straightforward. Dogs like walks, they like attention, and they like seeing their parents happy and hugging. But how about the people? A marriage proposal is a daunting thing. You only have one chance to create the story that (hopefully) you'll be telling people for fifty years. In a big moment like a proposal, a dog is there to calm your nerves, take some of the edges off the fumbling for the ring and flubbed lines of your rehearsed speech. But more important, they're there because they're a crucial part of a couple's life and shouldn't be absent from such a momentous occasion like asking to spend the rest of your life with someone. Also, how could you say no to a dog? (In a happy coincidence, New York is one of the nearly thirty states that allow dogs to be official witnesses on marriage certificates. If a dog brings you together with your partner, maybe reward the dog with this privilege.)

I first met my fiancée, Sam, when I was much younger. We went to the same high school and even had overlapping social circles, but it was strictly platonic back then. We lost track of each other in college and then, through a few chance encounters on the streets of NYC (we lived in the same area, coincidentally), we reconnected in our late twenties. That time, things accelerated quickly—it turned out we had romantic chemistry. That also skittered out quickly. I wasn't ready to commit. Dogs were a factor, in a strange way—The Dogist had started to get some traction, and that meant that as a single guy dating in New York, I had a special added cachet. When I went on dating apps—and I went on most of them—I would subtly code my profession: "Photographer," I'd say. But I always made sure my photos were full of puppies and dogs, a classic dating app cheat code. In my case, there was nothing insincere about it. Many of my first dates would play coy: "You take pictures of dogs? Wow, that's so cool!" or "Wait, I think my friend has heard of you" or "Do you think Coco can make the cut?" Those who were less shy about admitting that they knew what I did for a living were often surprised to discover that I had a relatively modest demeanor. "I thought you were going to be a total douchebag, to be honest," they'd say. (I guess that's what they call a backhanded compliment?)

That was a fun, chaotic time—a series of quick relationships, each of which had its own greatness but none of which had enough to last. Honestly, I can't think of one bad date I went on (okay, maybe one or two). I didn't have a dog of my own yet, but it made me think about how dogs might function in relationships. I experienced all the things that Leigh later mentioned. When I met a woman, I considered whether the two of us had a legitimate attraction that might last, but I also thought about her "dog energy"—about her relationship with dogs, or her own dog, and whether I could see myself *having* a dog with her. If I was out with a woman and discovered that she didn't have a dog, I'd make sure our second date was in a dog-populated area, so I could see how she engaged with the dogs we'd meet. A canine litmus test. If I was out with a woman and discovered that she didn't like dogs, I kept it to one drink, hugged her goodbye, and spent the rest of my night trying to determine how she figured we could possibly have a connection given the clues I'd dropped in my dating profile. (Did they think they could convert me to becoming a non-dog person?) During that time, I thought back to my early twenties, when my girlfriend at the time, Naomi—coincidentally, the first-ever Dogist follower—celebrated my birthday by getting me a number of standard presents and then one decidedly nonstandard one. She borrowed her friend's dog Raisin, a brindle French Bulldog that looked like one, to spend the day with us. It will forever stand as one of the best birthday presents I've ever received, and one of the funniest.

When I did meet a woman with a dog, it felt like a prepackaged deal. I briefly went out with a woman who had a Toy Poodle. I liked her. She was smart and funny and we were attracted to each other. And of course, despite her dog not being exactly what I had pictured on my Future Dog Mood Board, I liked her dog too. But I wasn't thrilled about the way her dog fit into her life. For example, if we were in bed, the dog would be in the bed. If anything were to happen in bed, the dog would stay right there. I realized she didn't have the heart to draw a clear boundary with her dog, and that unnerved me a bit. And as much as I love dogs, I do think a little privacy and space are important sometimes.

Beginning to see my dates and girlfriends through the prism of their dog energy helped me hone in on the qualities I was looking for. But dating apps also traffic in volume, which means that there's always another new picture to swipe on, which means that the concept of settling into a long-term relationship is an uphill battle against your animal mind. That's why Sam's and my first dalliance came and went so quickly. I remember running into her once in the neighborhood while she was walking her father's dog, a big Golden-doodle named Barry White. We had a nice talk, I snapped a picture of Barry for The Dogist and posted it, but it didn't solidify into anything more meaningful. I knew I cared about her deeply, but I just wasn't ready for something serious.

Then came COVID. I have written elsewhere about my escape from the city (heartbroken friend, too much avocado toast), and how it connected me to a Husky-mix named Elsa. When I returned to my apartment in the city, I was a changed man. I was no longer just The Dogist, no longer just a dog enthusiast or canine evangelist. I was a dog owner. This changed my dating life drastically. At first, it just brought more of the same. Having Elsa by my side certainly didn't make things more difficult. (It was partly that it broadcast my capacity for love and commitment, but also partly just the fact that everyone loves a beautiful dog, and Elsa is certainly that.) Soon enough, though, I realized that Elsa had changed the way I thought about the women I was dating. They didn't just have to be compatible with me, they had to be compatible with her as well.

One day, out of the blue, I got a text from Sam. We had been talking a bit during the beginning of COVID, but I was in the proverbial doghouse after going radio silent. But I missed her, and her text came at a time when I was feeling a bit lost. She had a friend named Erika who had just gotten a Golden Retriever puppy named Cow-boy. The dog, she said, was gorgeous, and she was wondering if I would consider photographing it. I met them while they were at brunch at Sadelle's in SoHo. Sam was right. The puppy was gorgeous. But the meeting also gave me a chance to remember that she and I had a unique chemistry. It wasn't just that she was smart, funny, and attractive. It was that she was way ahead of the pack in all those categories. She made me laugh more than anyone I had ever met, and most of all, I felt I could just be my doggone self around her. For the first time, I felt my future with someone could be really exciting.

When I realized that she was the only one I really liked spending time with, I made sure not to let things go to the dogs. Or rather, made sure that I did. A week later she invited Elsa and me over to her father's house in Philadelphia (where both our parents live) to swim in the pool. Elsa wasn't interested in the pool, but she and Sam's father's dog, Barry White, got to run and play in the yard (they did get into a little scrap over whose food was whose, but we'll gloss over that detail for posterity's sake). What really stood out to me was Sam's dog energy. (There's a great Bill Murray quote about this: "I'm suspicious of people who don't like dogs, but I trust a dog when it doesn't like a person.") The way she spoke to them and cuddled them really struck a chord with me. We weren't just a match as people, we were a match as *dog people*. We three have been together ever since.

As Sam and I rekindled our relationship, I was impressed at how great of a dog mom she was to Elsa. She fed her, and rolled around on the floor with her, and was okay with her (insane) shedding. Soon enough I trusted Sam to take her on "walkies," just the two of them—she even excelled at picking up Elsa's shit and reporting back its shape and consistency in overwhelming detail (as most good dog parents do). She also laughed at my canine ventriloquism, the way I would look at Elsa and say, in her childish, raspy voice, complete with a dog lisp, "I say we go ow-thide. In-thide niyth, but ow-thide, REAL niyth." She laughed, and would add her own thoughts to Elsa's inner monologue! If she didn't think my dog voices were funny . . . well, we'd have a problem. But the laughter was only part of the equation. Sam and I were able to get more serious with each other in part because Elsa made the whole thing more than the sum of its parts. It wasn't just about my capacity to love anymore, or Sam's. It was about the actuality of it.

Sheriff, Lab/Golden-cross (8 months old),
Chelsea Market, New York, NY • "He took his
first subway ride today—the 6 and the L. He's
the seventh puppy I've raised for Canine
Companions. He's laid-back, easygoing. One
of our dogs became the first courthouse dog
in the state of Maryland."

CHAPTER 15

THE FOUR-LEGGED CHILD

S am and I are engaged now. We'll get married soon and then, after that, we'll talk about starting a family. But that's paradoxical because we already have a family. Elsa is the third member in our relationship, our child in some ways—what some dog owners call a fur child or fur baby (we call her our "dogter").

When I told an older friend that I was writing about fur babies, he furrowed his brow. "Like an especially hairy baby?" he asked. I assumed he was joking. To be fair, upon seeing the term used online, I rolled my eyes too. It suggests dogs should be treated like human babies, instead of, well, dogs. But if you can bear with the term for a minute, we'll arrive at a purpose, at least. When I did a little research, I found that the term has only been in wide circulation for fifteen years or so. Fur baby refers to a pet that is an integral part of a household, to the point where it serves as a kind of substitute for—or, just as often, a prelude to—a human baby. A couple raises their fur children, but they also train the couple by teaching them about responsibility and love, not to mention helping them to deal with stress and adjusting their expectations regarding the ups and downs of developmental milestones and frustrations. Did you think that your dog would become housebroken overnight? When it didn't happen, did you let your emotions get the better of you? How do you feel about the fact that your boyfriend lets the dog whine for ten minutes before taking her for a walk? Do you blame the dog for being impatient? Do you think your boyfriend should make it a priority over watching the ninth inning of the Yankees game? Does your girlfriend invite your dog into the bed, while you think of the bed as a dog-free zone? Your fur children ask these questions and force you to answer them, or at least come up with a first-draft answer in full view of your partner or spouse. You both come to see that you're in this together.

A dog as the third member of a relationship does more than foreground questions of responsibility and care. They background questions of the ego. This happens when you meet a prospective partner, of course, but more slowly—you have to determine if you really plan to have this person in your life for the long run. And even then, there's a bit of a dance. *Oh, you want me to spend three nights a week at your place even though it makes my commute longer? Hmm: I am gratified that you want so many nights together, but it also seems . . . what's the word . . . selfish. My bed is more comfortable anyway.* When you have a dog, you don't have the luxury (or the sadness) of constantly revising your thoughts about whether they will be in the equation next week, or next month, or next year. You can't break up with a dog once you've committed. I mean, people do. Barring some legitimate extenuating circumstance, you can't just decide that a dog is suddenly incompatible with your lifestyle because they, say, are a threat to your furniture, or free time. That's just immature and irresponsible. When you bring a pet into your life, you're making a real commitment. That happens when you are a single dog owner, and it happens even more when you are a couple with a dog. Sam and I must constantly escape the gravitational pull of self-interest, because we're focused on this amazing four-legged being in our family who depends upon us for everything. I've heard somewhere (probably

TikTok) that you don't truly become an adult until you learn to put someone else before you.

The entire world shifts conceptually, in the sense that basic philosophical concepts are now seen through the prism of relationships. I see space differently now. Our sofa is only big enough for two of us. Do I yield to Elsa when we want to watch a show, or do I bribe her off the couch with a treat? (I recently had a breakthrough of putting Elsa's bed right on top of us while we're on the couch. It might be a bit lumpy for her, but we're definitely all happier together.) I see money differently. (Is any expense too great? Do we really need every shot and lab result that the vet recommends? Where is the line between pleasing your pet and spoiling it, and when can that start to be counterproductive?) These are all questions that we'll be asking each other over and over again as they relate to children, and Elsa gives us a chance to hash them out. Those kinds of negotiations, and the discussions around them, are a daily occurrence for us now. Maybe most important, they don't happen in a conspicuous, we're-having-an-important-discussion kind of way. There's no patting ourselves on the back for being so mature that we now consider multiple factors as we proceed forward in our relationship. It's just our life and how we are living it, as predictable and as necessary as a morning or an evening walk.

Dogs will even retrain your speech in ways that are good preparation for a human child. Research shows that people have a certain tone when speaking to their dogs; raising pitch, going to a singsong cadence. You might think of it as baby talk, but it is just as accurate to think of it as dog talk. And a recent study at the University of York demonstrates that dogs like it.

Researchers carried out a series of speech tests with adult dogs, where they were given the chance to listen to one person using dog-directed speech containing phrases such as "you're a good dog," and "shall we go for a walk?," and then another person using adult-directed speech with no dog-related content, such as "I went to the cinema last night."

Can you guess which speaker the dogs preferred? The study found that adult dogs were more engaged by "dog-directed" speech and "dog-related" content. When neither of these two things were present, dogs lost interest. That seems . . . unsurprising. But the study went on to mix things up, using doggish speech but non-doggish content and vice versa. The final conclusion? That "adult dogs need to hear dog-relevant words spoken in a high-pitched emotional voice in order to find it relevant." So remember, there is a specific canine version of baby talk, which also means that nobody can make fun of your goofy dog talk anymore (or mine!). There's a quote often attributed to Nietzsche: "And those who were seen dancing were thought to be insane by those who could not hear the music." If you're new to dogs or feel absurd pandering to your mischievous Vizsla who won't drop your shoe, I recommend turning the music up. That dog in your family needs to hear from you.

I fully expect that Sam and I will be together until we are very old people, so old that I can't even remember the name of the wonky-eared Husky/Chihuahua–mix I ran into in Cobble Hill who joined me in a howling a cappella duet. That part, I will remember, but his name may escape me by then. (Current me remembers fine: it was Davey, and he had a particularly prominent malocclusion, aka an underbite.) But not all relationships pan out. When they don't, couples divide whatever they shared when they were together. This means that someone's going to get the dog. In cases where the dog belonged to one of the people before the relationship existed, the outcome is typically more straightforward. In my case, I adopted Elsa before Sam and I were together, so if something were to happen with us, Elsa would stay with me (though Sam likes to joke that she would get custody). But what about situations where people get a dog together and then break up? My mind always goes to the televised court scene of the judge suggesting that the couple go to opposite sides of the courtroom and let the dog decide who they prefer. Talk about a moment of truth (I would suggest eating a hot dog before that hearing). There's a major tension to deal with during a breakup on top of the heartbreak of losing one if not two people (your dog). Naturally, both parties will feel bonded with the dog, though perhaps one more than the other. Perhaps a person might want to start fresh and move on from whatever reminds them of the other person. On the other hand, they are both going to need to heal, so ending up with the dog might be a very necessary panacea.

When Britney Spears and her husband Sam Asghari broke up, I paid special attention to the story, not because of my love for Britney or her music (though when "I'm a Slave 4 U" comes on, you may think otherwise), but because of my concern for Britney's dogs. According to the *New York Post,* Asghari not only requested that Spears cover his legal fees during divorce proceedings, but he also requested something called "separate assets." Spears and her camp were worried that—or at least told the press that they were worried that—those assets would include the two dogs the couple shared, a Doberman named Porsha and an Australian Shepherd named Sawyer. Porsha was a present from Asghari to Spears from early in their relationship, while Sawyer was adopted in Maui at Spears's request. Spears also owned a number of dogs that preceded her relationship with Asghari, including a Yorkie named Hannah.

When the news broke, I spent a few days researching how courts handled dog custody. I learned that most jurisdictions across the United States treat dogs as property. Only a few states have started to come around to seeing dogs as family members. Alaska was the pioneer. In 2017, it amended its divorce laws to take into account the "well-being of the animal," which governed marriage dissolution proceedings and also permitted joint ownership of pets. In the wake of Alaska's law, other states followed suit—Illinois, California, New Hampshire, Maine, New York, and Delaware. Britney was in California. What did that mean for Porsha and Sawyer?

I followed the story fairly closely at first, but the press seemed to lose interest after the marriage ended. The next I heard about the dogs was in December, when Britney had to rush out of her birthday party to deal with a canine medical emergency. The reports didn't say which dog was sick, or what the emergency was, but it did contain a few important updates about the custody battle. Evidently, Porsha had gone with Asghari, and Spears had acquired another dog, a Maltese named Snow. Good to see that everyone landed on their feet, or paws. (There are other cases, celebrity and otherwise, where a dog doesn't outlast the relationship, but predeceases it— a shared dog dies, the relationship falls apart of its own accord, and both of the people in the relationship recognize that the dog, as it turns out, was the best thing in the relationship, the only thing holding it together.)

Jasper, Dachshund (2 years old),
Bleecker St. & Bank St., New York, NY ·
"He knows where everything in the house
is that you don't want him to find. His
preference is tissues. He can also hear things
that we don't (which prompts the barking).
You know, the 'ghosts' in the house."

CHAPTER 16

THE FAMILY DOG

S o far we have looked at the way that dogs can bring single people into the world, the way that they can bring single people in
contact with other single people, and the way that they can help to
cement the relationship between those two people. There's an even
more common way in which dogs strengthen and deepen human
relationships: the family dog. Its name was Riley, or Max, or
_____ (fill in the blank—each of you will have a different
name here). Most of us experience this in our youths. We beg for a
dog. Our parents say no. We beg more. They say no some more. And
then, to our delight, one day either Mom or Dad cracks and comes
home carrying a little ball of fur, or the whole family takes an un-
planned drive out to a place in the country, or maybe it's something
theatrical like a box in the middle of the living room with a giant
bow.

Whatever the setup, the result is the same: a dog comes into the
family. And the second that it does, everything changes. Kids immediately take to playing with the dog, to running around outside,
to throwing a Frisbee or a ball, to coaxing the dog into sleeping in

their room with them at night. Dad, who may have initially been apprehensive about the whole thing, has decided to fashion a custom doggy-door for access to the backyard, with a custom "Bruno" engraving on top (so the raccoons know to use a different door?). The kids also (hopefully) begin to take on some responsibilities: making sure that the dog gets fed and has a full water bowl, for starters, then walking the dog around the neighborhood, using a pooper-scooper in the backyard or poop bags on the street. Dogs teach sharing. Dogs teach coexistence. Dogs teach anger management and the importance of alone time. Dogs instill in children a profound awareness of a life that is not their own. You could make the argument that all pets do, but a dog offers a few more degrees than a lizard or a guinea pig. Think back to your first puppy, or the first time you saw a kid with a puppy: snuggling up to it to feel its body heat, sensing its heart beating within, understanding that it is a living being with its own impulses and desires, its own emotions. Something that can experience happiness and pain. This is an awesome feeling, in the precise sense of the word: it is inspiring but also a bit daunting. And above all, beyond all these complex and nuanced lessons, there is one simple and powerful one: dogs teach love. This is not to say that children don't understand love without dogs. Children have parents they love, siblings they love, stuffed animals they love. But pets, and especially dogs, accelerate and deepen this process. They radiate love. Josh Billings, a famous American humorist and a contemporary of Mark Twain, has one of the best quotes on this subject: "A dog is the only thing on earth that loves you more than he loves himself." I know I'm supposed to be keeping The Dogist Pledge, but here's another scholarly quote by John W. Stephens that may make for a good mug or fridge magnet: "Be the person your dog thinks you are."

People like to talk about the birds and the bees, but really it's the birds and the Beagles. Dogs are the key factor in helping many kids unravel the mysteries of sex. I remember our family taking our Lab Ruby to the breeder, which we jokingly referred to as the stud farm. She was a purebred Labrador and, with my veterinarian aunt's oversight, we wanted her to have a litter of other Labs. Coming from a family of scientists, my parents wanted us to learn about reproduction, along with the joy of offering the puppies to people we knew who wanted a dog. After we dropped Ruby off, my siblings and I giggled about what would soon be happening to her. We were very young, still in elementary school, which meant that we chattered our way through a series of guileless thoughts about biology, romance, puppy names, and genetics. One of us wondered if Ruby would be getting married and what her husband's name was. One of us wondered about the physics of it, and essentially whether dogs really did it "doggy style." My mother confirmed this, but also explained that they would additionally use a "turkey baster" (artificial insemination) to increase the odds. About six weeks later, my mom showed up at my elementary school for my turn at show and tell, escorting a fully pregnant Ruby. And about a month after that, Ruby came back to class with a bunch of puppies and her uterus in a jar of formaldehyde— we had decided to spay her. I'm not sure if anyone's parents called in upset about that.

That breeder visit and classroom follow-ups occupied the sophisticated end of the spectrum when it came to learning about sex from our dogs. There was also a street version, courtesy of Ruby's sister Snowy. Snowy was also not spayed, and one summer we were at our house in Woods Hole when she was in heat, which meant that she was attracting every male dog in the neighborhood. They could smell her a mile away. One of those dogs, a chunky Lab named Max, somehow got out of his yard and into ours. One afternoon we heard screeching and ran outside to see them "tied" together butt to butt, Max locked inside Snowy. The screeching was coming from him: he was in terrible pain, as anyone getting their penis stretched out might be. Finally Snowy relaxed and unclamped and Max scampered off down the street, with his bits basically touching the ground.

I remember the faces of Henry and Isabel, my younger siblings, shocked by the noise, but also suddenly older, as if they had been given access to a deep mystery. Snowy didn't seem fazed.

Snowy technically was my cousin's dog, and Ruby was technically mine. As my family got older, my parents decided that they wanted Henry and Isabel to have dogs of their own too. That got them thinking, which got them asking, which got them looking, and eventually it got them driving home one day with two more family dogs: a Pug and a Brussels Griffon that had been relinquished from their owners. The Pug, intended for Henry, was named Whistle. The Brussels Griffon, earmarked for Isabel, was named Mousie. My parents figured that soon enough, each of the three of us would have a dog to care for and love. They figured wrong. For whatever reason, within a few hours of their arrival, Whistle and Mousie were bonded to me. When I sat down on the couch, they sat with me. When I went up the stairs, they followed (I would not entirely eliminate the possibility of foul play, i.e., me currying favor with treats). The plan to get dogs for Henry and Isabel fizzled quickly. On top of that, Whistle had a habit of depositing turds at various locations throughout the house. My mother would come home from work and discover these gifts in the living room, the kitchen, the laundry room. "Goddamned dog," I'd hear her mumble. My mother didn't curse very much, so this was noteworthy.

One day a couple from the neighborhood was over and was introduced to the new additions to the household. They were well-behaved that day, sprawled on the couch with my brother and sister. "Oh," the woman said. "What are their names?"

"Mousie," Isabel said, pointing at Mousie.

"Goddamned Dog," Henry said, pointing at Whistle.

Mousie and Whistle didn't stay with us for much longer. Within a few weeks, my parents started asking around to find a potentially better home for them. They were good dogs, but not a good overall match for our family. Soon enough they found an older lady family friend who "absolutely adored" them. We said goodbye to them as they happily hopped in her car. It probably took a few months for my mom to stop watching every step she took around the house to avoid a turd surprise. As far as we know, Whistle and Mousie lived for many happy years with the other family.

Not too long ago, I was approached by a toy company that wanted to explore the robotic dog market. The meeting was interesting, but the psychology behind it was even more interesting. The conversation included a history of baby dolls. I had always thought that they were a way for young girls to feel a greater sense of maturity. I was right, but imprecise in how I understood the appeal. Young girls wanted baby dolls because they mirrored the infant care they witnessed being given to younger siblings by their mothers, or people they knew. That explanation not only made sense but created a demand for lifelike, interactive dog dolls, particularly in the wake of the pandemic. Quarantine changed everything about modern life. Sweatpants replaced dress pants. Takeout and cooking at home replaced dining out. And the borders between office life and domestic life collapsed. This boosted the presence of dogs. Their presence was increasingly accepted. Their care was increasingly prioritized. (I work in the dog world, and even I remember the first time that I was on a business video call during the pandemic and a dog in the background of one of the windows started barking. At any earlier time, someone may have spoken up: "Excuse me, Gerald, could you put Bailey in another room so that he doesn't disturb us?" But as quarantine wore on, the presence of dogs in business meetings became less and less the exception and more and more the rule.) Not only did dog care become a central part of daily routines, but it often happened in full view of young children, who were not going to school classrooms. That created a desire in children to imitate, which in turn created a desire for a dog (or another dog). But families couldn't just add an extra dog without considering the consequences. Was the apartment big enough? What if Mom or Dad's work schedule shifted again? The toy company wondered if highly advanced dog "dolls," canine robots, might suffice as a real dog alternative. It was an interesting question, but I eventually decided it ultimately wouldn't work. You can do amazing things with wires and circuits, but there is no substitute for the magic of a real dog, shedding, pooping, chewing, and all.

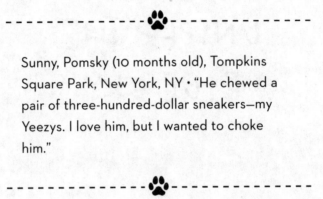

Sunny, Pomsky (10 months old), Tompkins Square Park, New York, NY • "He chewed a pair of three-hundred-dollar sneakers—my Yeezys. I love him, but I wanted to choke him."

CHAPTER 17

UNDER THE BLUE SKY

It was terrible weather, days and days of rain in the Northeast, a downpour causing floods that in turn caused delays in traffic, in public transportation, in everything. I was on a train that, miraculously, seemed to be the only one leaving on time, heading from New York to Philadelphia. I had gotten a message from a friend the night before that a friend of hers had gotten bad news. She and her partner had rescued a dog from a shelter. The dog, a Pit Bull–mix named Blue, had lived a hard life before it had come to them. It had been neglected and abused before being abandoned at the shelter. They did months of rehabilitation to work on Blue's temperament, spending lots of time and money, or rather converting their time and money into loving Blue. At the end of that time, the dog, which had started off as an emaciated nervous wreck, had regained its weight, health, and good nature. Blue regained his faith in people. The life he led in their house in Philadelphia was great, better than anything he could have imagined. Their summerhouse in Cape May was an extra cherry on top. They worked through the pandemic with a special focus on giving their dog a new life, a better life. The devotion with which they designed this was inspiring, and anyone who encountered it understood this—they even got some publicity for it on the Philly news, local couple rescues mistreated dog, that kind of thing. Philly does love an underdog story.

Then, in 2023, as the pandemic was waning, the couple had a difficult year. They suffered through some loss and some upheaval. On top of that, they started to notice that Blue was in pain. They went to the vet to see why. The vet ran some tests and then came back to them with grave news. The diagnosis was terminal, inoperable cancer. Amid everything else happening in their life, they were told that they would have to euthanize their dog. In fact, the cancer was so advanced that the vet seemed to be on the brink of recommending that they do it as soon as possible, before Blue's condition further deteriorated and his pain became unbearable. The couple wrestled with this unimaginable dilemma, and bore upon the vet to reconsider. The vet suggested a farewell plan to give Blue a heavy course of sedatives and give the couple an additional seventy-two hours—a full weekend—during which they could give Blue all his favorite foods and go to all his favorite spots. They let their close friends know, and one of their friends let me know. I knew it was an important story to tell and something Blue's family would value deeply. We came up with a plan and I booked a train to Philly for the next day.

I spent my time on the train composing myself and contemplating ways I should act differently or treat them differently because they were going through something tragic. But then I reminded myself to think of it more from the dog's perspective. Sure, Blue was in pain, but he was surrounded by his family, whom he'd grown to trust. The family who fed him, and gave him a bed, and scratched his belly, and sang to him, and took him to Cape May—his favorite place. He knew they'd always have his best interests in mind, and that's one good reason to be happy. My top-line goal was to get some nice pictures, aware that the family would be melancholy, aware that Blue would be sedated. I wanted at least one picture that captured the love that had surrounded the dog, and that despite Blue's time being cut short, he had found his people and they gave him their whole heart.

When I arrived, I greeted Blue's parents, and despite the obvious sorrow they felt, we couldn't help but feel a sense of joy too. We give everything to our dogs—Blue came back from being skin and bones to being a big ol' happy boy. And still, God (or whatever higher power you believe in) sometimes has other plans. We don't always learn the lessons we're expecting. Blue was in surprisingly good spirits that day. He was excited to meet me and sat down as soon as he smelled the treats in my pocket. I was struck by how handsome he was. His parents made sure he took it easy so as not to exacerbate his condition. Every moment of the remaining hours that they all had together was priceless. I took several portraits of Blue in a regal pose, and then, upon seeing his dad sitting on the bench, the dog decided he had the strength to get up there one more time to join him. "That's their favorite spot," Blue's mom said, fighting off tears. I snapped a few of the two of them together on the bench, and then all three of them. I could tell the sadness was welling up for Blue's dad, so I asked Blue's mom about what his favorite things were. "Piggy," she said, referring to his favorite stuffed animal. "And he likes when I sing to him." I hesitated, but asked what song he liked and if we could hear a refrain. She looked at Blue, but we had reached the limit of sorrow for the day. "I . . . don't think I can," she said. That would have to wait for Cape May.

Of all the dogs I have met, this is the sentiment that keeps returning to me most deeply, the feeling that I am helping to create a singular and heartwarming keepsake for people that they can have forever, even after their dog passes. Sometimes that moment is far away. Sometimes, as with Blue, it is only a weekend. While losing a dog is among the hardest things anyone goes through, I feel that through my work, I'm able to immortalize them in a way. Each dog's image and story is seen by millions of people who are able to appreciate (and often completely fawn over) them, even though they may never meet that dog in person. I genuinely believe that people feel like they "knew that dog." Even after a dog crosses the rainbow bridge, their stories and images live on in perpetuity, continuing to make people laugh, smile, be inspired, or sometimes cry.

Whenever I do a photo shoot like the one I did with Blue, I think about my first year as The Dogist back in 2014. I was out west photographing dogs around Los Angeles and spent a day near Santa Monica. When I returned, I posted the photos from the trip, and then a few days after that, I got an email from a woman named Elisabeth. It started like many others.

Good morning,

I am writing to you about the beautiful photo you took of Cooper and my son Oliver—

I remembered Cooper, a Labrador/Australian Shepherd–mix. I had photographed him in a sitting pose, wearing a red harness. I remembered Oliver, too, a kid of twelve or thirteen. He had been shy at first but had opened up, obviously proud of his dog. I assumed that the rest of the letter would tell me that he had shown the pictures to kids in school or that a teacher had seen them online and that Oliver and Cooper were enjoying a moment of celebrity. I assumed wrong.

I have very sad news to share, as Cooper passed away unexpectedly yesterday. I have found comfort at looking at this beautiful photo—just showing my son and his best friend doing their thing, being together. Cooper looks so proud! He would have actually smiled for you—he did that.

She ended with a question: Could she order two prints of the photo? I sent them out immediately.

Elisabeth's note answered many of the questions I had floating around my head at the time. My new job was only a year old, and I wondered constantly if I was doing something real—or if I was doing anything at all. Was my entire project silly? Was it reaching people in any important and sustainable way? Elisabeth's note instilled a deep sense of meaning and purpose in what I was doing. Being The Dogist wasn't just a novelty. I had helped an entire family grieve. I had helped them cherish the memory of their lost pet. Over the years I would receive many more notes like this from the families of the dogs I met. And yes, I cried like a baby at each and every one of them. Sometimes I would post a memorial for the departed dog, usually in black and white, letting my audience know that Rowdy or Cliff had passed and linking back to the original post. That became part of the rhythm of the site, red-and-blue harnesses leading to black-and-white photos. Did those memorial posts make a lot of people cry at their desks at work? A hundred percent. And plenty of those people posted heartfelt comments underneath those tributes, which in turn consoled the owners by demonstrating to them that their dog, even in death, was in many ways still there.

I have withheld my own story on purpose. It's not easy to tell, even after all these years. I graduated high school in 2006 and headed off to college at Boston University. It was a big adjustment in all the ways that going to college is an adjustment—not exactly homesickness but a vaguely queasy feeling that I was leaving the place where I felt most comfortable and would have to learn how to be comfortable in a new place. I had traveled solo before, but this was different, more permanent. It was hard to leave my parents and my brother and sister, and it was also hard to leave Ruby, my dog.

By that point, Ruby was around twelve. I think I probably knew that Labs had lifespans of between ten to fourteen years, but I knew it only in the sense that I would have guessed it correctly if it was an answer on a multiple-choice test. But if I was assigned an essay about dogs and end-of-life planning, I would have come up blank. Those kinds of thoughts were not top of mind. I was doing what I was supposed to be doing, which was to be wildly distracted by the terror and excitement of graduating high school and heading off to college and all that entailed: girls, procuring beer, not losing my $120 textbooks. I wasn't putting too much mental energy into thinking about my aging dog, who slept more than she ever had, though I remember coming home at Thanksgiving and going right to her for a belly rub and getting a smile at the corner of her cheek, like the good ol' days.

Then it was second semester. Henry, my brother, is two years younger than me, which means that he was still in high school at the time. One Saturday morning he went downstairs to the dining room and saw Ruby lying there, nothing out of the ordinary. He then reached out to pet her, but she didn't move. More specifically, she was stiff. Henry didn't know what to do, so he went back upstairs. He didn't say anything right away, but after a little while he told my dad, who went down and confirmed (as one of the two physicians in the house) that Ruby had died. I got a phone call early that afternoon.

"Elias, we have some news," my dad said. I could tell from his tone that it wasn't good news. "Ruby died."

That was, for me, a formative trauma. It wasn't like I became unraveled, dropped the phone, and started bawling. I was sad, but I didn't know how to process it immediately. She had slowed down in her final years, and I had been distracted by all the fun life had to offer an eighteen-year-old. I took the logical approach: "She was old. It was expected. She had a good life." All things that were true, but I buried my emotions a bit. I felt guilty for not giving her more attention in her final years, and I wasn't there with her at the end. As a teenager, I couldn't yet grasp the concepts of mortality and the finite nature of life in any real way. A numbness washed over me. I thought about the belly rubs I didn't give her. The steak tidbits from my plate she didn't get. The paws on my leg she would've given me. Not being there to see the final spot she chose for herself on the floor. Had she been wondering where I was? (Please feel free to take this as a cue to go pet your dog.) I would never be able to make up for any lost time or get an answer to that question. She was gone.

A few hours later, my dad called me back. He sounded a bit out of breath and I could hear my brother in the background, along with some birds chirping. "We wanted to let you know that we're planning to bury Ruby in the backyard." They had already started digging a grave.

"No," I said. The tone of my voice surprised me. It was firm, formal, as if I was her power of attorney. "We're not burying her. We're going to cremate her and scatter her ashes at Dog Beach in Woods Hole." That beach was the source of many of my memories with Ruby, summer vacations that brought together not just the people in the family—cousins, my parents' brothers and sisters, grandparents— but their dogs too. If a dog somehow escaped from the house, which would happen sometimes in the welter of activity, Dog Beach was usually where they'd be. Snowy, Ruby's sister who died much earlier of cancer, was already waiting in a box on the mantel in Woods Hole. I knew they would've wanted to go for one final swim together.

There was a long pause while my father considered my terms. I figured that I had an advantage. My parents are both physicians, which means that they have never been especially sentimental when it comes to bodies. In their training they had to pick apart cadavers. The mysteries of life reside elsewhere for them, and a dead body is just a decomposing husk. In fact, my grandparents and even great-grandparents had been cremated, which was still a relatively new and relatively rare practice in Judaism, where return to the earth is the dominant thinking around death and burial: the temple of the body is returned to God as he gave it to you. But we were never very religious and interpretation was always something my parents encouraged. This evolution of thinking seemed to have taken hold with my parents. My mother always talked about how she would like to have her ashes scattered off Nobska Lighthouse overlooking the Vineyard Sound. I wanted Ruby to have that as well.

"Okay," he said. I could hear my brother's shovel stop in the background. Ruby was cremated, as per my request/demand, and we partly scattered her ashes on Dog Beach that summer, along with some of Snowy's ashes. Many years have passed since then, and currently the rest of their ashes—along with a few of our other dogs' over the years—are still in the cardboard boxes that they came from the crematory in, with their names handwritten on the outside in Sharpie. They're nestled together above the CD player cabinet in our dining room in our Woods Hole home in what has become a makeshift canine mausoleum. (I really want to say "pawsoleum," but I won't.) They still watch over each of our meals, as they had. Each box also has their original collar and leash attached to it. My aunt Alice, the vet, who has a good (and persistent) sense of humor, would occasionally take them down for a walk if we were around, dragging their box across the floor. "Come on, Ruby," she'd say. "Let's go. Good girl." I think Ruby would be happy to know that she was making us laugh even after she passed. What dog doesn't like to go for a walk?!

Ruby and Snowy were from my early childhood, but there are other dogs there too. Down the shelf from Ruby is Matilda, the chocolate Lab we got for my siblings to make everything fair. After Ruby passed, Matilda started to slow down too. One day, she eventually stopped eating entirely. My mom called us all and let us know it was Matilda's time. My mom and my aunt Alice then went for a ride with Matilda and her vet bag that contained a vial of pentobarbital, the euthanasia drug that puts dogs to sleep. They went to the beach on Surf Drive in Falmouth, where, with Alice's help, Matilda, overlooking the ocean in the back of my mom's Volvo station wagon, transitioned to her next state of being.

Helping a dog out of its suffering, especially once it has become unendurably painful, is noble. I think not only of my aunt but of a piece in *The New Yorker* in 2022 about a Colorado man named Steve Greig, who opened his home and his heart to something like a dozen senior dogs, caring for them as they approached the ends of their lives. The quote I remember was perfectly attuned to what it means to care for a dog, with an awareness of the disparity between canine and human lifespans: "The joy I get out of it far outweighs the pain," he said. "It's hard knowing that it's a short time, but that's what the purpose is."

And yet, that pain accumulates. In fact, veterinarians, the people who spend the most time caring for dogs, do it at a great cost to themselves. It's a profession with an alarmingly high suicide rate. Male vets are twice as likely as the population at large to commit suicide, which seems like an alarming statistic until the second shoe drops: female vets are four times as likely. A recent BBC article noted that nearly 70 percent of vets have had a colleague die by their own hand. There are many explanations for this sad truth, though they boil down to a few main factors. First, there is the psychological strain: though the intent of aspiring to and becoming a vet is to help animals, the reality of the job is that much of it involves helping animals die. This wears on them, and in a different way than it might wear on an oncologist. Dogs are purely trusting. They put their fate in your hands. They can't communicate clearly about the pain they are feeling, can't articulate whether or not they are at peace with the final chapter that is being plotted out, so the burden falls squarely on the shoulders of the vet. And when something goes wrong with someone's pet, and inevitably something will, pet owners often pin the full blame on their vet, who often is operating a small practice without the benefit of colleague support and the stability of a larger hospital institution. It may not take much to have their career take a rapid turn. Add all of that to the fact that vets have access to the tools of assisted suicide—pentobarbital and knowledge of the proper doses by weight—it's no wonder so many fall victim to suicide.

I had seen it close-up, in faraway places. I remember driving around with the Crijojo Trappers in Aruba, responding to reports of stray dogs and dogs in distress. One day, we got a call from the police department: it was about a dog under one of their cars at the station. When we arrived, one of the women lay down on the ground next to the car to get a visual on the dog. When she arose, the look on her face was one of gloom. She looked at her colleague and shook her head. They understood that the dog was beyond saving, and they conveyed this to us. They were able to get the dog out from under the car. But it was hardly a recognizable dog at that point. It had gone under that car to die. We were all silent as we rode to the nearby veterinary facility with the dog covered from the sun in the bed of the pickup truck.

When we arrived, one of the women went in, and within a minute a young female vet came out in her white coat and with her medical bag. She knew the Crijojo Trappers by first name—it was clear this was not an uncommon occurrence. I stood there rapt with a mixture of sadness and demoralization. This dog, covered in mange and open lesions, didn't even have the strength to lift his head. The women comforted him with their voices and pet his paws and head as the vet drew a dose of blue liquid into her syringe. I had never seen anything so graphic before, but I felt it was important for me to witness. One of the women sang something calmly to him in Dutch as every muscle in his body simultaneously relaxed and he laid his head down one final time. He was gone, and we were all crying, of course. I could sense that despite having to do this so often, it was always hard on their souls. While nine out of ten dogs may make a recovery, some are just too far gone. The vet went back inside, and two men came out to take the dog, wrapped in a sheet, around to the back of the facility to be safely disposed of. We all got back in the car in a quiet state of shock. I remember reflecting on the fact that despite his dire condition, he was lucky we found him. Who knows for how much longer he would've languished in the heat under that car. Releasing him from his suffering and filling his last moments with love was something I think he truly appreciated. I could see it in his eyes.

Back in 2014, almost a year after launching The Dogist, I ran across a news item about Dr. Sophia Yin, a renowned vet in Davis, California. Yin was not just a practicing vet but also a canine behaviorist who had served as president of the American Veterinary Society of Animal Behavior. She appeared on television, wrote a column for the *San Francisco Chronicle,* and even invented a positive-reward dog training system that could be operated remotely. But in her late forties, she started to feel as though the work was more depressing than rewarding. The overwhelming darkness closed around her and wouldn't open back up, and she took her own life at the age of forty-eight.

Colleagues of Yin's founded an organization called Not One More Vet to highlight her memory and bring attention to the mental health crisis among veterinarians. I have worked with similar organizations, including the Veterinary Mental Health Initiative, which was based in Boston. Dr. Alett Mekler, a vet who has a special interest in canine end-of-life issues, posed for me back in 2021 with a five-year-old Chihuahua named Fig. It was a rare Dogist post in the sense that it gave the dog and the human equal billing. In the caption, Mekler reviewed some of the bleaker statistics around vet suicide and talked about yet another reason that pressures on vets mount: They are under intense stress from the moment they enter veterinary school. The profession not only requires rigorous training at institutions that have low acceptance rates but awards internships and residencies to only the highest achievers. That leads to a life of competitiveness and isolation, where it's hard to make friends because the people closest to you are also the ones standing in the way between you and a stable career. And even those vets who do succeed are denied the same respect afforded to doctors with human patients. Vets are the ones who help us keep our dogs healthy, or who help them to leave us when the time comes. We should not only value their work, but we should help protect them from the harsher realities of their profession.

Mister, German Shepherd (6 years old),
Washington Square Park, New York, NY ·
"He's new to the city from Portland, Oregon.
He's a softie—he craves attention in a very
un-Germanic way."

CHAPTER 18

THE MAGIC OF DOGS

I have always been a tennis fanatic, and after unknowingly photographing her dog, I came to know Camera (Cam) Ashe, Arthur Ashe's daughter. (She got the name because her mother was a photographer, another point of contact between us.) One year she hooked me up with tickets to the men's final at the US Open. I wrote to thank her but I didn't hear back right away. Finally, she replied: "Sorry," she said. "My seventeen-year-old Dachshund had a catastrophic stroke." That was a third point of contact between us.

No one gets to the point where losing a dog is okay. You feel like you let it down. Partly that's because dogs age seven times more quickly than we do. Some breeds, like Bernese Mountain Dogs, Dogues de Bordeaux (French Mastiffs), and Irish Wolfhounds, have exceptionally short lifespans, between five and eight years. Along with Great Danes and Saint Bernards, they are sometimes known as "heartbreak breeds" because they can go at a young age suddenly, without warning. At the other end of the spectrum are breeds such as Chihuahuas, Toy Poodles, Schipperkes, Manchester Terriers, and (name-dropping a breed you've probably never heard of) Löwchens ("little lion dogs," once the rarest officially recognized breed in the world), which all routinely live upward of fifteen years, still only a fraction of the human lifespan. For the most part, the dog we bring into our life will leave that life long before we do.

Over the last few months, I have read a few articles about experimental treatments to prolong the lifespans of dogs. The impulse is understandable. It seems like when it comes to a dog's years with us, more is better. *If only I could have had another year with her.* Makes sense, right? But there's a narcissism to it, a prioritization of our human needs over the needs of the dog. I don't believe that dogs consider the future and their mortality in the abstract way that we do. They experience their existence when they are here, for themselves and for us. They live their lives fully in the moment. Their eight years, or ten, or twelve, are just as powerful to them as our eighty or ninety are to us, if not more. Extending an individual dog's life so that an owner can have more time with it disrupts part of the beauty of dog ownership: to have, to hold, to love, to lose, to mourn, to reminisce.

A dog's passage is sad, yes. It is also part of the magic of dogs. They give us access to time-lapse wisdom. A dog's life occupies a phase of our life. We have one dog when we are growing up, another when our kids are growing up, maybe a third in retirement. Maybe you're lucky enough to have ten (or thirty)! As sad as it is to say goodbye to each dog, it is also the opportunity to say hello to another dog. Joy can be replenished, renewed. The advice that I sometimes give to people who I sense have a particular closeness with their pets is that when their dog begins to decline, they should consider welcoming in a second dog before the first passes. Not only does this help soften the grief of loss and bypass a state of doglessness, but I believe there's something special about a dog that knew your past dog. At the risk of sounding superstitious, I believe making that connection imbues a piece of each dog's soul within each other.

Sometimes, when a dog goes, the instinct is to replace it immediately with an exact successor: a Beagle leaves the family, so a new Beagle must arrive. The logic makes sense. A family wants to pay homage to the past dog. Why would we not get the same dog? Here, the rejuvenation takes on a dimension of reincarnation. (Or is that reincanination? Okay, never mind.) I have found in my Dogist travels that certain breeds lend themselves to this principle. Golden Retrievers, for example, exude such a sense of unbridled joy and "galoopiness" that owners cannot imagine their house without a Golden Retriever galooping around. I have found the same to be true for Pugs. I get the sense that once you're in the "Pug Club," losing your membership card (a Pug) is not a viable option. (This is likely true for many breeds, but for whatever reason, those two examples stick out for me.)

As The Dogist, I have photographed three-month-old puppies that have just arrived in a family, and I have photographed gray-faced, arthritic dogs on their way out. I have also talked to countless owners about how they experienced their dog's passage. What I've consistently gleaned from those conversations is that their dogs maintain their drive to be emotionally centered within the family, even as they are fading physically. They'll always hobble over and roll over for a belly rub or want your help getting on the couch or bed, or give you their best attempt at puppy-dog eyes when you're eating steak. When cats are at the end of their lives, they often wander away. Whether it's out of shame or pride, no one can really know. Dogs tend to do the opposite. They stick close to their people. I've heard many people say that their once-standoffish dog became a total lovebug in their old age. People should learn from dogs. They should lean into love. An ending dignified in this manner is as important not just for the being on their way out but for everyone who's sticking around for a while longer in their absence.

One final note on the current climate and how it's framing matters of life and death, dogs and grief. In 2024, as the election season heated up and various international conflicts refused to cool down, Jon Stewart announced that he was returning to *The Daily Show* as host—he would sit behind the desk Mondays only, but it was still a major story. The first week, Stewart talked about the ages of the two presidential candidates (at that point, Biden and Trump). The second week he talked about Tucker Carlson's interview with Vladimir Putin and Carlson's strange appreciation for Moscow supermarkets. The third week, Stewart's main story was about the Middle East, but he ended the episode by paying tribute to his three-legged Pit-mix, Dipper, who had just passed away. I had met Dipper back in 2015 when I was invited to photograph him. The Stewarts had found him while volunteering at Animal Haven, a shelter in Manhattan: Dipper had been hit by a car somewhere in Brooklyn and lost a leg. The Stewarts brought him into their house, and into their hearts. In 2024, speaking from behind the desk, Stewart couldn't get through two sentences about Dipper before getting choked up. "He was ready," Stewart said. "But I wasn't. And the family, we were all together—thank goodness. We were all with him. But boy, my wish for you is that one day you find *that* dog—that one dog that is just the best."

The next day, his analysis of Israel and Gaza got some coverage, but most of the social media energy around the *Daily Show* episode was reserved for Dipper. Dipper's death unlocked every loss-of-dog meme: the rainbow bridge, of course, but also pictures of fans remembering their dogs as puppies, fan art of fields of dogs awaiting a new arrival in dog heaven, and more. It sent older fans scrambling for older clips, like Jimmy Stewart's 1981 *Tonight Show* appearance where he read a poem titled "Beau," about his own dear departed pet (one I personally can't watch without a box of tissues). Other fans remembered that on his first show after 9/11, Stewart (Jon, not Jimmy) had ended the episode by holding a puppy in his arms. Animal Haven got more than $35,000 in donations within a week. In a month of wrestling with the world's biggest news, Dipper's departure was somehow the biggest news of all. That's what dogs do. They get into your soul and they don't disappear, even when they physically do.

Usually, people outlive their dogs. But when dogs are in close prox-imity to human illness and death, they can also play a fascinating role. I have never watched the popular TV medical dramas like *ER* or *Grey's Anatomy* (though I loved *Scrubs*). Both my parents were doctors, remember, so whenever those shows came on, they would roll their eyes, explain why whatever was happening was very dra-matized, and then change the channel. *Jeopardy!* was my dad's favor-ite (he would always get every question), but his second favorite was *The Planet's Funniest Animals*. That would make us all laugh more than anything else could. As long as programming was *real*—trivia, animals, sports—we were encouraged to watch it.

Recently, though, I was flipping channels and came across an epi-sode of a medical drama that involved an animal. This particular animal was a cat, whose nickname was "death cat." The cat lived in a nursing home as an uncontroversial mascot, comforting the elderly residents. Then, over the course of a month, everything changed. Rather than curling up in a corner of the office, it started sleeping in the beds of patients. And not just any patient. It would pick one pa-tient in particular and camp out there for a few days. Then it would move on and select another bedmate. Each patient the cat visited died in a day or two. One of the doctors in the show became ob-sessed with disproving that the cat was an angel of death. Was it? No spoilers.

But this isn't a cat book. I want to point to one particular conver-sation in the episode between two doctors. They were going down the hall arguing about whether or not the angel-of-death theory was plausible in any way. One of the doctors dismissed it outright as idiotic. He was walking quickly down the hall. A younger doctor who was walking with him slowed down and tilted his head. "Well," he said, "dogs can smell cancer." I was watching on my computer, and I hit the arrow to jump back ten seconds so I could hear the younger doctor again. Dogs can smell cancer? Was that true? I enlisted The Dogist Research Department to help track it down.

The first thing they found was a 2016 paper in the journal *Frontiers in Medicine*. It had a promising title: "Real-Time Detection of a Virus Using Detection Dogs." My kid-of-doctors brain knew that viruses and cancers are different, though certain viruses can lead to certain cancers. I read on: "We investigated the ability of two trained dogs to detect cell cultures infected with bovine viral diarrhea virus (BVDV) and to discriminate BVDV-infected cell cultures from uninfected cell cultures and from cell cultures infected with bovine herpes virus 1 (BHV 1) and bovine parainfluenza virus 3 (BPIV 3)." My eyes glazed over and I stopped reading for a little while. I took a moment to be grateful I wasn't a farmer whose cows had a highly contagious diarrhea virus, and then I found a few other articles that filled out the picture. These volatile organic compounds (VOCs), which were released by cancer cells, could be detected by dogs as a result of their superior senses of smell, which was somewhere between ten thousand and a hundred thousand times as powerful as the human sense of smell. This is a staggering fact that has always made me both envy and pity dogs. I guess it's great to be able to find a needle in a haystack, olfactorily speaking, but who wants to smell the world a hundred thousand times more acutely? Dogs could identify VOCs in urine or feces, in sweat and breath, and on skin, even when they were only present in parts per trillion, and that could in turn identify a range of cancers, including colorectal, ovarian, prostate, and lung.

That was impressive, but I was still confused. Even once it was established that dogs could detect cancers, how did humans know when that was happening? Had someone invented a talk-box that dogs wore around their necks that translated their various barks, grunts, growls, howls, and whines into spoken English? (I didn't know if that technology existed in real life, though I had seen it in the movie *Up*, which is admittedly animated.) Some cases, it turned out, didn't require anything that sophisticated. One man in his seventies went to the doctor after—and in part because—his dog kept licking at a spot behind his ear. It turned out that it was a malignant melanoma. In other situations, dogs in labs were trained to signal the presence of VOCs the same way dogs in airports would signal the presence of contraband or explosives (they're essentially trained to look for their toy that smells like the substance of interest). The studies cited ranged from equivocal (dogs could detect lung cancer from breath somewhere between 40 and 70 percent of the time, which is a wide range and not entirely convincing) to nearly definitive (one smaller study had results that suggested that dogs could identify breast cancer from urine samples 100 percent of the time).

Most of the articles ended with clarifications and disclaimers. The techniques are new and not yet well understood. Doctors don't know if certain breeds are better at detection across the board or whether certain breeds are more attuned to certain kinds of cancers. And the training, still in its infancy, has not yet established the best ways to teach dogs to communicate what they detect. Still, employing dogs as a tool to detect cancers is noninvasive, low-risk, portable, and affordable, which makes it a promising avenue of exploration. It's also an amplification of the core promise of dogs: they can change your life by helping you to keep it.

In 2017, I posted a photograph I took of a drawing of a dog by a six-year-old girl. This particular six-year-old girl, Catherine Hubbard, should have been eleven years old, but she had been killed in 2012 during the Sandy Hook Elementary School shooting in Newtown, Connecticut.

Parents remember all kinds of things about their children's early years, but in the Hubbards' case, one aspect of their daughter's life came into special focus. "Our daughter was a lover of animals," her mother, Jenny, told me. "I don't know why she loved animals so much. It's who she was. She had a little purple mouse, and my husband said that was the start of it. All of her clothing had animals on it." When Catherine and her older brother Freddy were just beginning elementary school, they made themselves business cards. Catherine gave herself a workplace and a title: she was the "Caretaker of Catherine's Animal Shelter." Her caretaking wasn't just theoretical. The family had feral cats in their backyard, and Catherine brought them food. When they were vacationing at the beach, she would collect hermit crabs, but she was always careful to return them to the sea.

Catherine loved all animals, but her dog, Sammy, was close to her heart. "She and Sammy would always hang out underneath the dining room table," her parents told me. On the day of the massacre, the news traveled from person to person, and was also understood by Sammy. "Sammy knew when Catherine didn't come home. She was sad. She'd look at us like, 'Where's Catherine?' There was something about Catherine's spirit—there was that special bond."

The Hubbard family built their recovery from grief specifically around Catherine's love for animals. "When Catherine died at Sandy Hook Elementary, we could've certainly crawled into a hole, and it would've been understandable. But Catherine deserves more than that." Instead, they channeled their grief to active ends. They founded an animal sanctuary in Catherine's name and hosted an annual event, Catherine's Butterfly Party, which featured more than a dozen tristate rescue organizations, including the ASPCA and ARF.

"As sad as it is for us that she's gone," her mother told me, "we're not unique in losing a child. What's unique is the outpouring we received. We've created a sanctuary for a six-year-old who loved animals. We're sharing her life and what she stood for. Everything we're doing is about making her legacy live on. We don't want people being sad and heavy. There are still parts of Newtown that are still very hurt, unfortunately. That's why we're so adamant about having an afternoon that's innocent and carefree. Maybe for those few hours you can experience what Catherine experienced."

When I looked at all the pictures of Catherine her mother shared with me at their dining room table, I kept thinking one thing: *I was just like her as a kid.* I had been that child, shy except when it came to animals, eager to protect animals and curate experiences around them. I felt like we would've gotten along. She probably would've really enjoyed The Dogist.

It is impossible to say what she would have become, but easy to see that her parents kept alive one of the best parts of her spirit.

Before I left, I photographed their family's two chocolate Labs, Zachary and Brownie, in the front yard. "We haven't touched anything in Catherine's room," Mrs. Hubbard informed me, "but Brownie always goes in there and takes out all of her toys, and we're like, 'Catherine would've loved that.'"

Years later, when I visited Catherine's 2024 Butterfly Party, her mother took me aside and told me something that reached a depth of my soul I wasn't prepared to reckon with that day.

"I want to tell you . . . I truly believe you and Catherine are kindred spirits," she said with unwavering eye contact, her hand on my arm, as though she could sense a part of her daughter present within me.

I welled up behind my sunglasses and struggled to articulate a response. She had confirmed that thought I had been carrying with me since first learning about her Catherine—that she was like me.

"I . . . feel the same way," I finally responded, doing my best to not lose it in public.

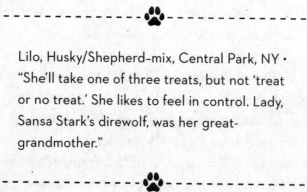

Lilo, Husky/Shepherd–mix, Central Park, NY ·
"She'll take one of three treats, but not 'treat
or no treat.' She likes to feel in control. Lady,
Sansa Stark's direwolf, was her great-
grandmother."

CHAPTER 19

RESTORING HUMANITY

A few years back, I was working on my site when an email popped up in my inbox. It was from a group called Puppies Behind Bars (PBB), and I have to admit that my first reaction was visualizing a cartoon of a little dog in a striped prisoner's uniform, looking out from its cell. That wasn't what the email was about. Puppies Behind Bars, as it turned out, was an NYC–based organization that had been founded by a woman named Gloria Gilbert Stoga, a Yale grad whose early career had been located at the intersection of economic opportunity and activism. She had served on the city's Youth Empowerment Commission and also worked with UNICEF. In the late nineties, she started teaching inmates at the Bedford Hills Correctional Facility, New York State's sole maximum-security prison for women. She wasn't teaching math or literature. She was teaching them to raise and train service dogs, often for police officers and soldiers who had been psychologically or physically wounded in the line of duty. The organization wanted to know if I would be interested in creating a video series with some of their members, both human and canine. I had featured a different prison program in my second book, which was purely photographic, so with this opportunity to tell an even more in-depth account of something so fascinating, I was eager to go back to prison (does that make me a canine recidivist?).

I was nervous. I had been to a Level III security prison in the past, but this experience would have me entering medium- and maximum-security prisons, typically reserved for people who've committed higher and more violent crimes. I didn't know if it would be dangerous—or rather, how dangerous it would be. Gloria told me that I needed to catalog everything I planned to bring into the facility, "down to the paper clip." The list I sent them included my "boxer-brief underwear." Even my choice of pants was scrutinized: I wasn't allowed to wear green so as to avoid being confused with the incarcerated by prison staff. And I was to adhere to Puppies Behind Bars' preferred nomenclature of "incarcerated individual," rather than "inmate" or "prisoner." This made sense and was in line with their mission of restoring a sense of humanity to people in a very inhuman environment. On top of all of that, I didn't know the specifics of how I would interact with the men in the program. I would be visiting two facilities: Fishkill Correctional Facility in Beacon, New York, and Eastern NY Correctional Facility in Napanoch, New York, a maximum-security prison located about two hours north of New York City in Ulster County. I assumed that there would be big, tattooed "tough guys," hardened by time served. Was there anything I could say to them that wouldn't highlight the difference and distance between us in ways that would make the conversation irretrievably awkward?

When I arrived at the outer reception area the morning of our shoot at Eastern, I was instructed to go over every item on the checklist I had sent them, pointing to every cable, lens hood, and camera strap. It was like being selected for "extra screening" at a TSA checkpoint, with one exception: everyone kept saying hello. Many of the guards knew who I was, or at least knew my site. One of the guards stood there patiently while I finished my paperwork, and then asked if he could take a selfie with me. "My daughter is a big fan," he said. As strange as that moment was, it was also familiar, the kind of thing that could have just as easily happened at a coffee shop or a park. It put me back in the normal world, up until the point when they buzzed us through the first door, into the sally port (a holding space where one door closes before the next door can open, just like the entrance to a dog park) and any semblance of normalcy quickly evaporated. I started picturing scenes from shows like *Oz*, where a nervous outsider walks down the hall as all these tatted-up guys are yelling from their cells. "Fresh meat!" they'd say. Or "Come over here and let me see you." Or worse.

My imagination couldn't have been more wrong. The route we took didn't pass through long corridors of cells. Instead, it was like walking through a large, mostly empty high school. Eventually we came to a room that looked like a classroom and went in. This was Puppies Behind Bars. About a dozen guys were sitting there, and they didn't look like prisoners at first. They were wearing at least one item from a uniform, something drab green to mark them, but otherwise they had on a variety of T-shirts and sneakers—some of which were quite trendy. I was introduced to the group by their PBB instructor, Carl, a tall, muscular bald man who you might assume was once in prison himself (you'd then be amused to learn that he was actually a former pastry chef). I wasn't told anything about the men ahead of time, and there was a very specific reason for that. Learning anything about what these men had done to put them in Eastern might well have interfered with my ability to interact with them normally. If I had known that any of them were convicted murderers or arsonists or kidnappers, could I have kept that out of my mind in my conversations with them? Probably not. I could tell that the mere subject of "their crimes" was taboo, and I made sure to refrain from asking them any questions related to it (though I was informed that anyone convicted of a sex crime was automatically ineligible for the program). I had been told one thing about these particular men, which was that whatever they had done to put themselves in prison, they had responded to their incarceration better than most. In order to be eligible for the program, they had to have a flawless history of good behavior during their time served. Furthermore, they had to show an interest and aptitude to learn and be open to new concepts and experiences. One of those new experiences, at least that day, was me. While I had been told to keep my curiosity under wraps, the prisoners weren't as guarded, pun intended. They had a genuine curiosity about who I was, like I was an alien from another planet. After all, many of these men had been incarcerated for decades, and the simple things we take for granted, like the latest iPhone, what's trending on Netflix, and social media, are often completely foreign to them. Upon learning that I lived in the Village in Manhattan, one of them wanted to know if a restaurant he used to frequent was still open (it wasn't). I tried to answer a few more questions as broadly as possible—I'll admit that I wasn't too thrilled about the idea of convicted criminals at a maximum-security prison knowing where I lived or my fiancée's name.

Because I didn't know much about their lives, and because I didn't come forward with too many details about my own, much of the conversation revolved around dogs. What was clear immediately was that they were, to the last, extremely proud to be in the Puppies Behind Bars program, though their continued membership was not guaranteed, not by a long shot. If they got one ticket—those were citations for even the most minor infractions—they were immediately kicked out of the program. That kept them on their best behavior.

The more we talked about the program and the men demonstrated their training skills and knowledge, the more I saw that training the service dogs was only half of the equation. The other, and possibly more remarkable half, was that the program was clearly training the men as well. Early on, before anyone would be assigned a dog, the men were taught something called "jollying," which basically boiled down to dancing around and speaking in baby talk for the puppies. This was a human version of galoopiness with a very specific purpose. Prison froze these men, kept them watched and watchful, locked up and pent-up. Jollying helped to thaw them, to let their hair down (metaphorically; very few of them had any hair) and give them an opportunity to smile and do something fun for a change.

That trend continued. One of the men who had been incarcerated for more than two decades (he looked no older than forty), told me that "depression was par for the course," which wasn't surprising. In prison, he said, you have to "shut your emotions off so that you don't overly miss your family." Even if you felt like connecting with another person, in prison you can't just ask for a hug without seeming vulnerable. The dogs started to reverse that. "Being in Puppies Behind Bars," he said, "you have to open your heart back up. There's no way you can successfully raise one of these puppies without allowing yourself to love them, and to receive that love." Without the dogs, the men led lives nearly devoid of any humanness and emotionality. With them, they found an opportunity to be human again, to be loving and accountable and present. In that room, I saw so much sincere affection pass between the men and their dogs, even more than I would typically see on the outside. Another man told me that when he first went in, more than a decade prior, his daughter was a baby. Incarceration had robbed him of the ability to be a father to her as she got older. His absence from her life pressed on him more and more, not just because he was missing milestones—school graduations, soccer games—but because he didn't know what it felt like to have that paternal responsibility to another being. He told me that his dog, Zeus, gave him that chance.

When I left Eastern and posted the photos, the comments were mixed. Some people criticized the program, arguing that these men don't deserve to have good things. How was playing with dogs punishment? How was it holding them accountable for what they had done to others in society? Other people understood that the dogs were acting as a rehabilitative force. At some point, these men were going to be released, and it seemed better for them to reenter society not as hardened, dulled, cold products of an impersonal institution but as people with an active capacity for empathy, communication, and loyalty. In the end, the support outweighed the objections. In fact, of all the programs I work with, Puppies Behind Bars struck the deepest chord. When we launched our fundraiser for them, we reached our initial ten-thousand-dollar goal within an hour. I increased the goal, and we met that one too. And while the negative comments didn't go away—there were still some people who thought that we were shining a light on people who deserved to stay in the dark—most people were inspired by the philosophy of the organization, which is that dogs can unlock a person's humanity, no matter how deep it's buried or how resistant they are to opening up. I understand why people don't believe in magic, but this program makes a pretty compelling case that dogs can create it.

Barrett, German Shorthaired Pointer
(3 months old), S. 16th St. & Walnut St.,
Philadelphia, PA · "He's a country dog in the
city. He loves hiking and peanut butter and
he's named after Syd Barrett of Pink Floyd."

CHAPTER 20

POLITICAL ANIMALS

I n 2022, the city of New York elected its first honorary dog mayor. The election process did not bear much resemblance to a human election. For starters, there were no debates. Instead, sixteen dogs representing all five boroughs of the city were seeded in a bracket, March Madness–style, though the contest took place in late summer and early fall. Most of the voting was done online, by humans, though there were publicity photos released of dogs trotting toward polling places, ballots in their mouths. The contest eventually came down to two finalists: Sally Long Dog, a Basset Hound from the East Village who had worked as a therapy dog, and Riley, a Golden Retriever from Staten Island. The decisive vote was a real tail-biter at first, as Riley took the lead, fell back as Sally surged forward, reclaimed the lead, lost it again. Midway through the contest, Sally started to pull away from Riley, and in the end Sally was elected the city's first honorary dog mayor. Riley became the first deputy honorary dog mayor. In a scandal all too common in our divisive age, Riley also claimed that the election was stolen, along with his prized tennis ball, which he left in the park and which was definitely his. (That last part I may have made up entirely.)

So what were Sally's duties, apart from just continuing to be a dog? She—often with Riley at her side—appeared at important city events, such as the New York City Marathon, and more generally she tried to focus the city's attention on pressing canine issues: the importance of volunteer and service animals, adoption advocacy, and park maintenance. Sally also kept her ears to the ground about New York's small businesses, and not just on dog-related issues but in general. And in a long feature in the *West Side Rag*, an online publication, Sally graciously attributed some of her newfound fame to a young man named Stephen Calabria. Calabria, formerly a political reporter for *HuffPost*, had observed the downward trend in national politics away from open and forthright communication and toward a kind of toxic cynicism. Dogs seemed like they could function as an antidote to this cynicism, reengaging voters with the idea that the city should ideally serve the needs of all its inhabitants. Sally's first administration went smoothly, and in October 2023, during National Pet Wellness Month, she met with the city's human mayor, Eric Adams, and took a tour of city hall. Despite attempts to reach Sally for comment, her office responded that she "doesn't want to comment but is open to being bribed." (That last part I definitely made up.)

On a national political (paw-litical?) level, dogs serve a different purpose. Rather than running for office themselves, they act as loyal companions to the candidates who own them, humanizing their owners and helping them to connect with potential voters. Take Fala, the Scottish Terrier who lived with Franklin Delano Roosevelt in the White House from 1940 until Roosevelt's death. Fala was originally named Big Boy and was given a new name by FDR: Murray the Outlaw of Falahill, after a Scottish ancestor of the Roosevelts. Fala was a nickname for that long, unwieldy name. The dog was trained, did tricks, and became something of a staple in media coverage of the Roosevelts, the first presidential dog to become a celebrity. Fala wasn't the first presidential dog, of course. Jefferson bred dogs. Calvin Coolidge—who famously said that the business of America was business—operated like the business of America was pets: he owned many dogs, including a white Collie named Rob Roy, and even more non-dogs (a donkey named Ebeneezer, a bobcat, a wallaby, a raccoon, and a pygmy hippo). But FDR was an institution, so it was inevitable that his dog would rise above all previous dogs. There was even a Fala scandal, a rumor that the dog had been accidentally left behind on an island and that a naval craft had been sent, at immense cost to taxpayers, to retrieve him. FDR spoke to the controversy directly, centering his dog: "These Republican leaders have not been content with attacks on me, or my wife, or on my sons. No, not content with that, they now include my little dog, Fala. Well, of course, I don't resent attacks, and my family doesn't resent attacks, but Fala does resent them."

FDR's skillful use of his dog as a means of influencing public opinion was echoed by Richard Nixon less than a decade later, when he spoke out against accusations of improper campaign gifts by both addressing the allegations and defiantly insisting that he would keep one gift.

> The day before we left on this campaign trip, we got a message from Union Station in Baltimore saying they had a package for us. We went down to get it. You know what it was? It was a little cocker spaniel dog in a crate that he'd [a man] sent all the way from Texas, black and white spotted. And our little girl Tricia, the six-year-old, named it Checkers. And you know, the kids, like all kids, love the dog and I just want to say this right now, that regardless of what they say about it, we're gonna keep it.

Dogs as presidential pets, dogs as political pawns—the lines crossed and the borders blurred. As we went through the sixties into the seventies, eighties, and nineties, presidential pets were reliable places for the press and for voters to go when they wanted to see their chief executives in a more human light. George H. W. Bush had a Springer Spaniel named Millie who wrote a children's book. (Hold on: I am hearing from my canine fact-checkers that Barbara Bush may have in fact written it. Believe what you want.) The Clintons felt like cat people, mainly—shout-out to Socks—but they also had a Lab named Buddy. George W. Bush returned to the spaniel spot with Spot, who was Millie's daughter, and he also nodded to Fala with a pair of Scottish Terriers. Barack Obama had Portuguese Water Dogs, including Bo, who enjoyed a kind of celebrity of his own, even (sort of) writing a piece about his first hundred (dog) days in office for *The New York Times*.

During that administration, I was already The Dogist, and we were in touch with Obama's team for a while to see if there might be an opportunity to photograph Bo and Sunny. It never quite panned out. Donald Trump, who succeeded Obama in office, was a radical departure—as this is not a political book, we are referring solely to his pet ownership, which was nonexistent. (This wasn't just a minor deviation from the norm. There are only a handful of presidents who did not have pets. James K. Polk didn't. Andrew Johnson, who is frequently compared with Trump for reasons both good and bad, did not officially have any, either, but he found white mice in the White House and took to feeding them.) After Biden won the 2020 election, we got back in touch with presidential staffers, many of whom were Dogist fans. COVID put everything on hold, but at the beginning of 2022, Biden's staff sent out The Dogist Bat-Signal. They wanted to let me know that Major, the president's German Shepherd who had been recently making headlines for biting people, was going to leave Washington, and that they would be debuting a new puppy, also a German Shepherd, named Commander. Traditionally, I had stayed away from political work. Elizabeth Warren's team had gotten in touch with me during campaign season, and I had said no (I would've totally photographed Bailey any other time of year). But this was different. It was a sitting president, not one who was campaigning, and as it turned out, they wanted me to create a photo series for National Pet Day on April 11. It felt less like political speech and more like a general act of patriotism. Being invited to the White House is one of the highest honors for a human or dog photographer!

I had nothing but questions. Would I just be photographing Commander? Commander and the Bidens? Would I really get time with the president? They couldn't give me definitive answers on everything. As they explained, a note of humor in their tone, in a day filled with national security meetings, writing tax bills, calling legislators, the president posing with his new puppy was one of the lowest priorities, even though for me it was the highest. Still, they gave me a tentative date at the very beginning of March. As it got closer, their mood got better. Biden's first Supreme Court nominee, Ketanji Brown Jackson, was nominated in late February. Shortly after that, I took the 6 A.M. Acela from New York to D.C., sticking fairly close to the White House right up until my scheduled 3 P.M. meeting. I passed much of the time at a restaurant bar nearby, checking my phone between spoonfuls of tomato soup. And then, right on schedule, I got a text summoning me to the White House. I had been COVID tested in advance and prescreened by the Secret Service, so my name was on the gatehouse list. I went through a TSA-type security check and was immediately greeted by my contact from Biden's staff, who gave me a little tour: the North Lawn (I took a selfie), the press room, the China Room.

We ended our tour in the Rose Garden, where Commander was waiting with his handler. He was a ten-month-old German Shepherd, a substantial dog—ten-month-old puppies have pretty much arrived at their mature size. I had photographed many before. But this was the president's dog, in the president's house. I couldn't do my normal schtick, chatting with the owner, collecting funny stories. Everything was planned down to the second. I had nine hundred seconds (they said fifteen minutes, but I heard it even more precisely) to get some portraits of Commander on his own, then nine hundred more seconds with the president and his dog, where I could photograph the two of them together. Secret Service agents stationed around the garden reminded me that every move of mine would be watched, which removed the rest of the spontaneity from the session.

I got a bunch of great portraits and action shots of Commander running through the garden and the colonnade with his ball. In those photos he looks just like any other young dog. Sixty seconds before my 3:30 P.M. appointment with the president, I saw Commander's attention fix on something in the distance. I looked where he was looking and saw Jill Biden, the First Lady, walking down the South Lawn with some other people. When I turned back to my subject, I saw a blur of fur and then Commander's butt as he raced toward his mom. To me, this was more normalcy—a dog running giddily to its family—but my staff contact had a distressed look on her face. We needed Commander for our session with the president, which was happening imminently.

Fifteen seconds later, President Biden stepped out from the Oval Office onto the colonnade. He saw his dog and his wife down the way, raised his fingers to his mouth, and produced a high-pitched, extremely loud dog whistle. Commander turned and started running back to us. It was a good first impression—for Joe, certainly, though Commander got halfway to us and then doubled back to Jill, requiring handler intervention.

By the time we sorted out the dog, we had about ten minutes left. President Biden came around the hedges, shook my hand, and asked what I wanted him to do. "I want to get some shots of you and Commander, some close-up and some from afar," I said. The president relaxed a bit. All I wanted him to do was to have fun with his dog? Easiest work of the day. He hopped to it. He had good dog energy and a real rapport with Commander; I could tell he had grown up with German Shepherds. The close-up shots of the two of them were heartwarming and brought out Joe's younger self. Those remain unpublished thus far. His team chose to post a great classic portrait I got of the two of them sitting on the steps in front of the Oval Office.

It was released on National Pet Day, along with a quote: "Commander settled right in at the White House. It helps that he thinks he runs the place."

In the years that followed, Commander himself, despite his good looks and charm, followed in the footsteps (or is that toothmarks?) of his predecessor. He took to biting, too, to the point where he was removed from the White House in October 2023. A few months after that, CNN "obtained documents" that suggested that there may have been two dozen separate incidents, and they brought on Marshall Mirarchi, who handled several presidential dogs, to discuss the matter. He suggested that twenty-four separate biting events was a surprisingly high number. I agree. But I also believe that when you put a high-energy dog like a German Shepherd in the position Commander was put in and fail to train him properly and consistently, you're going to get that kind of result. A White House dog is at the mercy of greater forces of scheduling than the average dog. People are always moving the dog from one place to another, probably without much regard for its own desires of comfort. And, of course, the president's dog will never have any real awareness that it's the FDOTUS (First Dog of the United States), only that the vibe around it is constantly tense and packed with people and activities. In fact, a dog like Commander may think that it's responding exactly appropriately by showing teeth or nipping, that it's protecting its turf from the new guy who has been transferred in from the campaign staff to hustle it to a photo op.

On top of that, I doubt that Biden's dogs' bites were the first in presidential history. Hoover had a shepherd, as did Kennedy. FDR even had one named Major, a police dog he inherited from the New York Police Department, though his Major got nowhere near the ink that Fala did. But those dogs lived in the White House long before the twenty-four-hour news cycle or social media, so any transgressions probably got swept under the rug (likely along with a lot of shed hair). In the end, Commander proved what Major proved before him, that all dogs—even those thrust into the public eye, even those bearing a large symbolic load, even those replacing problematic predecessors and expected to act better than them—are still just dogs at the end of the day.

------------------------- 🐾 -------------------------

Umi, sato-mix (1.5 years old), Greene St. & Morgan St., Jersey City, NJ · "We rescued him from Puerto Rico. He's a really funny dog. We got him in December, and he's eaten through two full comforters. We woke up in the middle of the night, and the feathers inside of the comforter were all over our face. We look down and it's just holes everywhere. So yeah, everything's ruined, but we love him."

------------------------- 🐾 -------------------------

CHAPTER 21

PUP CULTURE

P ro football doesn't have many teams named for dogs. The National Football League is largely big cats and birds of prey (along with some left-field choices, like the formidable Packer). The Cleveland Browns use a dog as their mascot, but the team is named for a person—Paul Brown, the founder of the franchise. Ask people about dogs in the NFL and the first thing that most people will think of is Michael Vick, the star quarterback for the Falcons and Eagles who served jail time after a conviction for dogfighting. Vick is an uncomfortable and tragic story, maybe for the same reasons that we don't want to see dogs as NFL mascots: football is a violent sport. Why would we want our best friends to get involved in that? (I went to see the Vicktory dogs, the pets that were seized after Vick's arrest, some of which had ended up in Kanab, Utah, with the help of Best Friends Animal Society. Their energy was still intense; I photographed Meryl on a leash ten feet away and Tug through a fence.)

So why are dogs so prominent in college football? There are Huskies at the University of Washington and the University of Connecticut. There are Terriers at Boston University (my alma mater) and Wofford College and Carnegie Mellon. The most common canine college mascot, of course, is the bulldog. Bulldogs represent no fewer than fifteen universities, including Gonzaga, Fresno State, Georgetown, Butler, and Citadel.

The two most famous college Bulldogs, arguably, are the University of Georgia and Yale University. I have had the opportunity to perform Dogist duties on both campuses. I visited Athens, Georgia, in September 2019. The football team, ranked third in the country at that point, was playing Arkansas State. No one thought the Red Wolves would give the Dawgs much trouble. I was happy to watch the football game, which turned out not to be much of a game— Georgia was up 34–0 at the half and went on to win 55–0. But I wasn't there for the dog-over-wolf action. I was tasked with one very specific slice of the on-field activity: the presentation of the school's mascot. Like every other Georgia mascot since the 1950s, the dog was named Uga (after UGA, the abbreviation of the university). While many dogs have off-duty names—the first one was Hood's Ole Dan—they all perform in public as Uga.

The dogs don't just share a stage name. The university has a requirement that every Uga must be part of the same bloodline. It's part of a general sense of royalty that extends from birth to death— all previous mascots are buried inside a mausoleum near the front entrance of the football stadium. But this bloodline requirement has significant downsides. As we have discussed earlier, narrow breeding isn't generally to a dog's advantage. It compounds congenital problems, and bulldogs are no picnic to start with. There have been eleven Ugas in sixty years, which has at least something to do with imprudent breeding and overall health. When I went to Athens, it was to photograph Uga X, also named Que. It was a hot weekend in early fall—too hot for Uga. There was concern that he would not be able to breathe well through his nose, a common worry for brachycephalic animals. They gave us a tour of the stadium, where we got some shots of Finn (at the time our foster puppy, now my brother Henry's dog—more on him later), and gave us tickets to the game. When they handed over the tickets, they let me know that there wouldn't be an opportunity at that time to meet Uga "behind the hedges," as they say. He was to appear for fifteen seconds on his way into his air-conditioned Uga-themed doghouse on the sidelines. I wouldn't be able to get a photograph, especially one of him panting. Everyone cheered when he made his appearance, and the staff told me I was invited back anytime to try again when the weather was more suitable for a photo shoot. They had Que's best interest in mind, which I completely understood and respected.

In 2023, I was asked to photograph Handsome Dan, the mascot of Yale University. Handsome Dan differs from Uga not only because he has slightly different athletic responsibilities, but also because he is not subject to the same bloodline requirements. The only stipulation is that he be a bulldog, which he satisfies. In fact, Kingman (i.e., Handsome Dan XIX) is an Olde English Bulldogge, which means that he is free of some of the health problems that bedevil his southern cousin, who is an English Bulldog. Handsome Dan circulates around the campus, meeting incoming freshmen, making people feel at home—sometimes literally, as they miss their own pets. Campus dogs in general act as their dog away from home, helping all students to feel a sense of unity, and during COVID, many universities expanded their campus dog programs, since students were returning from quarantine and extended periods during which they had bonded strongly with pets old or new. Dogs that they could hold for a few minutes before moving back into their dorms were a gentling force, and a way of holding the community together. (A brief pawnote: Que, aka Uga X, was retired in April 2023—he was succeeded by a dog named Boom, who immediately went to work as Uga XI. Que passed away at the age of ten in January 2024. Sometimes on The Dogist I will post memorial tributes to dogs I have photographed. I dedicate this section to Que.)

Earlier, we discussed how dogs die, and in dying teach us about death. Mascots like Uga and Handsome Dan perform an opposite function in some sense. They carry tradition across generations in defiance of the passage of time. In that sense they are more like Lassie. Lassie, of course, is a female Collie whose TV show aired from 1954 to 1973, which is nearly twenty years, and almost six hundred episodes. All but two of those years were on a major network, CBS. And yet, today, if people know about the show at all, they know about it from a brief scene in which Lassie runs up to an adult and starts barking, after which the adult says, "What is it, girl? Timmy's trapped in the well?" As far as I can tell, this never actually happened. There was a Timmy in the show, and he did get into trouble, and sometimes that trouble involved tight spaces, but never a well. The only clip I could find involving a well was a scene where Lassie pushes a bad guy into a well for trying to mess with Jeff, another boy on the show. The guy was also a land thief, so he may well have deserved the bottom of the well. Lassie frequently "saved the day" by biting people or causing them harm (FDOTUS Commander probably would've been a great Lassie). I never met Lassie, of course, but I did photograph her star on the Hollywood Walk of Fame, along with Rin Tin Tin's star. The Dogist respects Hollywood history.

What interests me most about Lassie isn't the Mandela Effect around the well scene. It isn't Lassie's impressive intelligence as a Collie either. It's the fact that the same dog persists over time. Lassie was played by a succession of dogs, but the studio never made that apparent. As a result, Lassie never truly died. There are fictions in which dogs die conspicuously: *Sounder* and *Old Yeller* and *My Dog Skip* and *Where the Red Fern Grows*. Those narratives are a pop culture version of the mourning rite of passage we discussed earlier. They create a bond with a fictional dog and then activate the power of grief. But Lassie goes on and on, like a canine James Bond.

We don't have our own Lassie today, not exactly. We don't have our own Benji, the small Golden-mix who starred in movies like *Benji* and *Oh! Heavenly Dog* in the 1970s and early 1980s. People around my age grew up with Beethoven, the Saint Bernard, who hung around for eight movies with diminishing returns. We grew up with Eddie, the Jack Russell Terrier, who was part of the comic ensemble of the original *Frasier*. And then we had our own favorites. For me, the most significant fictional dogs were Milo (the Pug from the Japanese-to-American film *The Adventures of Milo and Otis*, voiced by Dudley Moore), Skip (a Smooth Fox Terrier from *My Dog Skip*, a film version of Willie Morris's memoir), Hooch (a French Mastiff from *Turner & Hooch*, where he surrendered top billing to Tom Hanks), Chance and Shadow (an American Bulldog and Golden Retriever from *Homeward Bound: The Incredible Journey*), and The Beast (an Old English Mastiff from *The Sandlot*). And I have a special place in my heart for Sparky, the main character in Tim Burton's *Frankenweenie* (a film that exists in two versions, the short that launched his career and the feature-length remake in 2012). I watched *Frankenweenie* repeatedly partly because of my love of Tim Burton's dark style but also for the love it illustrates between a boy and his dog. Sparky, the boy's Bull Terrier (a very Tim Burtonesque breed), is sadly hit by a car and goes to the rainbow bridge. But the boy doesn't give up. He uses lightning to reanimate Sparky. Watching it as a child, I wondered if that might someday be possible. Even as a metaphor, it's still a powerful illustration of how love can exercise its power from beyond the grave.

Pop culture dogs not only come from scripted movies and TV shows, of course. They are in ads, like Spuds MacKenzie and the Taco Bell Chihuahua. Those are the dogs that bond us, the dogs that we, in a way, own collectively. Like our own pets, we can rely on these partially fictitious dogs to connect with others, to process our emotions, to laugh at their goofiness and worry when they are in jeopardy. But pop culture can, as we have discussed, disrupt and imbalance the dog culture. When Disney released *101 Dalmatians*—not the original cartoon from 1961 but the 1996 live-action remake with Glenn Close—animal-rights activists were concerned that it would make every kid in America clamor for a Dalmatian puppy. Their concern turned out to be well-founded, as I explained above. Shelters strained at the seams with Dalmatians that had been taken into the home for the wrong reasons. There was a similar mastiff boom after *Turner & Hooch*. Brussels Griffons had an uptick after *As Good as It Gets*. The Husky population spiked after the popularity of the *Game of Thrones* direwolves. I'm somewhat conflicted about this one because, alas, Elsa very likely entered my life because of this phenomenon. Indeed, when I showed a picture of Elsa to the *Game of Thrones* star Nathalie Emmanuel, she confirmed Elsa would've made a great direwolf on the show. Breed booms may be waning. These days, we are in a time of dogversity, where the trend for brands and cinema is not to project or promote one specific breed or even breeds in general. A rescued mutt is the most PC canine character to get behind. I commend the industry for it, and the millions of dogs in shelters do too.

I'm no *Game of Thrones* or *101 Dalmatians,* but as The Dogist, I do have some pop culture influence, and over the years I have seen how I can put my finger on the dog scale. One afternoon I was out in New York, springtime, Sunday, Riverside Park near Seventy-Second Street. People talk all about the skyscrapers and museums and restaurants, but one of the best benefits of New York City is that you're basically swimming in dogs wherever you go. I can just stand on a corner and see dozens an hour. But I don't generally stand on corners. I'm on the move, scanning the block ahead of me for a dog I can track down and photograph. If you think this seems like a form of stalking, you'd be right. This particular Riverside afternoon, I saw a young couple with a child in a stroller going for a walk. They were facing mostly away from me, but I glimpsed the dog's profile (and butt—always the butt). I couldn't ID the breed exactly at first, which made me even more intrigued. I noticed its tall, slender build, which made me think it was a Whippet, but then I noticed longer wisps of gray and white hair, which made me think it was something else.

The process of elimination for a medium-size sighthound doesn't leave you many options once you've ruled out Whippet. It was too big to be an Italian Greyhound, so I settled on either a Saluki or, less likely, a Silken Windhound.

I caught up with them and delivered my standard opening line: "Excuse me, may I take a quick photo of your dog?" The man replied, "Sure."

"What's his or her name?" I asked.

"Enzo," he said. I couldn't suppress a grin. Who doesn't love when two of their favorite things cross over? Dogs and Ferraris, in this case.

"Is he a Saluki?" I asked.

"He's a Silken Windhound." I admonished myself internally for not taking the riskier guess on the rarer breed. I would've seemed way cooler to him—and The Dogist audience watching the video later—had I nailed the identification. Enzo was an apt name. Sighthounds are among the fastest breeds on earth. They are capable of speeds of forty miles per hour. This one was going about zero, standing calmly by its owners, considering me.

"I think I've only met one other Silken Windhound before, in Texas," I said. "So Enzo's the second."

The woman corrected me. "The third, actually."

"What do you mean?" How could a random woman in the park know The Dogist archive more completely than I did?

"You photographed our friend's dog. Sadie."

I got out my phone and searched for past Dogist posts of the breed.

The first result was for Sirrus, a dog from Austin, Texas, that I met in 2017. That's the one I had remembered. He was under a year old and sat on the sidewalk at the corner of Guadalupe and Second Streets downtown. His nickname was Lover Boy, the owner told me, because he aimed to please. Since that had been my first Silken Windhound, the owner had to educate me on the breed, explaining that they were a cross between Borzois and Whippets. But the woman was right: there was a second one, Sadie, from Washington Square Park. Now it came back to me: not only did I remember Sadie, but I remembered Sadie's owner telling me that she had discovered the breed through the Sirrus post.

"Yup, that's Sadie," the woman said.

"My best friend's dog," the man said. "That's why we got Enzo."

So a New York owner had discovered the breed from my original Austin post, and had in turn passed on a love for the breed to real-life friends. It was a canine triple play, Sirrus to Sadie to Enzo. Enzo's parents also informed me that there was another silken in the neighborhood named Porsche, which added another layer of transmission (for once a car pun instead of a dog pun). In the spirit of transparency, I need to say that Sadie's caption also included a lovely anecdote about Sadie eating the owner's potty-training niece's poop. The Dogist does not endorse this behavior, but it also recognizes that dogs will be dogs.

The Silken Windhound circuit started me thinking about the mystery of breed selection. As I go out into the world to create more Dogist posts, I am constantly on a search to discover which kinds of breeds line up with which kinds of owners, and why. Sometimes it seems like a matter of appearance. People want dogs that reflect back to them the way they think they look. Maybe that means a more muscular dog, a more aerodynamic form, a prettier face. Other times, owners submit to practicality: which dog fits the living space, not just in size but in temperament. So what had brought these three owners to silkens? I couldn't detect any common characteristics, other than maybe an appreciation of the breed's personality and a pride that's connected to its rarity.

One thing I can be sure of—what these owners had in common was The Dogist. And I process that realization with intellectual curiosity rather than with ego. The American mathematician Edward Norton Lorenz, writing in the *Journal of the Atmospheric Sciences* in 1963, proposed the idea of the "seagull effect," which held that a small event such as a single bird flapping its wings could in theory cause a large meteorological event weeks later. Lorenz continued to develop this theory, and was, luckily, persuaded by friends to replace the seagull with something more visually pleasing: a butterfly. The Butterfly Effect, as it came to be called, was not exactly a new idea but one that elaborated upon early work by thinkers such as Fichte and Poincaré, who looked at chaos and disruption in systems. But Lorenz branded it, and the notion that a butterfly flapping its wings could affect a much larger system became installed in the popular imagination. This was not quite that. I couldn't prove that running into Sirrus all those years ago had caused, say, Hurricane Ian. But there was a related principle at work. My run-in with Enzo in Riverside Park was a perfect illustration of the mysterious gears that are always turning behind the simple act of walking a dog. In this case, one chance meeting with a Silken Windhound in Austin in 2017 led to multiple families seeking out the breed, only for me to then photograph each of those dogs by pure chance, 1,800 miles and five years apart.

In 1993, a man named Peter Steiner had an idea. Steiner, a pleasant-looking gentleman in his early fifties, had always had ideas. It was his job; he drew cartoons for *The New Yorker*. In one, a boardroom of executives are all in their seats, each reviewing the printed report they had been given. "The starred items are hot and spicy," he says. In another, two people on a desert island—one of those tiny desert islands with a single palm tree that's ever present in cartoons—are being circled by sharks. One of them turns to the other. "Could we talk about something else?" he says. In a third, a group of surgeons stand around a patient on a table. One of them is holding a dark cylindrical object. "Fresh ground pepper?" he says.

You may or may not know these cartoons. But you certainly know at least one of Steiner's. It is set in a home office, where a large black dog is sitting in a desk chair in front of a computer. A smaller dog is on the floor next to him. The larger dog is typing and talking. "On the Internet," he says, "nobody knows you're a dog." This cartoon first appeared in 1993, which is a bit hard to believe, in part because very few people were on the internet yet. According to a *New York Times* article published that year, the number stood at around 15 million online. But it wasn't paradise so much as a parking lot, or at least a busy street. "Jams Already Appearing on U.S. Data Highway," the headline read.

According to Steiner, the cartoon wasn't designed as a commentary on the online world. The drawing of the two dogs came first, and then he added the caption. But fortune had smiled on him. He had hit on one of the essential truths of the new medium, that it allowed users to assume any identity they wanted. As the internet exploded—users had increased tenfold within five years and a hundredfold more ten years after that—the cartoon felt more and more prophetic and profound.

The cartoon was innovative in many ways, but not in its use of dogs. Dogs are a staple in American comic strips—think of Marmaduke and Odie and Dogbert (my dad's personal favorite). The most famous, of course, is Snoopy, one of the marquee stars of *Peanuts*. Only Charlie Brown gets higher billing. Snoopy is a classic American creation, a marvel of whimsy, rue, and charming selfishness. He is a Beagle, of course, though for years I didn't think he was an especially good drawing of one. Then someone sent me a picture of a Beagle photographed sitting up on its hind legs waiting for its bowl of delicious food to be put on the ground, tongue slightly out tasting the air. The shadow cast on the wall in the image was nothing but Snoopy.

New Yorker comics are a more specific form—usually single panels rather than strips, captions rather than dialogue bubbles. I've always loved them for their succinctness. Some of my favorites include (and I'll do my best to depict them) one from Arnie Levin, where a dog is in between his owners in the living room wearing a tuxedo, bow tie, and top hat. The caption: "Howard, I think the dog wants to go out." Another, from Shannon Wheeler, has a cat and a dog playing Scrabble in the kitchen. "'Grrr' is not a word," the cat says. One from Mike Twohy shows two dogs looking at a door that one of them has completely scratched up. "All of my work deals with the theme of exclusion," the dog says. There's even a Lassie cartoon in two panels. In the first, a drowning man calls out to a Collie on the shore. "Lassie!" he says. "Get help!!" The second panel shows the dog in a psychiatrist's office, stretched out on a couch.

These cartoons use dogs as stand-ins for human relationships in all their neurotic glory. Sometimes the joke works by layering human self-consciousness over dogs. In a recent cartoon by Amy Hwang, two dogs exchange presents. One sees that it is receiving a bone wrapped in a ribbon. "I got you the same thing," it says. Sometimes the joke works in the opposite direction—in a 1999 cartoon by Charles Barsotti, a dog waiter approaches a dog diner at a restaurant, dragging a full garbage can behind him. "The special, sir. Shall I spread it out or will you knock it over yourself?"

You can't see any of these cartoons here, though a quick Google search would remedy that. Luckily, there is a parallel genre that achieves the same aims: the talking-dog joke. I know a guy who is a kind of connoisseur of them. He'll text me with new ones, by which I mean old ones that I haven't heard yet: the talking dog at the bar, the talking dog at the airport, the talking dog at the racetrack. The jokes, like the cartoons, reveal truths about the ways in which we behave: our vanity, our fears, our lack of impulse control. Canine protagonists liberate us to practice honesty. We employ them as avatars to talk about ourselves. Here is one:

A man is driving when he sees a sign in front of a house that says, "Talking Dog for Sale: $5." He stops his car and knocks on the door. "I noticed your sign," he says to the woman who answers. "Do you really have a talking dog for sale?"

"He's out back," she says. "Go see for yourself."

The man goes out onto the porch. A shaggy-looking white dog is resting there. "Uh," the man says, "I feel stupid, but here goes: Hello?"

"Hi there," the dog says.

The man gasps. "You can talk?"

"Sure," the dog says. "I've always been able to talk. When I was about a year old, I met this guy named Sam. He was in the CIA, and he trained me as a spy. I learned something like nine languages. I helped him bring down some bad types. The lady in there is his ex-wife. She kept me when Sam died. I slowed down, but I didn't stop. Now I'm learning calculus."

The man goes back inside the house. "That dog is amazing," he tells the woman. "But can I ask you a question? Why is he so cheap? Five bucks is nothing."

"Sure, he can talk," the woman says. "But what a liar."

Human suspicion, human vanity, human self-doubt: they're all wrapped up in this talking porch dog, which is why it works as a joke.

Daisy, Foxhound-mix (4 years old), Battery Park, New York, NY • "She's our first dog—we didn't know that big paws equals big dog. She's about four times bigger than what we expected. 'The dog that kept growing.' I pictured carrying her up the subway stairs. No cabdrivers stop for us. We love her."

CHAPTER 22

AN EPIDEMIC OF LONELINESS

If the *New Yorker* cartoons are highbrow and the talking-dog jokes a little less so, you have to keep dropping lower to get to one of my favorite sites of dog humor. Because of my parents' love for David Letterman, I saw Letterman's Stupid Pet Tricks, a segment that featured ordinary people introducing their pets and demonstrating weird stunts. There was a horse that could open a refrigerator, a pig eating mints, a rabbit dozing off when rocked like a baby. People love looking at animals, always, because they elicit something primal within us, but the best were always the dogs. There was a dog named Elsa (not mine, but an earlier, stupider-pet-trickier one) that flipped a biscuit off its nose to another dog sitting behind it. The segment was revived as a full-length show in 2024 with Sarah Silverman as host, and for my money it leans a little too hard on exotic animals— a camel!—at the expense of good old dogs. Even now, it's the dogs that get the strongest response, because they're the pets that are closest to our hearts and souls.

I grew up, as did many people my age, with *America's Funniest Home Videos*, the ABC television program hosted by Bob Saget

(RIP). *America's Funniest Home Videos* created the idea of viral before the idea of viral existed. They would show one short video clip and within the day everyone seemed to know about it. Maybe it was twin toddlers fighting over a pacifier. Maybe it was a dad slipping and falling in the snow.

Many had animal content. One of my earliest and sharpest ambitions was to get on the show. I was already filming plenty of content starring my dog Ruby, some of which involved tricks that I had taught her. One of those tricks (though arguably not really a trick) was eating corn right off the cob. I would hold it out and rotate it as she munched away at the kernels. It was hilarious. I filmed her on my dad's video camera and sent it in to the post office box they put at the end of the show. I knew it was funny, though I knew Ruby would be competing with everyone else's dogs. I had a good feeling about it, though. About six weeks later my parents handed me a package that had arrived in the mail with the AFV logo on it. To me, this (retrospectively) felt like the equivalent of opening up a college acceptance or rejection letter. I opened it up. The letter inside told me that they had received Ruby's corn on the cob video and had decided, after careful consideration, that it was going to be aired! Also in the package was an AFV T-shirt.

The letter also told me the air date, but to be completely honest, I don't remember seeing it on TV. I must have had baseball practice, or something. Just knowing Ruby made the cut was all that mattered to me.

These days, families don't cluster around the TV anymore. Everyone's head is down in their devices more than not. Where the internet used to offer a break from reality, now reality offers a break from the internet. And though the internet when Peter Steiner made his cartoon was very different, the message is still just as relevant as it was then.

The internet has changed everything about humanity and society.

It has changed the way we shop. It has changed the way we work. It has changed the way we check the weather. The most conspicuous shift is also the most fundamental, which is that it has changed the way we communicate. I am not that old, in the scope of things. Still, my earliest memories come from the floppy-disk and dial-up era. I remember my yellow Sony Walkman that I mostly used to listen to Stevie Wonder on cassette tape. I am also old enough to remember the time before cellphones, when PDA meant "personal digital assistant" (like a PalmPilot) instead of canoodling with your boo on the street corner. I remember a time when people still mostly called and had conversations instead of just texting each other. I remember a time when people emailed funny pictures to each other instead of DMing them over social media. Instead of writing friends to describe your recent vacation to Italy or telling them in person, now you just put up some posts on Facebook or Instagram or you tweet about it while you are there, and your friends like those posts and maybe add comments of their own. On Peter Steiner's internet, nobody knew if you were a dog (or a leprechaun, for that matter). On today's internet, you portray the type of person you imagine or want yourself to be, even if you're still a dog. We're often just as masked as we were before, but now have the delusion of thinking our social personas fully align with our offline selves.

At the beginning of this section, I talked about going to a Halloween party with Sam, and how liberated people felt when their masks/costumes were still on. The internet has a related effect, though often a detrimental version of it. Our anonymity online allows us to be unrestrained, which sometimes allows us to genuinely connect, but at other times makes us feel empowered to lob grenades at each other—to be "keyboard warriors." Much of the behavior is critical, with a conspicuous shortage of empathy. Moreover, social media has gotten really good at getting under our skin and changing our mood quickly. When I see friends in person, we often spend a good deal of time venting about a recent experience or something crazy we saw on social media. It's a detox process that brings us back to the baseline, where we no longer feel alone and frustrated and under siege, and can proceed with conversations about things that happened off the internet. More than ever, we live in a time of alienation and anger, a desperation that comes from the fact that we have so many more ways to connect with others, at least in theory, but feel less and less like we're actually engaged. Our masks make us free, but the lack of physical interaction frees us from the consequences we'd other-wise face. It can bring out the best, but it often brings out the worst aspects of being human. The funny and poignantly sad reality of Steiner's internet is that it would be much better if everyone were, in fact, dogs.

And yet, I, too, live on the internet. I live there in my private life, like everyone else. But it's conclusively where I live as The Dogist. I have lived there since the early days of Instagram in 2013. My first Instagram posts from my personal page were about all your typical mundane things—meals, trips, friends. People liked them enough for me to keep going. But when I posted a photo of a dog I met while on a trip to Vienna, the interest ramped up to a whole new level. That's when I got the idea to post only dogs, and to create a new on-line identity as The Dogist.

Over the years, I have built a large online community. I post my pictures and videos on various social media platforms, whether Instagram or TikTok or Facebook or Twitter, and what binds them all together is the people who come to see them. People talk to each other about the dogs that I have photographed, and this leads natu-rally into conversations about their own dogs, about their cares and concerns and appreciations they have for their dogs. This commu-nity is bound together by a common interest, and for the most part, it avoids the pitfalls of the larger internet.

In fact, I often consider it to be an antidote to the rest of the inter-net. Much of the internet makes you feel jealous, envious, angry, self-conscious, lazy, or stupid. The Dogist was created to be a breath of fresh air. Something real. Something you could breathe in deeply, even if it made you smile or cry. I once posted a photo series with a woman who had just gotten a puppy. I took pictures of her six-month-old rescue mix, Willa, on Lafayette Street in SoHo. The woman started by saying that she was on the brink of solving the mystery of what kind of mix Willa was: "We're about to get the DNA results back," she said. She went on to say that the dog brought her incredible joy and headache both: "Seventy percent of the time amazing, thirty percent of the time she's trying to ruin my life, but I love her so much." I added a little prompt at the end of the post: "What percentage of time is your dog amazing?" The responses to that post were representative of the kind of positive energy that The Dogist can generate, the way that it not only encourages people to come forward in unselfconscious happiness, but also the way it can forge and reinforce relationships between people. Commenters, hundreds of them, rushed in to empathize with the woman, to relate their own stories about having new puppies in the house. The 70/30 ratio was acknowledged, but the 70 was what people talked about. The overall vibe around that post was so nourishing and supportive, an example of the best kinds of human relationships, and the way that they create warmth and humor.

Recently, I posted a video of my encounter with a rescued medium-size mixed-breed named Milo. The owner said he was some combination of Chow, Miniature Pinscher, and Cocker Spaniel. What caught my attention was his distinctively fluffy tail (a "hat on his butt" is what I called it; she called it a toupee). Aside from that, he was just another great, cute dog walking around New York City. When I asked if he had an Instagram account, she gave it to me and mentioned he "only had eighty-five followers." I turned to the camera and jokingly insisted that The Dogist audience needed to change that. Specifically, that our first milestone would be three digits, then four. I knew he would get to three, and likely four, but I was not expecting that in less than twenty-four hours he would have five digits. It's funny, sure, but it's more than that. People followed Milo because he was cute, but it boiled down to a universal principle all dog people hold dear: whatever goodness there is, dogs deserve it.

At times, the site has tipped the other way. I remember one post where the owner told me that her dog, a rescued English Setter named Rock, had come to her because the dog had killed a cat and been forced to leave its original home. I left that information in the post because to me, it was factually relevant to its backstory, and there was some dark humor to it. It was like a cartoon come to life: if not a *New Yorker* cartoon, maybe a *Far Side*. Something about primal animal nature, a lack of remorse from the dog, and how doing a bad thing ended up netting him a good thing. But when I published the photos of Rock, which featured the same elements of all my other posts—a beautiful dog in an environment where it was loved—people fixated on the dead cat in the story. One commenter told a story of how a childhood cat was killed by a dog in the neighborhood and warned Rock's owner, and by extension everyone else reading the comments, to keep the dog fenced in. Others criticized me for trivializing the cat's life (and death), for reducing it to a cat joke on a dog page. I spent the day questioning my judgment, and then the rest of the week considering how I might adjust my programming moving forward.

The same phenomenon happens every time I post a photo of a dog with cropped ears or tail, or a prong collar, or even a trendy breed hybrid like a Bernedoodle or Aussiedoodle—the comments section ignores the dog and instead turns into a debate about a hot-button issue in the dog world. And even that's okay. I am not against hosting debates about hot-button issues. I like to foster discussion. I don't want to sweep important conversations under the rug. But I wish that people's reactions weren't quite so knee-jerk and superficial. In this case, it's not fair to call training/prong collars torture devices. Context is always important. An older woman or man who nobly rescues a big dog from life in a shelter might find that the only way they can keep that dog under control on daily walks is with a prong collar. Is that ideal? Maybe not. Should the person just accept that the dog may pull them to the ground if they see a squirrel? No. Should that person then decide to relinquish the dog back to the shelter because they couldn't handle the dog's strength? Nobody wants that outcome either. So, a workable solution is reached. The dog gets to live a life of fresh air, walkies, and snuggling on the couch, and the person gets to keep their arm in their socket. There are cases where prong collars are improperly used or put on to seem menacing, but they are not inherently abusive. I generally hope to foster constructive conversations that allow people to learn and discuss things respectfully.

When these kinds of debates occur on my site, I think about Cesar Millan, the famous Dog Whisperer. I have no direct experience with Millan. I have never met him in real life. But my dad and I loved his show, the way it seemed to be about the relationships between people and dogs but was actually about the way that people understood relationships in general: how they understood self-respect and also tolerance, kindness but also firmness. We are similar in that regard, but there is a key difference. The Dog Whisperer required there to be something wrong that Cesar could, in his infinite wisdom, come in and fix. It was *Kitchen Nightmares* for dogs, a dramatic journey from a bad place to a good place. I don't have any inherent need for that initial bad place to exist. I'm simpler in that regard: I want to tell the true but optimistic story of dogs. The water-bowl-half-full story of dogs. I want to bring light into this world where there is so much darkness. And I want to take some memorable, meaningful, and hopefully funny pictures of dogs along the way. And in doing so, if I can help get some dogs adopted from shelters to homes, that's a fantastic cherry on top.

In the end, though, I am only one small corner of the internet. There is a vast world of dog content out there. In fact, I would go as far to say that *most* pictures are of dogs (I'm just pulling that out of thin air, but I have a good feeling about it). Most people are dog photographers, just like me (though they generally have fewer muses). I sometimes think dog content is the single strand of wire tethering our society to decency and sanity. For a moment, every dog you see is yours. I find no greater sense of joy and purpose in my life than when I'm crouched down photographing a dog. Dogs, in all their power, have turned one of the most alienating technologies ever invented into a channel of love, laughter, inspiration, and education, all while restoring faith in humanity. If Ruby were still around today, I would film her eating corn on the cob, but I probably wouldn't send it to *America's Funniest Home Videos*. I would just share it on The Dogist. In fact, if I ever find a copy of the VHS, I will.

------------- 🐾 -------------

Henry, mix (4 years old), Little West & 2nd Pl., New York, NY • "He goes by Hank, Henard, Henrico, and Hanklin, but Henry is his government name. The first week I got him, he locked himself in my bedroom. I had to break the doorknob to get him out."

------------- 🐾 -------------

PART THREE

OUR PURPOSE

CHAPTER 23

THIS DOG WILL CHANGE WHAT YOU THINK OF YOUR LIFE

I have written about the first time a dog saved my life: my grand-mother's dog, nosing me away from the street when I was a tod-dler. The second time was more conceptual, and also more profound. This was in the early twenty-first century, the century in which I was expected to become an adult. I was twenty-five years old, working in New York City for a marketing agency. I felt mostly uninspired, but I tried not to share that information with others at the company. I practiced go-along-to-get-along employment, doing a good enough job and trying to stay out of the line of fire. But the line of fire has a funny way of finding you.

About two years into my time there, my department had to put together a last-minute presentation for a big client. The guy I re-ported to was only slightly older than me, but he was fully dialed in as an employee and as a person, on top of things to an impressive degree. He had "upper management written all over him," as the Bobs from *Office Space* would say. But that particular week, he had a personal matter that demanded his attention, and so he, along with our mutual boss, proposed that I take the lead on putting the presentation together. "Of course," I said. My tone sounded enthusiastic, and for a minute there I think I might have even felt that way. I understood that if I did a good job, I could point back to the moment when the time came for raises, or promotions, or those conversations about where you saw yourself in five years. Would I take the lead on the presentation? Of course I would.

But the second I left the meeting, another thought flooded in. I, too, had a personal matter that demanded my attention that evening. Specifically, my best friend Adam's birthday party. It wasn't a normal party. It was a conceptual party, and I had designed the concept. When it came to my best friends' life events, I took them quite seriously. I used them as theatrical opportunities, with a comic edge, figuring out elaborate ways to prank and embarrass them as part of the celebration. My plan was to invite Adam to a bar and for him to arrive to see everyone else there in an Adam costume, down to his signature Elvis-style hairdo, his nerdy black glasses, and his trademark too-small teal shirt. It would be like *Where's Waldo?* in reverse. Look: He's everywhere!

I ordered the necessary supplies (glasses, shirts, wigs) and confirmed everyone's participation. It was not a hard sell. For weeks, I was consumed with the finer points of this plan. It would be one for the history books, or at least the history books that had a chapter on famous conceptual stunts designed for friends' birthdays. But suddenly there was a wrench in the works—in fact, the wrench was work. That day, while I should have been getting started on the deck, I was on the roof of my office spray-painting wigs to the exact brown of Adam's hair. (Elvis wigs, as it turns out, only come in black.) That night, when I should have been putting finishing touches on the presentation, I was leaving early to get a head start at the bar, both in terms of costuming and in terms of drinking. It turned out to be the perfect surprise party. Adam couldn't believe what he was seeing and blew a funny fuse upon arrival. There were drinks and toasts and more drinks and music and an all-around good time.

The good time extended beyond the point where I should have

been going home to get a jump on the project before bed. I went home to PTFO (you can google that if you want), slept a bit, and got to the office around 7 A.M. I did what I could before everyone came in. My colleague arrived around eight. "Okay," he said as he rounded the corner by my desk. "How are we doing?" I nervously showed him a few slides, and I could tell by his expression that he was having a minor panic attack. We raced to get everything sorted before the client came in for the presentation later that day. We did, just barely. The client loved it, but internally, I was a marked man. My director had a sense that I had let things go until the very last minute, that I had demonstrated a poor understanding of priority, and that we had all escaped by the skin of our teeth. While I was being reprimanded by my director, I was internally replaying every amazing aspect of Adam's party the night before in my head. The look on his face, him keeling over laughing, the pictures of us all together. Even though I kept my head down in the office that week, I felt something seismic within me shift. Most people would've been burning the midnight oil, making sure they did everything in their power to climb the corporate ladder and advance in their career. But I knew I couldn't end up like that. I knew making memories with the people who mattered to me transcended everything. Nobody would care about my Power-Point presentation for more than a day. Making fun of your best friend on his birthday—priceless.

A month or so after the presentation, I took a two-week vacation to go on my Birthright Israel trip. It was a blast. During that trip, I started floating the idea of a dog blog to others, with a great response. But I still had a job. When I got back to New York, the office was eerily quiet. I checked and there were no new projects for me. I asked around and many people seemed to be experiencing a similar lull. It had happened before, after big campaigns wound down and new business was still pitching. The time before the next big contract was like a company-wide inhale. The following week, on a Tuesday, maybe, I got an email from my group director addressed to me and another relatively new person in my department. The email was short, basically a summons to his office. We stood up and looked at each other. Maybe this was a new project, finally. We grabbed notepads and chatted excitedly as we walked to his office. When we arrived, the group director was standing. He didn't ask us to sit. "So," he said, "today will be your last day." I was stunned. She was stunned. We looked at each other again. We wouldn't be working together on a project, or any project in the future. Forty other people met the same fate that day in the company's downsizing.

The rest of that week was more than a little anxious for me. I had to call my parents and report what had happened. I had to break the news to my friends. But by the following Monday, the anxiety had mostly dissolved into relief that I wouldn't be spending the rest of my life in an office making PowerPoint presentations and coddling clients. I did what many people do, which is tell themselves that the loss of a job is a blessing in disguise, that the job had been a bad fit, a wage trap, a dead end disguised as the beginning of a career. But I also did what many people don't do, which was to believe in myself to try something on my own instead of going back to find the same job somewhere else. A sense of freedom was spreading inside me. I collaborated on a few projects with friends, writing some copy, helping craft mission statements, but each time I was more distant from the process and the version of me that was doing it—the collared-shirt-wearing, loafer-sporting, subway-commuting, laptop-toting Elias. Every day I felt more and more lackadaisical about "marketing" and more and more confident that I could turn away from that life into something that was both creative and entrepreneurial. I could use what I had learned about brand strategy to build a brand of my own.

I also had my Nikon camera, which was collecting dust in a bag.

And so, slowly but surely, I arrived at a solution to the problem of being laid off. My subject, I knew, would be dogs. What else? That was the thing closest to my heart, had always been, but it was also something I knew others felt the same way about. In the wake of losing my job, I traveled to Europe, and instead of taking a small point-

and-shoot camera, I took my Nikon—a proper DSLR—and began posting photographs to my personal Instagram. They looked much better than the snapshots people were taking with their phones. After posting several typical friends, food, and cityscape photos, I shared a few photos of some dogs that I had encountered and noticed that they were getting far more likes than anything I had posted on the trip. More than that, I felt the spark of creativity. I *wanted* to share those photos and checked Instagram incessantly to see people's reactions and comments. I felt like I was sharing my actual self through the dogs, whereas even posting a picture of me felt inauthentic. Narcissistic. I felt cosmically drawn toward dogs. Whatever I chose to do next, dogs would have to be involved. My friend Pasquale and I started creating videos featuring dogs in which we interviewed them about current events and new tech products.

I went to San Francisco to attend my cousin's wedding. While I was out there, I woke up at 3 A.M. in the hotel with a mild epiphany: *The Sartorialist* for dogs. The Dogist. A parody site that could be its own content, obviously, but more than that—a new identity for me. A little manic, I secured the handle on all available social media platforms and went back to sleep. That's when I went to Williamsburg and met the Frenchie. That's when I was asked what the photos were for, and when I said, "The Dogist." It sounded right, and that was that. I made my first post that day, October 23, 2013.

Soon after that, I started to solidify my online identity. I had a logo, or rather a mascot—based on a funny-faced Boxer I had photographed in Europe. To me, it represented all dogs. I called him the "everydog." The photo was taken at an angle that foregrounded the everydog's face and hid his left front leg. But that was all overwhelmed by the expression on the dog's face, which was perfect, so filled with curiosity and apprehension and humor. Boxers have kind of a permanent serious but goofy expression that I always loved. "I did him a spooky," I kept repeating in my head, giggling to myself. (Phrases like this, which are called DoggoLingo, are like an internet meme language used by dog owners to try to verbalize their dogs' thoughts and emotions. It's like an online crowdsourced version of my canine ventriloquism.) The photo was a perfect encapsulation of what I wanted to do with my photos, and eventually I had it turned into an illustration that became my logo.

The Boxer was an illustration of a dog, but it was also an illustration of how my life was changing because of dogs—and, more specifically, how I was extracting a new sense of purpose. In the process of training service dogs, you may hear the word "flunkie," which refers to the dogs that don't successfully graduate from the organization's training program and consequently don't go on to do the type of work that was intended. The term is mostly said in jest, but it suggests the dog failed at something it set out to do, that it fell short of its goal. (It's similar to the phrase "foster fail," which is used when a person fosters an adoptable dog and finds that they can't give the dog up to a potential applicant. It's a sarcastic way of saying "We fell in love.") While it's funny to suggest dogs have ambitions akin to a premed student getting accepted to medical school, the reality is that these dogs are not flunking anything. They are merely demonstrating that they would rather be a different kind of dog. Human life is often defined by expectations loaded onto us by others and by ourselves, and those expectations can be unreasonable, poorly designed, or ill-advised. Dogs, while certainly capable of incredible things, are not burdened by lofty, externally and self-imposed expectations. Canine life is guided by a set of intrinsic motivations, like the desire for company, love, and pleasure (they may also be motivated to get a bite of the piece of turkey that didn't stay in your sandwich, but everybody's gotta eat).

My midtwenties illustrated this shift for me. Or rather, it used me to illustrate this shift. I was—I am—the eldest son of two Jewish doctors. My dad is a pediatric hematologist. My mom is a prominent breast oncologist. My connection to medicine and science doesn't stop there. My mother's father was a famous biologist who literally wrote the textbook on histology. My paternal grandmother was one of the earliest female doctors in Philadelphia, and her husband, my grandfather, was a cardiologist. I grew up immersed in that world. During summers, when other kids were at summer camp playing Capture the Flag, I went to the Children's School of Science in Woods Hole (CSS), a pseudo-academic program where I spent my days collecting specimens, pinning bugs. I was a lifer there.

There was an expectation that I would be a professional in the same field. My parents didn't pressure me explicitly. But circumstance produced that expectation. And all along the way, I eluded it: subtly but stubbornly. The part of me that had other ideas kept surfacing. At CSS, my favorite course was photography. It meant more to me than anything else. It was the course everyone else wanted to get into, too, but it had limited spaces. I was a lifer at CSS, so while I was mostly expecting to get in, I was elated to find out that I did (I then went on to be the photography assistant teacher at CSS, another lasting source of pride). And while I took plenty of science classes in high school and did well enough in them to head off to college with at least the prospect of being premed, I ran into an obstacle my freshman year in the form of an introductory chemistry course. The reputation of the course was that it was a "weed out" class, one that was so difficult that it separated the kids who had a real commitment to being premed to those who were less committed. I revealed myself as one of the weeds. I just wasn't a good enough student. I was a procrastinator. I was smart enough to get by in class by cramming the night before, but the result was a B average.

So that put me off medicine—or put medicine further away from me. College kept going. I made more of my interest in art and in writing, which meant that when it came time to start working, I sought employment in those worlds. That meant New York City. Even though I was a Philly kid, my eyes were turned toward Manhattan. I was New York–obsessed through most of my adolescence. I wore a Yankees hat all through high school not because I was a Yankees fan, but because it was a kind of New York City uniform. My parents had bought a pied-à-terre on the Upper West Side, and that gave me a foothold, a place to stay if I got work in the city. And

I did. I had an internship at MTVU, the college-based offshoot of MTV, and my job involved running videos back and forth from Times Square. That led in some indirect way to my marketing job, which led in some direct way to my being without any job at all, which led directly to The Dogist.

I can't say this is a path for everyone, but there are some lessons that have universal currency. When I was a kid, imagining that I would become a dog photographer wouldn't have seemed real. But as time passed, the responsibilities I encountered—the academic ones, the professional ones—didn't seem any more real. Left to my own devices, I manifested a version of that original impulse. It didn't happen in a vacuum, of course. The growth of the internet, specifically social media, came just at the right time for me. If I had tried to be a dog photographer a decade earlier, I probably would have failed. I was not talented enough to be a print artist. I couldn't have gotten gallery shows or work in high-end editorial. I came up at a time when most of the pictures on the internet were "shot with a potato," as the meme goes. They were of poor quality and I represented a decided improvement over them. Timing and passion and luck all combined to bring me to a new and longer-lasting purpose. Dogs not only changed my life but changed what I thought of as life. The fact that I failed at being premed and failed at my marketing job and survived gave me the courage to take a bigger risk. As Jim Carrey (one of my favorites) once said in a 2014 commencement speech at the Maharishi University of Management, "You can fail at what you don't want, so you might as well take a chance on doing what you love."

Dogs were my purpose, but they were also my way into any discussion of purpose.

In 2018, I had lunch with my sister and brother in New York. They are twins, but their paths had diverged. My sister, Isabel, was at

Dropbox at the time, focused on doing well in the job and discovering where it led. She seemed happy with that outcome and motivated in that world. My brother, Henry, on the other hand, was laboring in ad sales, and I mean laboring. Every time we would talk, he would tell me what he was doing on the job, what he was learning, but the tone was always one of obligation. It didn't seem like him. He was getting by, like many people do, but I could recognize that he was in a similar trap that I had been in and there wasn't any obvious way to escape it.

By that point, I had been The Dogist for almost five years, long enough to know that it was working for me, but maybe not quite long enough to feel entirely secure. As a result, I was a bit of an evangelist for my own cause. At that lunch, I got up on a bit of a soapbox and started telling Isabel and Henry about the unprecedented promise of the internet, how it allowed you to locate your most central and profound interests and, through some technological alchemy, transform them into an actual career. I had gone to a New York tech conference where Gary Vaynerchuk told everyone to "Do your Smurf blog"—in other words, embrace whatever weird thing you care about, and the community of people with that same weird interest will find you and embrace you. I mentioned that and various other internet buzzwords and trending maxims at the time. I was a poster child for the social media blog boom, a true believer.

After about ten minutes, Henry interrupted my rant. "What am I supposed to do?" he said, throwing his hands up. "Make a dog blog?"

He was being somewhat mocking, but I took his frustration as a step in the right direction. As a newly activated Dogist, I wanted him to find his own -ist, whatever that was. After that lunch, I kept reiterating that theme, but less stridently, and Henry's resistance became less pronounced. He worked up the courage to quit his job, and then had the gumption to ask to borrow my old camera. His concept was to go to clubs like Terra Blues and Smalls Jazz Club and take photographs of the performers and the crowd. I gave him a lens and showed him how to use the camera. The photos were great, and he posted them to an Instagram page he called Scooter Jams, because he traveled to the venues on a scooter.

For a while, that satisfied him, but the while ran out. One day he called me. "I think I'm going to get a van." Again, I was encouraging. He got a Sprinter that already had significant mileage on it and started living the vanlife. This was a trend that took hold around 2018 or so, when ambitious and adventurous Gen Zers started doing their own version of what Jack Kerouac had done in the 1950s. Vanlife had its own rules and its own community, and Henry seemed happy there.

I had kept on as The Dogist, growing my content and growing my audience, and toward the end of 2018 a new project surfaced. It was in partnership with a luxury car brand and designed to draw attention to the sato dogs, the Puerto Rican street dogs that are all over the island and in need of happy homes. For the project, I got in touch with Chrissy from The Sato Project for a puppy to foster while driving cross-country, East Coast to West Coast, in search of its eventual adoptive family. Along the way, there would be an online poll to name the dog, and plenty of blog entries and photos. We picked one particularly cute brown puppy from a litter that had been born in a bush. We made arrangements to bring him to the mainland and start the project.

The journey kicked off in Boston, in part because I was there for my cousin's bat mitzvah. Henry was there, too, and I remember talking to him about what was about to happen. By that point, the naming poll had already closed, and the dog had been named Finn. "I'm going to take Finn west," I said. Then I either had a brainstorm or noticed something in my brother's expression. "Henry," I said, "do you want to come help me on this trip?"

We set out for Los Angeles in a new crossover SUV that had been loaned to me. The goal was to tell a set of intertwining stories—Finn's birth, The Sato Project, adoptions, and rescues—show Finn some of the best cities and sights in the United States, and to eventually find him a home. We met up with my aunt Alice in Bethesda, Maryland (she was an early candidate to take Finn in, but her dog didn't want the company). We went to Chicago, to Atlanta, to Charleston. We even made a stop at the Grand Ole Opry in Nashville—they have their own long-standing dog mascot, Ole Blu. Along the way, many people expressed an interest in Finn. He was the sweetheart of the internet, and much of the affection for him helped us in our fundraising for The Sato Project. Every thousand dollars we raised meant that another dog could be adopted: we measured our fundraising by Finns, and we were up to forty Finns, fifty Finns.

In New Orleans, we took a picture of Finn wearing Mardi Gras beads on Bourbon Street. That afternoon, after we got back to our hotel room, Henry came to me. "I think I want to keep him," he said. The announcement didn't shock me. Finn had been sleeping in Henry's bed. Still, it was big news to have a new dog father in the family. Suddenly, Finn had a home, Henry had a new purpose, and we were closing in on sixty Finns.

There was only one note of minor failure—given that we had satisfied the overall terms of the project, we weren't going to make it to LA. We pivoted. Henry had left his van in Flagstaff, Arizona, near where one of our cousins lived. We drove there. He and Finn went into his van. I called the car company and negotiated the change in plans, asking them if we could drop the vehicle in Phoenix. After they sorted it out, the three of us piled into Henry's Sprinter van, went to see the Grand Canyon (how could we not?), and turned around to head back east. That drive was quicker, with brief stops in Colorado and Chicago and some key educational gains (I acquired a new appreciation for public bathroom access and learned about the importance of parking on a level surface to avoid having to sleep at an angle).

We ended up back in Woods Hole, where we tried to come down from the high of our trip. It was hard, in part because it was clear to me that Henry and Finn were sudden celebrities. "Henry," I said, "are you going to create an account for him?" He put me off at first but came to his senses soon enough. Keeping Finn was the name we all landed on, and the first post both announced Finn's adoption and opened up a whole new door of opportunity for my brother. I remember crafting the post and caption, feeling emotionally overwhelmed at what I knew would be a flood of possibilities for Henry.

Overnight, he accumulated something like 75,000 followers: an instant dogfluencer. He started documenting his adventures with Finn in his van, which made for great travel writing and photography, but he also created a career out of rescuing dogs and forging important partnerships with both nonprofits and corporations. Oh, and he met his wife through his work. My family often thinks of Keeping Finn as a gift from me to my brother, but really it was a gift from dogs to me that I regifted to my brother. It was the gift of knowing that you could pursue a fulfilling career centered on something you loved. It was the gift of understanding that you could be your own boss and that you had the freedom to decide what you wanted to do with your short time here on earth. Above all, it was the gift of purpose. We have talked about how dogs help people to define and then refine their identities while deepening and strengthening their relationships. Once those things are in place, once people are acting more authentically and interacting with others more rewardingly, life throws up an entirely new set of better questions. What should we do with our time together? How should we spend our energy? What makes our life mean more to us as we move through it? Dogs are inspirational in this regard. My story—having my life redefined and reinvigorated by dogs—is echoed all over the world.

Ira, Dachshund (2 years old), McCarren Park, Brooklyn, NY • "He's an Aries. He's very fiery. He thinks he's the boss of the house. When he was a puppy, our neighbors had Huskies, and so I think he learned some of the howling from them. He's so smart, but he uses it for evil. He's mischievous, but he's a good boy deep at heart. He has a bent tail that he was born with, and it looked like a little pig curlicue when he was a puppy."

CHAPTER 24

DOGS OF WAR

When I got the call from Warrior Canine Connection, I knew it wasn't because of the warriors. The organization, which is based in Boyds, Maryland—a small community a few miles west of Germantown—was calling me to ask if I would create a photo essay about their program, which connected PTSD-afflicted vets to service dogs. "Of course," I said. The woman on the phone explained a bit about PTSD, how it causes emotional numbness, inexplicable nervousness, detachment, surges of frustration or rage during mundane tasks, and a crippling inability to sleep. "Of course," I said again, even though I hadn't known all those symptoms. What I did know—partly from my work with other programs, partly from the street photos I had taken—was that dogs make people's lives better. It happens every day, in a million different ways. This was a variation on that theme, and I wanted to see it firsthand.

The drive from New York to Germantown took about five hours. After I checked into my hotel, I went down the street to play Topgolf and then went to bed. I got to WCC's offices around nine. This was during the second winter of the pandemic, and the humans were all wearing masks. The dogs were not. The woman who greeted me gave me a list of whom I would be meeting with over the course of the day. The agenda went person, dogs, person. The morning would start with Rick Yount, the founder of the program. After I did what I had been brought to Maryland to do, photographing dogs—in this case a mother dog nursing a new litter of puppies—I would end the day by meeting with a veteran who was in WCC's program. I didn't quite catch the veteran's name—Chris? Tony?—and I didn't press the woman to repeat it. I knew that vets were reluctant to sit down and talk about their PTSD, and the honor of getting to tell this soldier's story, along with the pressure of wanting to get it right, made me apprehensive.

But that was hours away. First up was Rick, and not just Rick but his dog Cooper, an English Cream Golden Retriever. We sat in a meeting room and Rick, a friendly guy in his late fifties with a crew cut, outlined the program for me. WCC, Rick explained, employed a unique approach called Mission Based Trauma Recovery that framed therapy not as an indeterminate journey toward self-awareness and self-improvement but as a discrete time-limited process. In other words, a mission. That appealed to the military mindset, which had a built-in skepticism of open-ended processes. But WCC had to contend with one additional trait specific to PTSD-afflicted veterans, which was that they were notoriously reluctant to accept assistance for themselves. In their minds, there was always a comrade in arms worse off who needed help more than they did. That made PTSD devilishly difficult for them, a tightening noose.

To solve this problem, Warrior Canine Connection employed a brilliant bit of jiujitsu. Rather than giving veterans service dogs for their own use, WCC enrolled them into a program to train dogs for other service people. This made the veterans feel like instruments of someone else's deliverance, participants in an act of service rather than one of self-service. It was similar in some ways to a program like Puppies Behind Bars, except that the inmates in those programs understood immediately and fully how the dogs gave them back a missing piece of their humanity. Veterans were in some ways tougher nuts to crack. The program called this method the "Trojan Dog," which was a metaphor for how it snuck the therapy process into the minds of veterans (not to mention a time-tried military analogy).

The roots of the program reached back decades. In the early 1990s, when Yount was a social worker, he adopted a Golden Retriever puppy named Gabe that insisted on going with him to the office. "He gave me those eyes," Rick said. "You know: if you don't take me with you I might die. You can't resist those eyes." One afternoon Rick and his human partner went to remove a child from an abusive foster family. The home was unsafe for the boy, but it was still his home. "We showed up as two strangers taking a child away from everything he knows," Rick said. The boy thrashed and wailed. "When we finally got him in the car," Yount says, "Gabe put his head on his lap and he immediately calmed down."

Yount never forgot the Gabe effect, and in 2014 he founded WCC. A few months after he started, Walter Reed hospital asked him to work with its most challenging patients. One was a marine corps drill instructor with extreme PTSD; he had lost one of his best friends in combat and was suffering from survivor's guilt. The second soldier was severely depressed, unable to get out of bed. Yount began training them as dog trainers. A month later, Yount met with the patients for progress reports. The drill instructor went first. He told Yount that when he had started, his marriage had been in jeopardy, largely because his wife couldn't abide the way he spoke to their three-year-old son. He was brusque and impatient, a combination of military tone and inner turmoil. After his month as a trainer, he told Yount, he had a different pace and a new kind of patience. He thought that the program was saving his marriage. Moreover, the specific skills required for service dogs were immensely useful in addressing PTSD. That was no accident. "We teach the dogs that the world is a safe place and not to be scared of loud noises," Yount told me, "and that's exactly what the veterans learn too. They have to battle their intrusive thoughts to teach the dog. There are so many parallels."

The other soldier went next. His depression was severe, but his main issue was his insomnia. Doctors had told him that he had the worst sleep of any veteran they had treated in forty years. The night after he started working with his dog, he slept six hours straight. "I've had people ask me, how quickly can you see the positive effects of your program?" Yount told me. "The answer is: immediately."

The woman who had greeted me in the morning knocked on the door. It was time for the next item on the day's agenda. I went into the nursery and photographed a litter of Golden Retriever puppies with their mother, Devin, who was named in honor of Sergeant Devin Snyder, a twenty-year-old killed while on deployment in Afghanistan. Devin came to the edge of the whelping pen and sniffed me before allowing me near the litter. I must have passed the test, because she trotted back over to them, lay down, and started nursing her pups. Photographing newborn puppies is always adorable, but week-old puppies don't do much. I needed Devin's attention. I made puppy noises, and when she looked up to check if a member of her litter had wandered, I took a picture.

We broke for lunch and awaited the arrival of the veteran. The interview was scheduled for one o'clock, which came and went. I wondered out loud if the soldier had gotten cold feet. "It happens sometimes," Rick said. One thirty came and went too. Then a truck came up the long dirt driveway. "They're here," Rick said. We went out to meet them. A stocky bald man in his fifties stepped out of the truck, followed by a woman I assumed was his wife, and a Golden Retriever. Inside, we all shook hands and sat. Introductions still hadn't been officially made, and I was kicking myself for not remembering the man's name. Kelly? Jesse?

The couple was a study in contrasts. The woman was cheerful and chatty, a ball of energy, but the man was quiet, nearly still. This was what I had been worried about. Was the interview too much for him? Should I suggest a walk? I zeroed in on the dog, which was at the woman's side, and that's when it hit me. The dog was at her side because it was her dog. *She* was the veteran. The man was being quiet because he wasn't the one I was meant to talk to. "Elias," Rick said, nodding toward the woman, "this is Sandy Wilson." Sandy. At least I was right that it had been a gender-neutral name, which let me cut myself a little slack. Rick stood, as did the husband—his name, as it turned out, was Nick—and they left. Sandy and her dog, Barb, remained.

"So," Sandy said. "Where should I start?" She started at the beginning. Back in the seventies, Sandy had trained as a military police officer. She was part of the first class of women to graduate, and the training was grueling. "The first day I got there I got punched in the face," she said. In part, this was presented as a cull-the-herd strategy to eliminate weaker candidates, but it also illustrated the difficulty of being a woman in the military. "They really didn't want us there," she said. "Sixty of us started and only thirty graduated." The treatment also led to sexual harassment and worse. At one point, Sandy had to pull a weapon on another soldier to get him off her.

Sandy left the military, started a civilian career as a realtor, got married, raised a family. But over the years, she began to show classic symptoms of post-traumatic stress disorder. She shut down emotionally and had a hard time connecting with others. "I used to just stare at people," she said. "I wasn't always very nice to them." Like many vets in the grips of PTSD, she isolated herself, to the point where she didn't leave her house for two and a half years. During that time, someone mentioned service dogs. She liked the idea, in theory, but she didn't see it for herself. "I truly didn't believe I deserved a service dog because I don't have a physical injury," she said.

Eventually Sandy was connected with WCC and paired with Barb. Sandy started to train her for her public access test and get her ready for other veterans. Barb became not only a colleague of Sandy's but part of her family—she befriended Sandy's daughter's dog, spent time at picnics, and by degrees started to repair and restore Sandy's humanity. "Since getting Barb I'm open to meeting people," Sandy told me. "She helps me with every conversation. She opens my world up. It usually starts with a child who wants to pet her, and then I'm talking to their parents, and suddenly I'm out in the world. I feel like I've won—every day is a little bit better."

The benefits of Barb were apparent not just in Sandy's stories but in the room. The dog sensed tension in the way Sandy was holding her lead, and she kept coming in close to Sandy to give her supportive kisses. It was a beautiful dance—Sandy tightened up whenever she approached a triggering moment in her story, and Barb, fully in tune, knew just when to rub against her or put out a paw.

My drive home was filled with traffic and with thoughts: about how Sandy's optimism had been imprisoned by PTSD, about how Barb had liberated it. But Warrior Canine Connection was only the tip of the iceberg of programs pairing veterans with dogs. One of the best, and best-known, programs is America's VetDogs, which I have worked with several times across the years. In the summer of 2023, I met Seaver, a black Lab who was the second future service dog raised in partnership between America's VetDogs and the New York Mets. Seaver was named, of course, for Tom Seaver, the Mets' Hall of Fame pitcher, who won three Cy Young Awards while with the team. (The first dog, Shea, was named for the team's longtime field, Shea Stadium.) Seaver came to the team at the tender age of three months, attended games and community events, and generally hung out with the Mets while preparing for his formal service dog training. Or maybe it's more accurate to say that hanging out with the Mets was his training regimen. Spending time at Citi Field, where the Mets play, worked to his advantage. The clamor of the stadium flooded him with noise, with smells, with bright lights, all stimuli that he would have to learn to filter out to become a successful service dog.

The more dramatic the case, the more crucial a canine companion often is. Tyler McGibbon, a native of Toms River, New Jersey, joined the army straight from high school, and was in Kuwait in December 2014, helping to train troops to fight in Iraq, when the Humvee that was carrying him flipped and wrecked. Tyler was thrown from the vehicle and severely injured, with dozens of broken bones and multiple skull fractures. He died in the helicopter that was airlifting him to the hospital and came back to life, died again in the hospital and came back to life, was moved to another hospital in Germany, was moved to Walter Reed. He was in a coma for months. When he resurfaced into consciousness, Tyler received not only ongoing medical treatment but a host of therapies, from physical therapy to speech therapy to occupational therapy to music therapy—if his therapy sessions alone were totaled up, they would exceed 2,500 hours, or more than a hundred days.

In January 2016, still on his long road back, he was a guest of U.S. Representative Darin LaHood (R-IL) at President Obama's State of the Union speech. In 2019, he was a guest of the Seattle Opera for a new piece called *The Falling and the Rising*, based on a trio of stories of veteran rehabilitation. (The librettist of the opera, Jerre Dye, singled out Tyler, saying: "Tyler had this incredible story about what his coma experience was like . . . We leaned into that story right off the bat and knew that was going to be the arc of the piece: the idea of a liminal space inhabited by the mind of a soldier in an induced coma. It allowed us the freedom to interject different voices, different stories, different narratives.")

Tyler attended the premiere of *The Falling and the Rising* with Trooper, the Labrador Retriever service dog he received through America's VetDogs and perhaps his most important therapy. That's how I came to know the two of them. I traveled to his home in Toms River to document and share his story, and continued to do so on multiple occasions in the years that followed as Tyler's life and journey with Trooper progressed and changed. I got to know Trooper, who helped Tyler with mobility issues, like picking up items he had dropped, along with helping establish first contact with new people. The three of us even attended an NFL game together, the Philadelphia Eagles versus the San Francisco 49ers in late 2023. Tyler's family were the die-hard, tailgate-for-hours, season-ticket, bleed-green type. Tyler's father hadn't missed a single Eagles home game in—get this—thirty-nine years. His father's first question to Tyler upon waking from his coma was "What's your favorite NFL team?" (His father said he knew that Tyler would be okay when he gathered the strength to answer "Eagles.") At the tailgate before the game, Tyler took me aside. "So, I got a ring," he said. I knew what he meant immediately. I had met his girlfriend, Natalie. I congratulated him and gave him a well-deserved pat on the back. "I'd love for you to help me propose," he said. "Happily," I said.

The rest of the day wasn't as joyful. The Eagles lost 42–19 (and Trooper tried to steal my hot dog), but a few weeks after the game, I went to Toms River to meet Tyler and Natalie, under the pretense that I was doing another installation of man and dog. We went to the Ocean County Mall, took a picture with Santa, visited Tyler's mother at Macy's where she worked, built a new toy for Trooper at Build-A-Bear Workshop. Then we headed back to Tyler's place and set our plan in motion. Tyler had put the ring in a basket and put the basket in another room, and I had rigged a camera to capture video of Trooper retrieving that basket and delivering it to the happy couple. Trooper nailed his part, Tyler nailed his proposal, and Natalie said yes. After the excitement of it all set in, I asked Tyler whether he'd ever thought he'd be standing there with so many accomplishments and blessings—the incredible service dog that had been his companion for years and now an incredible future wife who completed the picture. "Never," he said. "Never." I posted a reel of the proposal on Christmas Eve 2023, the nine-year anniversary of Tyler's stay in the German hospital. People flooded the comments with well-wishes for Tyler, Natalie, and Trooper. Everybody likes a comeback story with a happy ending.

Asta, Kerry Blue Terrier (6 years old),
Houston St. & 6th Ave., New York, NY • "She's
named after the dog from *The Thin Man*
(1934). She enjoys chasing squirrels, skate-
boards, and cheese. High-quality stinky
cheese. She's not usually this furry—this is her
winter fuzz."

CHAPTER 25

THE EYES HAVE IT

Every Dogist series has a slightly different feel. Sometimes I feel like a journalist. Sometimes I feel like an explorer. Whenever I have been out to visit Morristown, New Jersey, I have felt a certain irony, walking around with my camera taking pictures of dogs whose entire lives revolved around guiding those who could not see. Morristown is home to a large training school for guide dogs—the oldest continuously operating such school in the world, in fact.

The story of The Seeing Eye stretches back to 1927, when a man named Morris Frank read a *Saturday Evening Post* article about blind World War I veterans who were using German Shepherds as assistance dogs. He was no relation to Morristown, New Jersey, which was named for Lewis Morris, the first governor of the colony of New Jersey. In fact, Morris Frank wasn't even in New Jersey at the time. He was in Tennessee, where he grew up. And when I say that he read a story about blind veterans, it's possible that he had it read to him, because he was blind, too, not from the war but from two separate accidents: he lost sight in one eye after a fall at age two and sight in the other in a boxing match at age sixteen. He had become proficient at piano tuning and worked to send himself through Vanderbilt University. Off and on, he was helped out by human guides, but he noticed that humans tended to lose focus over time, or had other business of their own. Frank was struck by the article about the veterans and their German Shepherds. He sent a letter to the author of the article, Dorothy Harrison Eustis, expressing his interest in obtaining a companion for himself. In her reply, Eustis explained that her dogs were trained in Vevey, a town on the north shore of Lake Geneva in the Swiss Alps. If he could travel to the training facility, they would give him a dog in return for his help popularizing the program at home.

Frank went overseas in 1928 and returned that summer with a dog named Buddy. (Renamed, actually: it had originally been named Kiss, but Frank told Eustis that he could not imagine walking around the streets of Nashville and calling out "Kiss, Kiss, come, Kiss.") When he landed in New York, Frank held up his end of the bargain immediately, staging an exhibition for reporters in which he allowed Buddy to lead him across a crowded Manhattan street. It made the papers all across the country.

Frank, who by that point worked in the insurance industry, secured the use of the Fourth and First National Bank in Nashville and converted it into a training and administrative facility. According to The Seeing Eye's charter, it would "provide for a model miniature city in which the dogs are trained, and whence they will be distributed at cost under Mr. Frank's personal supervision only to the deserving blind."

Frank opened it in January 1929, graduating his first class of dogs a month later. Two years later, the school moved from Nashville up to Whippany, New Jersey, and in 1965 to Morris Township. Along the way, the school also founded a breeding farm in nearby Chester, and added a second training facility in downtown Morristown. Frank passed away in 1980, having traveled the world with Buddy and Buddy's successors (also named Buddy) to spread the word.

In Morristown on an average day, you can see Seeing Eye trainers walking their dogs through the street. They stop patiently at traffic lights. They navigate the sidewalks. They learn how to go into buildings and out of buildings, how to get across parks. People come from all over to get their dogs and work with them before they take them home. There's the man in his early twenties who was blinded during a suicide attempt in his teens. There's the older woman who knew from her forties that genetic eye deterioration would likely get to her. Whoever they are, they need a new lease on life, or a new way through it. The Seeing Eye likened getting a dog to a teenager getting their driver's license.

I took pictures of Nemo, a year-old Lab, in front of the school's sign. I took pictures of Elroy, a two-year-old German Shepherd, in the parking lot. I took photos of Aspen, a three-year-old Lab, in the on-site restaurant, which was designed to help blind people and their dogs navigate a dining environment. "The dog should be invisible. If other patrons are surprised to see a dog emerge from under the table after the meal, that's what we want," the trainer told me. I took photos of Falcon, a two-year-old Golden Retriever, midway through his four-month training, learning to navigate an escalator (this particular escalator was installed solely for training purposes—it escalated to nowhere). One of the trainers told me something interesting, which was that while pairing with the first dog required intense effort, the second dog was even harder because comparisons with that first dog and its strong bond were inevitable. "They've got big shoes to fill," she said. I knew the owners would never see the pictures, but I figured someone from their camp would describe my posts to them in great detail.

There's another organization, similar if not quite as old—it was founded in 1954—that is headquartered in Yorktown Heights, New York, a town in far north Westchester County. Guiding Eyes for the Blind pairs dogs with the visually impaired, as well as finds dogs for people who have visual impairment plus another disability, impairment, or challenge, whether cognitive or motor skills or sensory. For example, I met dogs intended for people who are deaf-blind and communicate through ASL. The training for these dogs does not involve voice; rather, they are trained to respond to physical cues.

At one point, the idea started to be bandied around that I might have the opportunity to put a blindfold on and go for a guided walk with one of their dogs. This is not an opportunity afforded to most fully sighted people (I do not encourage you to approach a visually impaired person's guide dog and ask to take them for a spin). After one photo shoot session, the moment was upon us. A woman appeared with a blindfold—not one of my fantasies but exciting nonetheless. "Would you like to do the walk?" she asked.

"Yes," I said, excitedly but also nervously.

My dog for the day was Arby, a black Lab. I positioned myself next to him. I was on the right. He was on the left. Fun fact, did you know just about all guide dogs lead on the left side? Another fun fact: every guide dog harness is unique, designed to the height and preference of the handler. They are rigid, designed to give maximum information to the handler as to the dog's position and motion. I pulled down the blindfold and closed my eyes. Now all the lights were off. The trainer put Arby's handle in my hand and I felt a wave of feedback through the handle. I knew that I was on a paved walkway, but I immediately felt like this had the potential to go terribly wrong. I didn't want to trip and fall, and not just for safety reasons—this was all on camera, after all. I remember not knowing how to walk, literally. I wasn't sure which foot I should start with, and how quickly to follow with the other. "Forward," I said, and the train (Arby) left the station. I took a few tentative steps, trying to match the feedback coming through the handle, but I quickly realized in order for this to really work, I had to relax and let Arby take the reins. He did. We got up to a full walking pace and then, what I thought was most of a block later, he slowed to a stop. I could feel it through the handle like the brakes of a car engaging. Crosswalk? When the coast was clear, Arby started forward again, and so did I. We only went about a hundred feet in total, but it felt like a lifetime.

And it was: someone else's lifetime, and a chance for me to glimpse into it and see how this could restore confidence and independence.

On the street, shooting for The Dogist, I will sometimes run into dog-handler pairs. Like Al and Lloyd. Al was the dog, a black Lab. Lloyd was the handler, Lloyd Burlingame, a renowned Broadway stage designer who had lost his sight over the years due to macular degeneration. At eighty-one, he was nearly totally blind. His dogs, which came to him from Morristown, tipped him back into life. "When I had the white cane," he told me, "it was like I was a leper. But then they gave me a dog, and people were like, 'They're just out there trying to make the best of it!'" Lloyd told me that the dogs kept him feeling young, kept him from feeling vulnerable. Al was not his first partner—there had been Hickory first, and then Kemp, both of which were featured in a book that Lloyd wrote, *Two Seeing Eye Dogs Take Manhattan! . . . a Love Story*. Then came Al. When I photographed them, it was Al's fourth birthday. "Same as Mozart's," Lloyd said. "We like to call him 'Almadeus.'"

Dogs occupy all points of the compass. Morristown is west of where I live in New York City. Yorktown Heights is north. To the east is Garden City, New York, a village of about 25,000 people on Long Island. Telly Savalas was born there, as was the composer and TV host John Tesh. But the Garden City person who was high in my mind in the winter of 2024 was Anastasia Pagonis. Anastasia grew up on Long Island as a huge sports fan, especially hockey—she would watch Islanders games with her dad. Over time, the games got harder to watch, not because the Islanders were bad but because her eyesight was. It began to decline when she was eleven or so, and doctors diagnosed her with Stargardt macular degeneration, a genetic disorder where fat collects on the rear part of the retina. But the deterioration progressed so quickly that the diagnosis was revised to autoimmune retinopathy. By the time she turned fourteen, she was almost entirely blind. This changed everything in Anastasia's life, obviously. She had been a happy and outgoing girl. Now she kept to herself. She fell into depression. One of the things that kept her from a deeper darkness was swimming, which she had turned to as her sight faded. The pool was a controlled environment. "It's my happy place," she said during an appearance on the *Today* show. "It's the place where I feel like I don't have a disability and I feel like that's the only place where I feel free." Swimming wasn't only a safe space for Anastasia. It was a place where she could excel. She was good immediately and got better (and faster) fast. In a World Series event in Australia in 2020, she won a gold medal in the 400-meter freestyle and a bronze in the 200-meter individual medley.

Then came the pandemic, which disrupted events for a while. While she was at home, unable to compete, she got a call from the Guide Dog Foundation, an organization based in Long Island that trains companions for the visually impaired. They had a dog named Radar that they thought would be perfect for Anastasia. In a happy coincidence, the dog had been trained in part by the New York Islanders, where he served as an unofficial mascot. Radar came to her for additional training, and then stayed with her as a companion. He traveled with her to meets, where he helped her find the elevator or the door to the dining hall, not to mention that he was an icebreaker with the other athletes. "Having Radar has just given me so much independence and I'm literally in love with him," she told *Today*. "He's the best thing ever. We're a match made in heaven." With Radar at her side, Anastasia resumed her winning ways. At the Tokyo Paralympics, she set a world record in the 400-meter freestyle in a preliminary round and then swam even faster in the finals, winning a gold medal. At the 2022 World Championships in Madeira, she won gold again, this time in the 200-meter individual medley.

I knew I wanted to photograph her with Radar, but the winter I learned of her story was also a winter packed with everything else: long days for me working on the book, long evenings for me and Sam beginning to bring wedding plans into focus, long walks with

Elsa (that she wishes were longer still), and then the day-to-day of being The Dogist. I'll get out there soon enough, I expect, and I'm sure that the story will be all the things that I imagine: inspirational and joyful, with great insights into the way that adversity can focus the mind and dogs can focus the soul. In the meantime, I think about her every time I watch athletes perform at a high level, and I think about not just the guide-dog component but the overall relationship between dogs and humans, the way that athletes' lives are packed with pressure and moments of intense consequence and the way that dogs can lessen that pressure and create perspective around consequence. The U.S. Olympic women's gymnastics team was the center of attention through the summer of 2024, as Simone Biles and company picked up medal after medal in Paris, and one of the focuses was the team's relationship with its dogs. The one dog that stayed in the spotlight was Beacon, Team USA's principal therapy dog. Beacon was a four-year-old Golden Retriever who, as a result of his extremely chill personality and photogenic face, became a star alongside the team, collecting more than twenty thousand followers on social media. His official Olympic credentials said "Goodest Boy." He radiated love and support. At least some of the credit for the medals went directly to him, and all the athletes and coaches said so. I thought about him while Simone Biles was fighting through an injury in the team events, but I thought about him more later, in the individual events, especially the balance beam. Many gymnasts had trouble with it. The American team seemed especially unsteady. Both Biles and Suni Lee fell off the beam and missed out on medals. Both women were disappointed. You could see it in the grim set of their expressions. What I didn't see, but could imagine, was the way that their time with Beacon helped them survive the moment, helped them reach down and recover calm and resilience and a stronger sense of self.

Simba, Saint Bernard (1 year old), Prince St. &
W. Broadway, New York, NY • "Life is about
food. Food comes first, then Mom and Dad,
then sleep. Also shoes—he doesn't destroy
them, he just tightens the laces. He spends
hours tightening them, which makes us late
for work."

CHAPTER 26

THE PURPOSE-DRIVEN DOG LIFE

E arlier, we discussed dog intelligence, and how understanding it can unlock a broader sense of human intelligence. The same is true of dog purpose. Think about your own skills. What kind of training do you have? Do you think that what you do every day is a reflection of those skills? Dogs can inspire us by giving us purpose, but they can also inspire us when we watch them behave purposefully. Some of us are meant to help others in a one-on-one environment. Some of us are meant to inspire groups. Others are meant to venture into the unknown, certain that we will discover what we're meant to find there.

The range of dog purposes illuminates the range of human purposes, in part because dog purpose has been defined from the start through coevolution. The American Kennel Club's Working Group, for example, includes thirty-one breeds that range from the Akita to the Tibetan Mastiff. It includes a variety of shepherds. The dogs in the group are all designated for work, though the nature of the work varies. Each of these purposeful dog breeds is worthy of a documentary (or dogumentary) all on its own, but my time with them, spread out over my decade as The Dogist, has been more like an anthology series.

We have discussed dogs that bite: my friend Adam's childhood trauma with a Lab, the Chow that nipped at me on the street, Major at the White House. Some dogs are professional biters. I learned that while standing in a field with a sleeve on my arm in Stormville, in upstate New York, where police dogs are trained mostly for explosives detection work, but also protection work (this is a nicer way of describing an attack dog). The facility there is state-of-the-art, with mock city scenarios of all types for the dogs to train in—elevated street grates, a bus depot, even a few train cars. I photographed the dogs doing explosives search exercises, and then it was time for a protection demonstration. There was a wrinkle, which was that I wouldn't be watching. I would be participating. "Do you want to do a 'hit'?" the officer-handler asked me. He was referring to a "bite hit," when the police dog is sent out to neutralize the assailant by biting its arm. I would be the assailant. He showed me the protective arm sleeve I would wear. There was also a full body suit, which I asked about. "The arm sleeve is all you need," he said. "We won't give you a 'dirty dog.'" (That's a dog with a tendency to work its way past the bite sleeve.) We went out to the field where I met Vinny, a gorgeous short-haired German Shepherd with a sleek coat. We greeted each other, but that was the last of the pleasantries. The officer put the bite sleeve on my left arm. "When he hits you, you're going to feel some pressure," he said. "One thing you have to remember is to move around once the dog hits you. If you don't, he might let go and go for another part of you."

"Right!" I said, as if being The Dogist gave me some prior understanding of how to properly get bitten by a dog. (I had googled it before and found that Vinny's bite force could be nearly 300 PSI, but I didn't google more, so it was just a number, no context, no meaning.) The officer also explained that he and Vinny had a special shorthand between them. He would send the dog with a command, and then command the dog to release with a special phrase. There wasn't in fact anything special about the release phrase, but Vinny would only listen if it was given by his handler. Vinny had no ill will toward me or my arm. He was just trained to get excited about biting people's arms and rewarded for doing so. I grabbed my Nikon in my free hand, stood in the field, and braced for impact. The officer stood about fifty feet away with Vinny, seemingly whispering something in his ear, like a corner man giving advice to his prizefighter. Then the officer barked out a loud order and released Vinny. I dug in (and tried not to pee myself). Two seconds later, at full speed, Vinny leapt up, hit my arm, and latched on to the bite sleeve. I was relieved that Vinny's aim was good while feeling the pressure of Vinny's bite through the sleeve. (So that was what nearly 300 PSI felt like!) As instructed, I started moving around, which Vinny seemed to like, as he bit down harder. Once I was convinced the bite sleeve was working, I brought my Nikon up to my eye and started snapping shots of Vinny chomped down onto my arm, his eyes bulging out in excitement. (It was an amazing opportunity, but also an absurd one: Was there ever a person in the history of the universe who was trying for nice portraits while being chomped on?) After about thirty seconds, the officer came and commanded Vinny to release, which he did without hesitation. The officer gave Vinny his favorite toy, which was a partially shredded white towel (quite special, I know). I caught my breath and looked at all the officers, who had been watching as the guy from the internet got attacked by their star pupil. They were all smiling. I felt I had completed a rite of passage. I was good in their book, and probably Vinny's too. (Later on, I continued with my research, and learned that a gorilla has a bite force of more than 1,000 PSI, a crocodile of up to 4,000, and a T. rex of up to 10,000. I had gotten off easy, or at least easier than The Crocodilist and The Dinosaurist.)

Vinny was an American expert, but his training was rooted in Schutzhund protocols. "Schutzhund" is a German word that refers to a sport that combines tracking, obedience, and protection exercises and transforms an average dog into a high-end specialist. Or at least it used to be the word. "Schutzhund" (the word, not the exercises) fell out of favor because of its Nazi-esque overtones (in fact, the training did trace back to that period), and the training process was rebranded, first as Internationale Prüfungs-Ordnung, which means "protection dog," and then as Internationale Gebrauchshunde Prüfungsordnung. Whether Schutzhund, IPO, or IGP, these pioneering methods made their way around the world—including to American K-9 officers like Vinny—and so in the spirit of international exploration, I made my way back to Germany to see their original home. In Munich, I conducted my regular Dogist business, photographing a Pug at Karolinenplatz and a retriever at the Englischer Garten, and then I visited a special canine training facility. My host for the day, and the director of the facility, was a young American man who had married a German woman. We started off by talking about the dogs they used, all kinds but largely Malinois and German Shepherds. What was the difference between the two? "*DRIVE*," he said, with such emphasis that it was like he was speaking in all capital letters. He elaborated. "German Shepherds make great service dogs because they can think and make decisions. Mals are better for police work. They don't have an on-and-off switch like German Shepherds."

The day I was there, he demonstrated with a dog that did have a switch, a German Shepherd named Drago. Drago started off by looking for a target behind a blind, meaning a man hiding behind a barrier. Drago was trained to seek the target, identify it, and alert bark until his handler arrived, at which point the handler could command the dog to attack (or not). Drago performed with speed and an almost frightening efficiency. The next exercise involved a bullwhip. I was confused as to what it was for, and frankly scared of the noise it made every time it was cracked. As it turns out, that's exactly what it was for: to simulate the sound of a gunshot. In the event a dog encountered a person with a weapon, it couldn't be gun-shy, like I was. Drago wasn't. The sound of the whipcrack was impossible to ignore, but somehow he ignored it (along with the sound of the handler yelling crazily), went straight as a missile, and latched on to the handler by the bite sleeve. He was rewarded with a hearty "Soopahh!" (my phonetic interpretation of "super" in a German accent). "He loves to bite the sleeve more than anything, but he also loves to cuddle," the handler said. I had to take him at his word about the cuddling, though we wrapped up the day watching a litter of about seven German Shepherd puppies chase a lure at the end of a long stick. That part was as cute as it sounds.

I have yet to photograph narcotics dogs—the drug-sniffing dogs that work in airports and seaports—though a TSA detection dog once alerted to me while I was standing in the security line at the airport. It wasn't because I had anything illicit or explosive on me, but because I was The Dogist. That's right! The dog recognized me from Instagram! No, no. It was because I was coming home from a shoot and was still wearing cargo pants loaded with biscuits, and more important, a dog-drool-seasoned squeaky tennis ball. The yellow Lab working at the TSA believed devoutly that it was *his* tennis ball, and that it needed to be seized immediately (by his mouth, preferably). I took the ball out. The TSA dog sat and looked at it with delight. When I explained to the human officer what I did, he laughed and said he understood, but he also said he had to take me aside to fully inspect all my possessions. I got to keep the tennis ball, much to the retriever's chagrin. Another time, I was at a dog park on the Upper West Side, Dogisting. I had my lens trained on a dog running around, but this one Labrador kept approaching and sitting down next to me. The owner eventually came over. "Do you smoke pot?" he said. "No . . ." I said, remembering the THC vape pen I had in my pocket that I occasionally used at the time. "Oh, okay," the owner replied dubiously. "He's actually a sniffer dog," he said. "I work with him at JFK to detect narcotics." The man and I smiled at each other, and I made my way out of the park fairly quickly afterward.

That dog was focused on his weed hunting even on a pleasant dog park afternoon, which is one of the great things about dogs—they can be single-minded in ways that humans can only imagine. My family has a friend named David in Woods Hole. He's a great guy who breaks the norm for the area politically and culturally, in that he's a wealthy Southerner whose politics lean right. After I photographed his Goldendoodle, Sam, we played some golf at the Woods Hole Golf Club and shared some of his favorite Pappy Van Winkle whiskey—we realized we had more in common than not. After a few summers, he invited my uncle Nathaniel and me down to Charleston to play golf and go hunting. Hunting?! The thought was almost comical at first. My uncle Nathaniel had never heard, much less held or fired, a gun in his life. I had gone to ranges and done some skeet shooting, but I hadn't ever used a gun for its intended purpose: to kill something. I had grown up fishing, which is similar in many ways, but guns were no doubt scarier.

We accepted Dave's invitation, booked our flights, and figured we would get the rest of the details when we landed (all the better, really, to avoid spooking any of the rest of our family). When we landed in Charleston and got into the car, Dave informed us that we would be quail hunting (as I suspected) and that indeed we would be working with hunting dogs (as I had hoped). The trip had just become an official Dogist trip, though I wasn't sure about posting photos to the feed. (I had featured hunting before, once at a field trial with English Setters and Pointers and another with Small Münsterländers and Nova Scotia Duck Tolling Retrievers doing field exercises with frozen foxes and ducks, respectively. People still got up in arms in the comments.) We went to Dave's office, where he showed us a beautiful case of hand-engraved Italian shotguns, fitted us with some "safety orange" outfits from his closet, and showed us around town. Then one morning, we left early, around six, and drove two hours into Georgia to go hunting. The hunting preserve was a property out in the middle of nowhere in the country, thousands of acres filled with tens of thousands of quail that had been purchased and released onto the property. We met with Frank, a big guy in overalls, who spit tobacco as he spoke and who helped run the place. He sent Nathaniel over to the practice range to learn basic gun etiquette and shoot a practice shot at a clay pigeon. He missed the clay entirely, as expected. But that would have to do. Frank pulled around a Jeep with a trailer attached. The trailer had a spot for us to sit, but also four kennel cages built into the back. I peered into the kennels, trying to get a closer look at our companions.

We secured the guns, took a seat, and went off down the dirt road. The drive to our first stop took only a few minutes, and when we got there, Frank let the dogs out: two Pointers and one black Lab. I clocked their breeds, but only that, because within seconds they had bolted into the field to start looking for quail. Nearly all the interaction I have with dogs is designed as meet and greets—groomed dogs, stylish leashes, cute names. Frank's dogs were named Fancy, Tex, and Smokey (fine, fine, they are pretty cute names), but they were not groomed or even handsome in the traditional sense. They were pure athletes, lean and muscular—real working dogs. Frank didn't care about how his dogs looked, and they didn't either. The focus was entirely on whether the dogs could hunt, and he had invested countless hours training them to do so. He called each of the dogs back to put on GPS collars so that when a dog spotted a bird in a bush (using its nose) and stopped to point, Frank got an alert with the exact location. "We got a point over here," he said, and we walked through the brush to find the Pointer frozen solid, only its eyes glancing to and from us and the quail in the bush, in a sort of *You seeing what I'm seeing?!* We took up position about ten feet away—Nathaniel, the least experienced, in the middle—and Frank sent the Lab in to flush the bird. The bird popped up, and before we could blink, Dave took his shot. A direct hit. When this happened, the bird came right down. Sometimes it got winged and flew farther before it fell. The dogs (primarily the retriever) fetched the bird no matter what. I was amazed at how focused the dogs were. They were fully keyed in, instinctively driven, happy all morning. They ran full speed into thickets, over logs, into swamps, always with unconditional commitment. Over the course of the morning, we got something like forty birds, all with canine assistance, and all of which would be cleaned and eaten. We then headed back to the main building for a lunch of fried chicken, okra, and mac and cheese. We sat with the next group of hunters, who were locals—the Southern accents were so strong that I was somewhat wary of speaking and sounding like an East Coast liberal. There wasn't a chance to say goodbye to the dogs, yet another reminder that it wasn't a touchy-feely encounter. The dogs went right back to the kennel for food, water, and rest, so they could recharge for another day of doing what they did best and loved most: finding and retrieving birds.

Dogs can retrieve quail that have been killed, and they can also retrieve humans who are fighting to stay alive. A few years back, I met a man named George Abraham who lived in the Poconos, on Tobyhanna Lake, with his wife, Kate, and their dog, Oakley—it had the same name as the dog that carried the Central Park proposal, but it was an extremely different dog. Oakley was a four-year-old Land-seer, a black-and-white variety of the Newfoundland dog. Like all Newfies, they are ideal water dogs. They have webbed paws, double coats, and an incredible swimming ability that enables them to pull up to fifty times their body weight through water. In fact, Oakley's owners told me that there had been a Newfie on the *Titanic* that had pulled a lifeboat for miles. Oakley (her full name was Oakley the NEPA Newfie—NEPA is the abbreviation for northeastern Pennsylvania) had put her skills to use for more than recreation. She was a water rescue dog, trained at the American Academy of Canine Water Rescue in Boston. When I met her, she had Level Two certification, which meant that she could deploy either from land or from water. Level Three involved jumping from a helicopter, and Oakley was beginning to learn how to do that, traveling to Milan, Italy, and training with an elite team at the Italian School of Water Rescue Dogs. If she finished the course, George and his wife told me, she would be only the second American dog ever to graduate. She did.

As a rescue dog, Oakley was trained to help a person in distress. But it was more than that. "There's a difference between saving themselves versus looking to save someone else," George explained. "She'll drown herself saving you." Oakley wasn't just a rescue dog but an ambassador for the idea of rescue dogs. She visited schools to teach water safety, as well as training other dogs to assist lifeguards by serving as force multipliers in water rescues. When I visited Oakley at the lake, I was able to capture her in action rescuing a volunteer drowning victim (her mom) by rushing in from the shore, and then jumping from a rowboat to do the same. On a separate trip, I met them all at a helipad in Jersey City. Oakley had done helicopter training before, but never with the doors off. The sound of the rotors can often overwhelm a dog. But not Oakley. I snapped a bunch of pictures of her in position while we hovered, and more as we landed and deboarded. Throughout, she was perfectly focused and perfectly unflappable. Bombproof, as they say.

A few years after I posted about Oakley, I got a message from George. Oakley had, tragically, died in her sleep. She was only six and a half. Newfoundlands, like other large dogs, fall into the heartbreak breed category, meaning that they're more likely to die at a young age, often suddenly. George put up a post on Instagram, letting everyone know that Oakley had been "in the best shape of her life, routinely running two miles a day, but in the end, heaven must also be having a lifeguard shortage." Oakley lived a life few dogs could match. She was a super dog, and though her time was shorter than expected, her legacy is long. George and Kate bought a specially designed water rescue boat and named it the SS *Oakley* in her honor. They had also gotten another Landseer the year prior, named Kelby, and they trained her as Oakley's direct successor, using her to continue to educate people on water safety, the power of dogs, and lifesaving techniques. It was as if George and Kate felt morally obligated to extend Oakley's life through Kelby. Their dogs had purpose, but also their purpose was to have dogs.

Magic, Shiloh Shepherd (3 years old), Pan Pacific Park, Los Angeles, CA • "I had a shepherd that passed away and I said I'd never get another dog unless it was just like him. I went to the shelter and told them what he was like and out of all the dogs there they brought out Magic. We left together."

CHAPTER 27

THE JOB IS LOVE

There are dogs in the field and dogs in the water, but some dogs can fulfill their purpose without even stepping outside. In 2019, I photographed Sully H. W. Bush. Sully, a two-year-old Labrador, had been George H. W. Bush's service dog in the final year of Bush's life. Sully was a calm and loyal companion, and his love for children was important to the former president. When Bush died in 2018, he left a request for Sully to be shared with others. When I photographed him, Sully was in the process of transitioning from his career as a single-handler assistance dog to a new job as a facility dog. As a facility dog, he would be trained to float freely, dropping in on rehab sessions, lighting up a room during family visits. Facility dogs are generally employed by hospitals, schools, and similar institutions: they produce the same levels of joy, but they distribute it across a range of human beneficiaries. A few years after that, after the former president's death, I paid a visit to America's VetDogs HQ in Smithtown, New York, and had the pleasure of meeting one of their newly finished facility dogs, named Maggie. Sully was also in the room, supervising.

I had heard the term "facility dog" many times over the years as a concept, but had never experienced the power of one myself. I snapped a few photographs of Maggie at my usual distance—five feet away or so. Being the photographer is obviously my default, but Maggie's handler suggested I put my camera aside for a moment and let Maggie demonstrate her training on me. I was intrigued, but figured, what could any dog possibly do that I hadn't seen or experienced before? The handler instructed me to get down on my knees. I did. She then gave Maggie a command: "Maggie, hug! Yeah, go get him!" Maggie came right up to me and put her front legs up on my legs and then my shoulders. This was more than a typical dog cuddle. It was a full-fledged professional dog hug. It wasn't hasty or erratic in any way. She approached me slowly, engaged me with extreme eye contact, and then carefully went in for the hug. I was suddenly flooded with serotonin, the neurotransmitter that creates feelings of optimism and well-being. Ten seconds before, I had been in a somewhat tense mood. It could have been for any reason—the typical stresses of passing through an average week, some financial, some emotional, some medical, some creative. Maybe it was the ding on my car I noticed in the parking lot before coming into the building. It was life being lived, for better and for worse. But I hadn't even realized that I was in a mood until the dog came up to me and completely changed it. This dog functioned as a kind of emotional physician, both diagnosing and treating. I could see how someone in a senior home would absolutely love this, how it could fix what they didn't even know was ailing them. Maggie's handler described it like this: "If she knows you and she's hugged you before, she will force it upon you. She'll slowly creep up and slowly hug. She's like, 'Hi, I'm a hugger.'" Dogs like this are trained to stare at you and hold eye contact longer as well, to emphasize that you're the only one who matters in that moment.

I have my own version of that. It starts in my own facility, meaning my apartment, where every night at ten or so I take Elsa on her final walk of the night. It's her shortest walk, a nice peaceful moment for the two of us, not too many people around, not too many emails or texts to check (hopefully). Then we go home, where I give Sam a news bulletin account. "Did you hear what happened?" I say. "Everyone's talking about it." Sam confirms that she did in fact hear. Then I reiterate exactly how the events of the evening transpired: "Elsa did double pee pee *and* poo poo" (in Elsa's favorite baby-talk voice) as Sam rubs Elsa's belly and commends her the way a parent would if their kid's report card came back with straight A's. If we decide to watch an episode of something on TV, we'll sit on the couch. It's only big enough for two of us—that's one of our ambitions: to get an apartment big enough to get a couch big enough to fit all three. If Elsa gets up on the couch before I make it into the room (which she usually does), I have to go to her treat jar to offer a bribe in exchange for her seat. It works every time, which I guess means Elsa considers it a fair trade.

After the show or movie ends, Sam and I turn off the TV, go up the spiral stairs to our loft, get ready for bed, dim the lights, and lie down. Once Elsa senses that we're settled, she makes her way up to us. "I hear tap shoes!" Sam says, referring to Elsa's toenails clicking on the staircase. When Elsa hops into the bed, we make a fuss. "Oh no! It's a wolf!" we say. "Run!" But we're not running. We're rubbing her back and her head and trying to make her smile. Elsa loves this routine, but she doesn't stick around. Eventually she goes back downstairs to sleep on her own. Sometimes we will check the Google cam to see whether she's picked the couch, the floor, or her bed.

This ritual happens every night, which means that it happened every night while I was writing about working dogs: brave rescue dogs, laser-focused hunting dogs, guide dogs. Those dogs are impressive, certainly, but are they any more impressive than Elsa? Elsa, in fact, represents the majority of dogs, the so-called everyday dogs, whose purpose isn't herding sheep, saving someone from drowning, or stopping a bad guy with a gun but, rather, providing affection. Sometimes a dog's purpose is just to be a dog—a human companion, a sympathetic mirror, a source of comfort, a reason to smile. I think back to the day that I met Barb and Sandy. I started off my drive home thinking about the brilliance of the program, and that shifted into thoughts about the darkness that can fall over the lives of veterans, especially military nurses. It was heavy stuff and I felt increasingly bleak as I approached home. When I opened my apartment door, the first thing I saw was Elsa coming toward me, ears back, tail wagging. Even before I could close the door, she was at my feet, turning over for a belly rub. I didn't know if she missed me deeply or was just expressing her own needs, but either way, she knew that affection would make us both feel better. Dogs are emotional savants. If they sense sadness, or discontent, or end-of-a-long-day fatigue, they don't ask where you've been or why you're bothered. They don't chide you or give you alternative theories to fuel your work drama. They get up next to you, give you a paw, and bring your mind back to the present with simple love and joy.

I recently came upon a story about a seventy-one-year-old man named Rich Moore. In August 2023, Moore left his home in Pagosa Springs, Colorado, with his dog, a Jack Russell Terrier named Finney. Moore planned to climb Blackhead Peak, a twelve-thousand-foot mountain about an hour from his home. He didn't return that night, or the next day. Friends and family became concerned and alerted local authorities. They sent out search parties, to no avail. After a month or so, people began to fear the worst, a suspicion that was confirmed on October 30, when a hunter a few miles east of the peak discovered human remains. They were Moore's. Right next to them was Finney, who had refused to leave his side, but Finney wasn't dead. He had lost half his body weight but was otherwise fine. There's no way to know whether he would have left Moore's side eventually. All we know for certain is that he didn't. "It brings us all to tears, the loyalty of that dog," said one of the women who had participated in the searches. Finney was not a professional companion. He was a dog, in the purest sense. Staying at his human's side was his full purpose. Loyalty and love were the entire job.

As in so many other ways, dogs offer us a key to unlocking a greater understanding of ourselves. People have to be open to the idea that leading with love and being content where they are, when they are, can be central to our humanity. They have to be open to the idea that we should not pressure ourselves unduly to always go further and further, to find more and more ways of testing and seeking and wringing every last drop out of the washcloth of life to the point of borderline insanity. There's a *New Yorker* cartoon that illustrates this point perfectly. Drawn by Charles Barsotti, it shows a psychiatrist's office. Predictably, a man is lying down on the couch talking to his shrink. Unpredictably, his shrink is a dog. "Well," the dog says, "*I think you're wonderful.*" Being unconditionally loving and supportive, being unabashedly affectionate, being entirely present in the moment, this is a job as central to survival as searching and rescuing. In fact, it is a form of emotional search and rescue that takes place on your couch. It's as purposeful as anything else that a living being can do.

Jazzy, Pomeranian (1 year old), Washington Square Park, New York, NY • "No matter what happens during the day, he'll be there to jazz it up at the end. Little body, big personality. He weighs five pounds and is 90 percent fluff."

CHAPTER 28

THE FUTURE OF DOGISM

A few years ago, I met a girl named Zoey Henry. Zoey, who was eleven, grew up in Brooklyn, and during her childhood, picked up a nickname, Clumsy Zoey. It was not a cruel nickname thought up by playground bullies but an affectionate one that came from her own family: they bestowed it upon her because Zoey had a habit of bumping into things and falling down. It was funny until a 2019 fall changed the picture. Zoey took a tumble and got up, like a million times before, but the next day she had trouble staying on her feet, and when her parents tried to talk to her, she burst into tears. Through the tears, she tried to explain that she couldn't keep her balance, but even her mouth was unsteady: her parents described it as her face sort of collapsing on one side. They rushed her to the hospital, where she was diagnosed with a glioma, a brain stem tumor, inoperable in her case because of its location. Over the next year, she underwent chemotherapy to shrink the tumor, which it did successfully, though it left her with other lasting health problems—a drop foot (that's a neurological condition where a person has difficulty lifting the front part of their foot when they walk), along with emotional and memory regulation issues. But Zoey had strong family support and tremendous personal motivation, and she kept on going. Her two main interests were photography and dogs—she loved to take pictures, and one of her favorite subjects was the family dog. Sound familiar?

One day I received an email from the Make-A-Wish foundation, the group that helps children with terminal illnesses realize long-held desires. Zoey had met with them, and they'd asked her what she most wanted to do, and her answer wasn't "meet Beyoncé" or "go to Disney World." Her wish was to photograph dogs, especially dogs in need of homes. The foundation in turn found me, and I became the concrete version of Zoey's wish.

We met in Washington Square Park in late October. My goal, having been The Dogist for ten years straight without missing a day, was to hand over the reins to her for an afternoon. Her exuberance reminded me of myself when I first started the project. She didn't take the responsibility lightly. I could tell it was meant to be. I had picked the day for a reason: it was the annual Halloween dog parade day, which meant hundreds of dogs in costumes, some dressed to match their owners. One dog was a policeman, with a hat and a badge. Another one was a baby in a basket. We warmed up with a few dogs Make-A-Wish had arranged for us to meet. Zoey had come with her sister and parents, but without her family's dog, Diesel, and though she was a little shy at first, her excitement was palpable.

We started out reviewing the basics of dog street photography. Some of it was technical, extending the camera strap so that she could move the camera around more freely, picking the proper lens for her Canon (also a Make-A-Wish gift). But she was even more interested in the essence of dog street photography—the dogs. I explained that the principal skill was attentiveness, that you had to understand that dogs would give you their full attention with eye contact for a second or two before they went right back to looking at other things. I told her that her job as the photographer was to have her camera ready for that moment. She nodded and smiled. I told her about the tools of my trade and my Dogist methods: hold a ball around the lens, make a strange noise, let them know you have a cookie, whatever it takes to get them to focus on you and you alone. I took a couple of pictures, made some funny noises, and then Zoey was up. It was time to pass the torch in the form of one of my field-tested, heavily patinaed squeaky tennis balls. Zoey sprang into action, getting a low shot of the Australian Shepherd that had come to meet us. She was a natural, and proudly showed me the frames she got on the back of her camera. "Great shots," I said. I could sense the encouragement welling up inside her. She was off to The Dogist races.

We made our way to Tompkins Square Park, ground zero for the dog Halloween parade. It's the Super Bowl of dog content—I call it that every year because it's true every year. Zoey jumped in like a Lab into a swimming pool. I hung back, took some pictures of my own, and watched her circulate. She was easy to find in the crowd, partly because everyone was giving her space to get her shots, partly because of her bright blue Make-A-Wish T-shirt. What impressed me most wasn't how she stood out, though, but how she blended in. She was still a special case, brought to the park by her health challenges, but she was also just an eleven-year-old girl walking around a park enjoying taking pictures of the things that she loved the most. I lost sight of Zoey for a minute and then found her again as the crowd shifted. She was crouched down in front of a Chihuahua, moving the tennis ball around, smiling as she made the dog and the people around it smile.

A few weeks later we met up again at a shelter in New Jersey, where we got shots of some of the adult dogs in kennels. The place gave Zoey a sense of the complexities of dog adoption, and we finished up in the puppy room. There was no official place called that (though clearly I need to open a dog bar in the city one day with that name—I'm glad no one overheard my plan). Instead, it was a quiet room with some chairs and a door, where they could bring puppies in for us to photograph without them escaping down the hall. For me, it was nothing new. I wouldn't say that I was jaded, but I had witnessed and absorbed this level of cuteness many times. Zoey, however, was fully in puppy heaven. After I had gotten my shots, she seemed to just be getting started. I stepped out to speak with the staff, and we watched Zoey through the window, on the floor with the puppies, soaking up every moment.

That night I came home filled with good feeling. I had helped a young girl accomplish something beautiful even as she fought through something daunting. She went on to have a gallery show to feature her dog artwork a few weeks later, sponsored by Make-A-Wish. But I was also feeling something else. It took me a bit to distill my thoughts, but I eventually realized that what I was feeling was gratitude. Not for the honor of being able to grant a little kid's wish but for the honor of getting to live that wish every day of my life.

It wasn't until I was home that night that the significance of the day really settled on me. At a young age, Zoey had been shown the fragility of life, something that I am not sure that I fully comprehend as a man in his midthirties. Given the opportunity, she had the wisdom not to squander her time on something superficial. She followed her bliss. She chose her love of dogs, and chose to share that love with others, just as a dog would. Zoey and I still communicate regularly through Instagram, and I am delighted to see every new post she shares.

I know how lucky I am to spend my time on earth doing something I love. It is not lost on me. People tell me every day on the streets that I have a dream job. That may be true, but since I'm the one dreaming it, I occasionally need help to wake up—to step back and fully appreciate it. It's stories like Zoey's that make me appreciate the privilege dogs give me of making art from their likenesses and stories, inspiring joy and laughter and heartfelt empathy. It's tragic stories like Catherine Hubbard's that make me feel a deep sense of duty to help carry out the legacy of a little girl who loved dogs as much as I do. It's the ever-present reminders dogs give us every day: to go outside, to connect with others, to not be afraid of just being who we are. To appreciate and do our best to be happy in the moment we're in. They make us laugh and keep us company when we're feeling down. They restore our trust when we've lost all faith. Dogs give us more than we can ever quantify. They're one of the universe's great sparks, and we're incredibly lucky to share this planet with them. It has sometimes been hard for me to concisely articulate my mission as The Dogist. Recently a woman stopped me in the park to share her appreciation for the work I've done over the years. We spoke for a minute, and she departed with a simple compliment that was anything but: "You're doing what's important." To me, that's the truth, but it's not the truth about me. It's the truth about dogs. They know what's important. They know that beyond all the things in life that we use to distract ourselves and self-soothe and keep score, it's the relationships we have with ourselves and one another that truly matter. Dogs know instinctively that yesterday is gone and tomorrow is never promised—that the only time we ever truly have is now. Every dog I have met and shared with the world is a loving, snoring, shedding, cuddling example that life is just better with them. For me, along with the thousands of people I've met through my work (and I'm sure most of you reading), nothing has been more life-changing than dogs.

I want to finish by returning to my friend Angus. When we last left off, his dog, Opal, had arrived in New York and begun to reshape his life. She had helped him to be less self-conscious, less anxious, and less worried. A few weeks after Opal came to live with Angus, Elsa and I ventured out onto the streets of New York City to meet them. He had told me on the phone that he was relaxed and happier, and I was curious if I would notice. I did. He spoke and moved with greater ease, in part because he had a dog to take care of, and that responsibility both kept him out of his own head and helped him to take care of himself. He was, above all, living proof of what I had promised him when he first thought about adding a four-legged best friend to his life, and what had given me the title for this book: this dog will change your life.

- - - - - - - - - - - - 🐾 - - - - - - - - - - - -

Maverick, Golden Retriever (7 months old), Newport Polo, Portsmouth, RI · "He's goofy and crazy—that's why I like Goldens. He eats underwear. He swallowed a pair whole, but he threw it right up. He has no regrets—he did it again."

- - - - - - - - - - - - 🐾 - - - - - - - - - - - -

PART FUR

DOGIST RESOURCES

During my time as The Dogist, I have worked with many organizations, from stateside shelters to international dog rescue operations to organizations that raise and train puppies to become service dogs, along with organizations that train dogs to find lost hikers, skiers in avalanches, or victims of natural and man-made disasters. Below, I have listed some of the groups, charities, and initiatives I have had the privilege of working with. There's an East Coast bias, certainly, and more specifically a New-York-City-and-environs bias—that's where I'm located and where I've done the majority of my work. But wherever you live, there are sure to be similarly incredible organizations doing dog's work.

RESCUE AND SHELTER ORGANIZATIONS

Shelters and rescue organizations, whether international, national, regional, or local, make up the backbone of animal rescue in the United States and the world. Brick-and-mortar shelters are able to house homeless animals themselves (to their capacity), and rescue organizations often rely on their network of foster volunteers and local shelters to house dogs until they're able to successfully place them with families. This process is a complex series of steps that has many ups and downs. Shelters today are suffering from extreme overcrowding, in part because adoption rates are down. The tireless people who run these organizations are in a constant state of dealing with stresses from all sides, and their approach is more science than art. They spend every day trying to help dogs find their forever families, a process they know requires all hands on deck and a deft touch to achieve the desired result. Here are a few of the incredible organizations I've worked with over the years. There are so many more organizations across the country—if you are not in proximity to these groups and want to contribute, find the ones nearest to you.

American Society for the Prevention of Cruelty to Animals (ASPCA)

aspca.org

One of the premier national organizations when it comes to animal welfare, the ASPCA goes above and beyond to take in dogs from all types of situations—dogfighting and hoarding cases, puppy mills, natural disasters, police seizures, and strays.

Animal Care Centers of New York City

nycacc.org

The ACC is New York's largest city shelter and it is "open admission," meaning that it's required to take in all owner surrenders, not just of dogs but cats, rabbits, guinea pigs, and so on.

Animal Haven

animalhaven.org

In operation since 1967, the SoHo-based Animal Haven works in collaboration with many local and national rescue groups to give dogs the best outcomes possible, and you can also stand across Centre Street and see animals playing in the window (and maybe even Tiffany, their founder).

Badass Animal Rescue

badassanimalrescue.com

Since I began The Dogist in 2013, Badass has been a leading rescue organization in New York. They're based in Brooklyn but pull mostly from the South, a notoriously dog-overpopulated part of the country.

Best Friends Animal Society

bestfriends.org

One of the largest national rescue organizations in the country. Visiting their sanctuary in Kanab, Utah, was one of the most noteworthy rescue features I've done. Their motto, "Save Them All," is one of my favorite aspirational messages.

Bideawee

bideawee.org

An NYC shelter operating since 1903 that was instrumental in pioneering the concept of "no-kill." The name means "stay a while" in Scottish. I've photographed many a cute dog rescued from Bideawee.

Cunucu Dog Rescue

cunucudogrescue.org

Based in the Dutch colony of Aruba, this rescue organization flies dogs to New York, where they are likely to be adopted. Cunucu was founded by four Dutch women, and is named for the Aruban island dog.

Hearts & Bones Rescue

heartsandbonesrescue.org

Hearts & Bones is an end-to-end (snoot-to-tail?) rescue organization, with paws on the ground in Dallas and NYC. Whitney and Alicia walk the Dallas-based municipal shelters in search of dogs that they believe will do well living the city life in NYC.

Korean K9 Rescue

koreank9rescue.org

Korean K9 focuses on rescuing dogs from Korea that may otherwise be destined for the dog-meat trade, to U.S. cities like Los Angeles, Boston, and New York.

Muddy Paws Rescue

muddypawsrescue.org

Founded in 2015, Muddy Paws not only succeeds in dog adoptions but has built a large network of foster families who aid in adoptable dog turnover. They strive to educate about dog behavior and responsible pet ownership.

Nantucket Island Safe Harbor

nishanimals.org

Known on the island as NiSHA, this organization helps those looking to adopt a dog on Nantucket island find their match. They may not have to grapple with overpopulated shelters like they would in a city, but they're the go-to organization on the island to make sure that dogs looking for a home find one.

North Shore Animal League

animalleague.org

One of the world's most venerable and largest animal rescue organizations, the North Shore Animal League (the North Shore in question is on Long Island) has been rescuing dogs for eighty years.

NYC Second Chance Rescue

nycsecondchancerescue.org

The organization, founded in 2009 by Jennifer Brooks, does exactly what its name says it does—it concentrates on dogs and cats that need life-saving care, especially those that have been critically injured or seriously neglected.

Pilots to the Rescue

pilotstotherescue.org

Pilots to the Rescue helps bring dogs from overcrowded places in the South, transporting them north, primarily to the tristate area, where they've got a better shot at finding a home. While space may be limited in Michael's Piper Aircraft, nicknamed Paw Force One, puppies and senior dogs may fare much better on a quick three-hour transport flight than a ten-plus-hour transport in a van.

Sandy Paws Rescue

sandypawsmv.com

An awesome team spearheaded by Ashley, out of Martha's Vineyard, Massachusetts. Sandy Paws rescues dogs from shelters, cruelty situations, and owner surrenders, and strays from Texas, North Carolina, Georgia, and Florida. They provide assistance to families in financial distress, and help connect them with spay and neuter services to battle the overpopulation issue. Sandy Paws also happens to be my dog Elsa's alma mater (alma mutter?).

The Sato Project

thesatoproject.org

This Puerto Rican organization works tirelessly to rescue satos (Puerto Rican street dogs), which exist in numbers as high as 500,000 on the island. Their seven programs address issues such as rescue and rehabilitation, freedom flights, and disaster relief. Chrissy, their founder, is also a super featherweight boxer, and is not to be messed with.

Sean Casey Animal Rescue

nyanimalrescue.org

Sean Casey Animal Rescue is one of very few rescues that takes in the most difficult medical cases. Beyond dogs, SCAR rescues cats, hamsters, birds, snakes, iguanas, and fish from neglect, abuse, confiscation, illness, or otherwise unwanted situations, and facilitates rehabilitation.

SNARR Northeast

snarrnortheast.org

SNARR stands for Special Needs Animal Rescue & Rehabilitation, and as their name suggests, they take in dogs with serious medical conditions, such as paralyzed dogs, dogs with neurological deficits, and deaf and blind dogs. They pull dogs from high-kill shelters all over the country, with a focus on NYC and New Jersey.

Social Tees

socialteesnyc.org

Social Tees started in 1991 as a T-shirt company and transitioned to animal rescue. They are a foster-based system and do not keep any dogs or cats on-site; they believe when done correctly, a foster-based system is the healthiest option.

St. Hubert's Animal Welfare Center

sthuberts.org

Based in Madison, New Jersey, St. Hubert's is one of the largest animal-service providers in the region, offering everything from pet food banks to vaccine clinics to emergency pet boarding to training classes.

Street Tails Animal Rescue

streettails.org

Located in Philadelphia, Street Tails is a small organization with just two full-time team members who oversee every aspect of their rescue operation.

True North Rescue Mission

truenorthrescue.org

True North Rescue Mission is fully volunteer-run and foster-based. They partner with several other organizations, including Slaughterhouse Survivors in Harbin, China, where dogs are rescued from the meat trade.

TRAINING AND ADVOCACY ORGANIZATIONS

American Academy of Canine Water Rescue

k9lifeguards.org

The staff of this organization has been trained by the Italian School of Water Rescue Dogs in Milan, Italy, with the goal of reducing or eliminating deaths by drowning. The water rescue K-9 team patrols beaches and lakes, and also educates the public on water safety.

America's VetDogs

vetdogs.org

America's VetDogs trains and provides service dogs, guide dogs, and facility dogs to veterans, active duty service members, first responders with disabilities, and military and VA hospitals. All services are provided at no charge to the individual.

The Exceptional Sidekick Service Dogs

exceptionalsidekick.org

The Exceptional Sidekick Service Dogs is a unique organization that provides psychiatric service dogs to teens and young adults.

Guiding Eyes for the Blind

guidingeyes.org

Since its founding in 1954, Guiding Eyes has paired more than ten thousand dogs with seeing-impaired people, and done so at no charge to the recipients. They have several facilities dedicated to canine development and field training, and their puppy-raising regions stretch across the country.

PAWS NY

pawsny.org

PAWS stands for Pets Are Wonderful Support; NY stands for New York. The organization helps and protects New Yorkers who can't always help and protect their pets as a result of physical and financial obstacles, with a focus on lower-income older adults and individuals living with illness or disability.

Puppies Behind Bars

puppiesbehindbars.com

Founded a quarter-century ago by Gloria Gilbert Stoga, Puppies Behind Bars pairs incarcerated individuals with puppies to train them to become future service dogs, helping to rebuild the individuals' humanity by restoring their sense of responsibility and creating a positive connection with the world.

The Seeing Eye

seeingeye.org

Based in Morristown, New Jersey, The Seeing Eye is the oldest guide dog school in the United States, with a history that extends back a century.

Warrior Canine Connection

warriorcanineconnection.org

WCC connects vets to dogs, and has the additional wrinkle of using dogs that were trained by other vets in the first place. It's an ingenious way of involving veterans in both ends of the process.

ACKNOWLEDGMENTS

To begin with, I would like to acknowledge every single dog I have ever met. No two have been the same, and I'm never the same person after meeting a dog and letting them go on their way. Not to say that I become an *entirely* different person after each dog. But we are the sum of our parts, and each dog adds a little (or big) piece to my soul. I stroll away a slightly better person, even if they barked at me.

I would also like to acknowledge every dog's person who has let me capture their dog's photo to share with the world. Joy is becoming a rarer commodity these days, so to share your four-legged best friend with a stranger (me), and to let that stranger then convey the story of that dog and its likeness so that it inspires smiles and giggles and tears for hundreds of thousands of people—that is very likely actually making the world a better place, one dog at a time.

Lastly, I would like to thank the people in my life who supported me in writing this book and in my work as The Dogist. My family, who encouraged me to embrace my artistic, eccentric side; Sam, my future wife, who is the best dog mom to Elsa and who *gets* me like no one else does; my friends and colleagues, who have had my back through the ups and downs of life; and my co-writer, Ben Greenman, who helped me write this book (though I think he got a lot of help from his dogs: his Beagle, Sammy, and his crotchety old Australian Silky Terrier, Ozzie).

DOG INDEX

A

Abbi, Chihuahua, 74

Al, black Labrador Retriever (4 years old), 223

Arby, black Labrador Retriever, 222

Arlo, mixed breed (9 years old), 58

Arthur the Great, Norfolk Terrier (11 years old), 99

Asta, Kerry Blue Terrier (6 years old), 218

Astrid, Harlequin Great Dane, 27

Axel, Great Dane (5 months old), 64

B

Barb, Golden Retriever, 213–15, 240

Barrett, German Shorthaired Pointer (3 months old), 166

Barry White, Goldendoodle, 125, 126

Beacon, Golden Retriever (4 years old), 225

Beast, Old English Mastiff (in film, *The Sandlot*), 179

Beethoven, Saint Bernard (in *Beethoven* film series), 179

Benji, Golden Retriever–mix (in films *Benji* and *Oh! Heavenly Dog*), 179

Blue, Pit Bull–mix, 140–42

Bo, Portuguese Water Dog (President Obama's White House dog), 170

Boom (Uga XI), Bulldog, 177

Brownie, chocolate Labrador Retriever, 160

Buddy, German Shepherd, 220

Buddy, Labrador Retriever (President Clinton's dog), 170

Buddy Holly, Petit Basset Griffon Vendéen, 11

Bunny, Sheepadoodle, 81–82

C

Chance, American Bulldog (in film, *Homeward Bound*), 170

Checkers, Cocker Spaniel (President Nixon's dog), 169

Cheeto, yellow Labrador Retriever, 93–94

Clark, Afghan Hound (3 years old), 80

Commander, German Shepherd (President Biden's dog), 170–74, 178

Cooper, Labrador Retriever/Australian Shepherd–mix, 143

Max, German Shepherd, 110
Max, Labrador Retriever, 136
May, terrier–mix, 114
Miller, Boxer–mix, 99–101
Millie, Springer Spaniel (President George H. W. Bush's family dog), 170
Milo, mixed breed, 191
Milo, Pug (in film, *The Adventures of Milo and Otis*), 179
Mister, German Shepherd (6 years old), 151
Moonlight, mixed breed (7 years old), 63, 64
Morpheus, Pug (1 year old), 18
Mousie, Brussels Griffon, 137–38
Mr. Bigglesworth "Biggie," Labrador Retriever, xiii
Mr. Vinny, Pit Bull–mix, 54–55

N

Nemo, Labrador Retriever (1 year old), 221

O

Oakley, Chinese Crested Powderpuff, 121
Oakley, Landseer (4 years old), 234–35
Ole Blu, hound (Grand Ole Opry mascot), 207
Opal, yellow Labrador Retriever, xxi, xxii–xxiii, 246–47
Oreo, black Labrador Retriever, xi–xii, xvii

P

Piney, Pit Bull, 73
Porsha, Doberman, 132, 133

Q

Que (Uga X), Bulldog, 176–77

R

Raisin, French Bulldog, 124
Rico, Border Collie, 81
Rigatoni, Bernedoodle, 67
Rigby, Labrador Retriever, xiii
Riley, Golden Retriever, 167–68
Rob Roy, Collie (President Coolidge's dog), 169

Rock, English Setter, 192
Rosie, Australian Shepherd–mix, 94
Rowdy, black Labrador Retriever (13 years old), 92–93
Roxy, Rottweiler–mix, 107
Ruby, black Labrador Retriever, xiii, xiv, *xxv*, 78, 79, 105–8, 136, 144–47, 188, 194

S

Sadie, Silken Windhound, 182
Sally Long Dog, Basset Hound, 167–68
Sam, Goldendoodle, 232
Sawyer, Australian Shepherd, 132, 133
Seaver, black Labrador Retriever, 215
Shadow, Golden Retriever (in film, *Homeward Bound*), 170
Sheriff, Labrador/Golden Retriever–cross (8 months old), 127
Simba, Golden Retriever (2 years old), 114
Simba, Saint Bernard (1 year old), 226
Sirrus, Silken Windhound, 181–82
Skip, Smooth Fox Terrier (in film, *My Dog Skip*), 179
Snoopy, Beagle (*Peanuts* cartoon dog), 184
Snow, Maltese, 133
Snowy, Labrador Retriever, xiii, xiv, 71, 136–37, 147
Snugzz, Cattle Dog–mix, 63, 64
Sparky, Bull Terrier (in film, *Frankenweenie*), 179
Spot, Springer Spaniel, 170
Stella, Scottish Terrier (9 years old), 7
Sudan, Afghan Hound (3 years old), 80
Sully H. W. Bush, Labrador Retriever (President George H. W. Bush's service dog), 237
Sunny, Pomsky (10 months old), 139
Sunny, Portuguese Water Dog, 170

T

Takashi, Akita (5 years old), 48
Togo, Afghan Hound (2 years old), 80
T-Paws, Labrador Retriever, xiii
Trooper, Labrador Retriever, 216
Trumpet, Bloodhound, 11

U

Uga, Bulldog (University of Georgia Bulldogs mascot), 176–77
Umi, sato–mix (1.5 years old), 65, 174

V

Vinny, German Shepherd, 228–29

W

Wasabi, Pekingese, 11
Whistle, Pug, 137–38
Whiz, Yorkie, 98
Willa, mixed breed, 191

Z

Zachary, chocolate Labrador Retriever, 160

GENERAL INDEX

ABOUT THE AUTHORS

ELIAS WEISS FRIEDMAN is a *New York Times* bestselling author, photographer, producer, and the creator and namesake of the popular online platform The Dogist, which boasts more than ten million followers across platforms. Over the last decade, Weiss Friedman has photographed more than fifty thousand dogs and redefined dog portraiture through his singular style of humanizing his subjects. Weiss Friedman is known for his philanthropic work as an advocate for dog rescue and advocacy organizations throughout the country, raising funds for many organizations that support dogs and help people through The Dogist Fund. He is the author of the instant *New York Times* bestseller *The Dogist: Photographic Encounters with 1,000 Dogs* and *The Dogist Puppies*.

@TheDogist

BEN GREENMAN is a former *New Yorker* editor and bestselling author who has published both fiction (*The Slippage, Please Step Back, Don Quixotic*) and nonfiction (*Dig If You Will the Picture, Emotional Rescue*). He has also co-authored a number of books, including projects with Steven Van Zandt, Brian Wilson, George Clinton, Sly Stone, and Questlove.

ABOUT THE TYPE

This book was set in Caslon, a typeface first designed in 1722 by William Caslon (1692–1766). Its widespread use by most English printers in the early eighteenth century soon supplanted the Dutch typefaces that had formerly prevailed. The roman is considered a "workhorse" typeface due to its pleasant, open appearance, while the italic is exceedingly decorative.